FROM PHONICS TO FLUENCY

FROM PHONICS TO FLUENCY

EFFECTIVE TEACHING OF DECODING AND READING FLUENCY IN THE ELEMENTARY SCHOOL

Timothy V. Rasinski
Kent State University

Nancy D. Padak
Kent State University

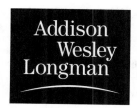

Addison
Wesley
Longman

New York San Francisco Boston
London Toronto Sydney Tokyo Singapore Madrid
Mexico City Munich Paris Cape Town Hong Kong Montreal

Publisher: Priscilla McGeehon
Senior Acquisitions Editor : Virginia L. Blanford
Development Director: Lisa Pinto
Supplements Editor: Jennifer Ackerman
Production Manager: Denise Phillip
Project Coordination, Text Design, and Electronic Page Makeup: WestWords, Inc.
Cover Designer/Manager: Nancy Danahy
Manufacturing Buyer: Al Dorsey
Printer and Binder: Maple-Vail Book Manufacturing Group
Cover Printer: Lehigh Press

For permission to use copyrighted material, grateful acknowledgment is made to the copyright holders on pp. 194, 224 which are hereby made part of this copyright page.

Library of Congress Cataloging-in-Publication Data

Rasinski, Timothy V.
    From phonics to fluency / Timothy V. Rasinski, Nancy D. Padak
        p. cm.
    Includes bibliographical references and index.
    ISBN 0-321-04903-9
    1. Word recognition. I. Padak, Nancy. II. Title

LB1050.44 .R28 2000
372.46'2—dc21   00-032262

Please visit our website at http://www.awl.com

ISBN 0-321-04903-9

    6 7 8 9 10—MA—03

The knowledge of words is the gate to scholarship.
—Woodrow Wilson

Give me the right word and the right accent and I will move the world
—Joseph Conrad

BRIEF CONTENTS

CONTENTS

CHAPTER 8

MAKING AND WRITING WORDS   84

CHAPTER 9

WORD BANKS AND WORD SORTS   96

CHAPTER 10

CONTEXTUAL WORD RECOGNITION   108

CHAPTER 11
THE LANGUAGE EXPERIENCE APPROACH AND WORD LEARNING   119

CHAPTER 12
WORD GAMES   134

CHAPTER 13
SPELLING AND WORD LEARNING   150

CHAPTER 14

BEYOND WORD STUDY: READING FLUENCY   163

CHAPTER 15

INSTRUCTIONAL ROUTINES FOR WORD STUDY AND FLUENCY   176

CHAPTER 16

ASSESSING WORD RECOGNITION AND READING FLUENCY   187

CHAPTER 17

INVOLVING PARENTS IN WORD STUDY AND READING FLUENCY INSTRUCTION   203

APPENDICES

PREFACE

One of the ongoing issues of twentieth century reading instruction has been the nature and role of word recognition instruction, or word study, in reading education. Throughout the century various methods for teaching word identification have come and gone. Also, throughout the century, the appropriate place for word recognition instruction has shifted—in some programs word study is the central element; in others it is hardly visible. These issues are likely to persist well into—perhaps throughout—the 21st century.

We enter this word study milieu by stating up front that competency in word recognition is absolutely essential to proficient reading. Moreover, although we believe that contextual reading is perhaps the best way to develop and consolidate word recognition strategies and skills, we also feel that direct instruction and ongoing coaching by teachers in word recognition are essential to optimal growth in reading. Not any kind of direct instruction and coaching will do however. Word study should be engaging and challenging for all students; it should be enjoyable and nurture a love of the written word among students, and it should be accomplished as authentically as possible so that students can see the application and importance of what they are learning.

One of the main purposes of this book then, is to provide you, the aspiring or veteran teacher, with workable approaches to word study that students will find authentic, engaging, and enjoyable. The approaches that we share with you are based on solid literacy theory, reading research, and/or actual classroom application.

From Phonics to Fluency does not stop with word study. Most word study books for teachers begin and end on the topic of words. Our book goes beyond words and explores effective fluency instruction. Indeed, our goal as teachers should not be readers who read accurately, regardless of whether meaning is constructed from the text. Rather, our goal should be fluent readers who read efficiently, expressively, and meaningfully so that meaning can easily be constructed by the reader. Fluency is necessary for good comprehension, and fluency is more than accurate word recognition. In this book we share with you many proven and effective instructional strategies for teaching reading fluency—strategies that can be easily and authentically integrated into other areas of the school curriculum, strategies that can lead to improvements in word recognition and comprehension, as well as fluency.

These two issues—engaging and authentic word study, and effective fluency instruction—are the topics that differentiate this text from many others on word identification instruction. We have also tried to give you, the reader, a sense for how these strategies have actually played out in classrooms by including the voices of real teachers who struggle with designing and implementing instruction for children every day. These teacher voices provide a real life context that helps even veteran teachers imagine how the instructional strategies may play out in their own classrooms.

The topic of this book is an old one. But our approach to the topic is fresh. The instruction described in this book, when examined and adapted by real teachers, new and experienced, for their own classrooms, will lead not only to improved word recognition, more fluent reading, and better reading comprehension, but will help nurture in many students a lifelong fascination with words and reading.

ACKNOWLEDGMENTS

We wish to acknowledge the many teachers we have met and worked with over the years who have shared with us their knowledge, their ideas, and their frustrations about word study and fluency instruction. In many ways, this is indeed your book. We are also indebted to reviewers of earlier versions of this book for their insights and suggestions. Many thanks go to Gwynne Ellen Ash of University of Georgia, Jean M. Casey of California State University at Long Beach, Jane Gordon of Eastern Michigan State University, Sherry Guice of State University of New York at Albany, Ann Hall of Southwestern Texas State University, Adrienne Herrell of California State University at Fresno, Nancy Horton of University of North Texas, Jeri Levesque of Webster University, David M. Lund of Southwestern Utah University, and Ramon A. Serrano of St. Cloud State University.

Finally, we wish to thank our editor at Addison-Wesley Longman, Ginny Blanford, who believed in our ideas about a new kind of "word" book for teachers and who provided expert guidance and support throughout the authoring process.

FOREWORD

It took a war—The Reading Wars—to bring the teaching of reading into balance. The Reading Wars were waged in the 1990's along several battle fronts: in the media, in legislatures, in school districts, and among colleagues. Media coverage, more often than not, dramatized the Reading Wars as a do-or-die battle between the proponents of phonics or whole language. Rather than view phonics and whole language on an instructional continuum, newspaper and television accounts of the Reading Wars only served to muddle the public's understanding of how to teach reading to beginners. Although the Reading Wars has pretty much run its course as we enter a new millennium, one of its unfortunate consequences is that it reinforced, and perhaps even perpetuated, a false dichotomy in the teaching of word learning skills: Either teachers of beginning readers initiate instruction by using letter-sound relationships (phonics) or by using "look-say" methods to teach words as wholes (whole language). This dichotomy not only mischaracterizes whole language as simply "teaching words as wholes," but it also narrowly portrays phonics instruction as the rigid, rote learning of letters and sounds. Neither characterization could be further from the instructional realities of today's classroom.

From Phonics to Fluency, fortunately, does much to repair the damage created by simplistic either-or portrayals of word learning in reading. Moreover, this important book underscores the relationships that exist among word study, fluency, and reading comprehension. Reading is about making sense. The only legitimate reason to teach word study to children is that they will be able to use decoding skills and strategies to better comprehend what they read. Children must be able to identify words accurately and quickly while reading. Tim Rasinski and Nancy Padak, the authors of *From Phonics to Fluency*, recognize that phonics is a tool needed by all readers and writers of alphabetically written languages such as English. However, they are not proponents of isolated drill, over reliance on worksheets, or rote memorization of phonic rules. They view phonics in the broader context of word study and support the use of contemporary instructional strategies that teach children what they need to know and actually do to identify words accurately and quickly. These strategies need to be taught explicitly in well-planned lessons, many of which are explained and demonstrated in this book.

What I like about *From Phonics to Fluency* is that it provides a balanced treatment of word study and fluency that draws upon both phonics and whole language perspectives. Phonics and whole language are grounded in knowledge and beliefs that can be supported by a body of research as well as common sense about the teaching of reading. Padak and Rasinski wisely avoid locking themselves into ideological shackles. Instead, they draw on what works based on research-supported practice on word learning. For example, they underscore the importance of authentic texts and the role of parental support in word study. Parents and teachers of beginners have mutually supportive roles to play in children's reading development. Both parents and teachers support and develop children's knowledge of words in early reading in numerous ways, including: reading stories, poems, and songs and discussing letter-sound relationships and patterns of letters in words that rhyme; encouraging children to listen for and identify sounds in words; encouraging children to spell the sounds they hear in words as they write; and comparing and contrasting letter and sound patterns in children's names, high interest words, and words drawn from the books children are reading, and the stories they write.

The core chapters of *From Phonics to Fluency* move teachers through a logical sequence of instructional strategies that will make a difference in the literate lives of elementary students: from teaching beginners to become phonemically aware; to instruction in the recognition of onsets and rimes; to making discoveries about words through word-making activities; to the use of word walls, word sorts, and word banks; to context-based strategies that help children cross-check for meaning; to strategies designed to develop children's reading fluency. Throughout each chapter, there are strong theoretical underpinnings to the practical strategies offered in this book.

I am pleased for Nancy Padak and Tim Rasinski. They have taken an old, beleaguered topic in the teaching of reading and given it a fresh approach. They have brought together the best of what is known about phonics and authentic word learning situations. Maybe The Reading Wars has some positive consequences after all.

by: Richard T. Vacca, PhD
Kent State University
Past President,
International Reading Association

1

WORD STUDY AND FLUENCY

It was two o'clock in the afternoon on Saturday, and everyone was tired. We had just completed another Saturday reading diagnostic clinic in which children from the surrounding area who are experiencing difficulty in reading are assessed to determine their reading levels and specific areas of difficulty. We make instructional recommendations to overcome those sources of difficulty. After the children leave, the clinicians remain to score and examine children's performance on the various assessments given. Two of the clinicians, Sandi and Tom, seemed perplexed.

Sandi and Tom had worked with a fifth-grade boy named Ted. According to the information supplied by Ted's parents and teachers, his major area of difficulty was in comprehension. He simply did not have good recall for any of the texts he had read in school or that were assigned for home reading. Sandi and Tom had anticipated looking into Ted's reading recall, his ability to make inferences from information provided in his reading, his understanding of words and concepts, and his study skills. They were surprised that these weren't the source of Ted's reading difficulties.

> "What we found was that Ted had trouble in word recognition. Even when we gave him a passage to read orally at the second grade level, he made a significant number of errors or miscues; over ten percent of the words he read were not what was written in the text. And, whether he read orally or silently, his reading was extremely slow and labored. Actually, when we asked him to retell what he had read we were surprised that he was able to remember so much. His recall was affected by his word recognition problems, but it wasn't bad at all. In fact, when we looked at his comprehension of text that we read to him and that he listened to, we had to conclude that his comprehension was a strength. It was his word recognition and fluency problems that made him appear to have poor comprehension."

This is a common occurrence among the children we see in our reading clinic. Students come in with a significant reading problem, and the problem is felt to lie in comprehension or overall reading achievement. But often, the comprehension problem is really a side effect of more fundamental problems—

1

problems at the root of many reading difficulties—difficulty in word recognition, word identification or decoding, and problems in fluency.

This book concerns that very important part of learning to read, namely, how to recognize words one finds in text. According to reading researcher Phil Gough, the process of reading can be summarized in the equation Reading $= D \times C$, where D refers to decoding words and C refers to comprehension of the words that are decoded. Gough's equation may seem simple, yet very little in the teaching and learning of reading is simple or universally accepted, Gough's equation for one.

For years, scholars have argued whether decoding actually needs to be taught at all, and if so, what are the best methods for teaching decoding. Jeanne Chall's seminal book *Reading: The Great Debate* (1967) intended to answer that question. Chall indicated that children did need to study the decoding of words and that phonics instruction is the most productive method for doing so.

At about the same time as Chall's book, scholars began looking at reading from a new perspective, a psycholinguistic perspective. One of the tenets of this approach, which evolved into reading instruction known as whole language, is that making meaning is the central act of reading. And, the act of constructing meaning can help students figure out (decode) words that they don't know. Consider the following sentences:

I ate lunch at McDonald's. I had a B___ M___, F___ _____, and a st_____ sh_____.

Of the sixteen words in the sentences, six cannot be decoded with certainty from the letters given. Phonics (sound-symbol) information is minimal. In this case, it is the meaning of the passage that helps the reader determine that the unknown words are *Big, Mac, French, fries, strawberry,* and *shake.* Meaning is the most significant factor in determining these words, not phonics or any other approach that uses the letters in the words to decode the words—in this case the letter information is minimal or nonexistent.

Whole language gained momentum throughout the '70s, '80s, and early '90s. In recent years, however, there has been a backlash against whole language. Critics have cited test score evidence that reading proficiency levels have dropped in the United States. Despite the fact that many whole language critics misinterpreted the data to begin with, the movement against whole language instruction has intensified.

Many reading scholars acknowledge that in some whole language approaches, phonics and word recognition were taught too indirectly for some children. It was often left up to students to see generalizations that existed in letter-sound relationships and other letter patterns in words. However, these same scholars recognized the exceptionally positive contributions made by whole language to reading instruction—the focus on real books and other forms of authentic texts, the focus on students and their needs and interests rather than the text as the focus for instruction, the recognition that understanding is the intended result of reading, and the need to read for real purposes, not for contrived purposes defined by the teacher or the reading textbook. With these contributions in mind, many reading scholars have moved toward an orientation called balanced reading.

Balanced reading instruction retains what is best from whole language—real reading for real purposes—and adds to it a limited amount of direct instruction in necessary strategies and skills for reading. Balanced reading, then, attempts to combine what is best from both worlds—learning to read for functional purposes, and learning key strategies and skills in order to be able to read for functional purposes. Among the most important reading strategies and skills are those related to word recognition or decoding, moving from the written form of a word to its oral representation.

In this book we approach reading instruction from a balanced perspective. We know that all reading instruction should be aimed at getting students to read independently in order to find satisfaction and enjoyment in reading. We also know that, for many children, reaching that point requires some direct instruction in words and how words work in texts. Thus, although we subscribe to the notion that learning to read requires attention to words and learning how they work, other principles guide our understanding of exemplary reading instruction. These guiding principles include:

- Teachers should maximize students' contextual reading. There is a fairly large body of research indicating that reading achievement results from lots of reading. Thus, at the foundation of our approach to reading instruction is the aim to increase the amount of real reading students do at school and at home.
- In order to maximize students' reading as well as their satisfaction with and motivation for reading, teachers and parents should create conditions in the classroom and home that will inspire students to read, for their own purposes as well as those assigned by the teacher. This means having plenty of engaging, authentic materials for literacy in the classroom, creating a pleasant and safe environment for reading, talking about reading and writing often, reading to students regularly, encouraging students to read and write, recommending books, and celebrating students' reading and writing.
- Teachers and parents should be models of proficient, life long, and engaged readers for students. Children emulate adults. They are most likely to learn those things that they feel adults value. Students need to see their teachers reading, during Sustained Silent Reading time as well as other times of the day. Teachers should share with students what they are reading, why they read, and how they read, so students know that reading is something adults do for real purposes.
- Teachers and parents should read to students daily. We mentioned this earlier in this section, and it is worth mentioning again. Another key to an exemplary reading curriculum is the need to *sell* reading to students. This is done through introducing students to the joy of reading by reading to students the best literature available, every day of the school year. Teachers should use the read-aloud session to introduce

students to genres of texts they may not read on their own—poetry, biography, fantasy, historical fiction, science fiction, etc.

- Again, it is well known that students who are read to regularly have better comprehension skills and larger vocabularies than children who are not read to. Teachers find that they can read more difficult texts to students than students could read on their own. Thus, through the read-aloud experience students negotiate more challenging texts with more sophisticated words and more complex πplots than texts they would read on their own. In addition, read-alouds help students develop an appreciation and love for good stories and, if teachers read to students in a fluent and expressive voice, they provide students with a direct model of what fluent oral reading should sound like.

- Students need to read for their own purposes. As teachers, we need to help students see that we don't read just because it is part of the school curriculum. Rather, students need to see that reading is an instrument they can use to solve problems; to learn about their world on their own; and to find enjoyment through stories, poetry, and other aesthetic texts. This can be done by integrating literacy into the school and life curricula. Teachers should help students see how important reading and writing are for learning about science, social studies, art, music, sports, and health. Teachers must also help students make literacy connections to their personal, family, and community lives. Students need to see that they can learn about themselves by keeping a personal journal; learn about their families through oral histories; and learn about their communities through newspapers, local publications, public libraries, the Internet, and book stores.

- In line with the notion of making connections, exemplary literacy instruction makes connections with students' homes. Reading growth is maximized when students read at home as well as in school. Perhaps the largest amount of time available for reading, assigned and pleasure, is at home in the evenings, on weekends, and during vacations. And, reading at home is most likely to occur when teachers make connections between home and school, encourage parents to help their children in reading, and support parents in their quest to do so.

- Exemplary reading instruction is comprehensive—it covers all the important aspects of reading. Here's that notion of balanced reading again. This means that teachers spend instructional time focused on reading comprehension, vocabulary (word meaning) building, spelling, sustained silent reading, and writing workshop; and through it all, word recognition and reading fluency are an important focus of instruction.

- Teachers of literacy should be informed decision makers (Spiegel 1998). Much is known from research about instructional practices that lead to reading growth. Still, it is up to the informed teacher to decide which instructional practices are best for students at any given time. Moreover, the informed teacher should make decisions that weave together varied instructional activities, some focusing on whole text reading, others focusing on individual words and word parts; some working with individuals, others working with small and large groups; some allowing students to read for their own purposes, others requiring direct instruction by the teacher, into a seamless whole that allows students to maintain sight of the end goal of reading instruction—life-long and meaningful engagements with texts.

Kathy subscribes to a balanced literacy approach. In her first grade classroom students do plenty of reading and writing for their own purposes. But she also provides time for direct individual, small group, and some whole class instruction in reading. We asked Kathy to talk about her approach to reading instruction.

> "I would like to say that real reading with real children's literature and real writing define my reading program. I read stories to my students two or three times a day. They read on their own for SQUIRT (super quiet uninterrupted reading time) every day for at least 20 minutes. We have whole class shared reading with big books and language experience stories and we have literature discussion groups with books that small groups of readers read together. My students also write in their own personal journals and literature response journals, and they write their own stories during our writing workshop time."
>
> "But I have to tell you that I also spend some time, nearly each day, teaching my students what we used to call phonics, decoding, and other skills. Actually, I like to think of them as activities that promote reading strategies. I will spend up to a half hour a day teaching these skills or strategies to my students. My students keep word banks, and they practice their words with a partner daily. They also sort their words into categories I give them a couple of times each week. We keep new sight words that we are learning on our word wall, and we read the wall every day. We cover at least two word families a week, and the word family words that we make go on another wall in our room. We make words and we play word games too. The students don't mind these activities. In fact, I think they like them. I keep these lessons fast paced and interesting. I think my students see that what they are learning during these word recognition skill and strategy lessons helps them immediately in their real reading and writing."

This book is indeed about teaching word recognition, going from printed symbols to meaningful oral representations of words and reading fluency, reading with expression and meaning. We have our own ideas about how word recognition and fluency ought to be taught. In reading this book you will find that we subscribe to particular approaches to word recognition and reading fluency, sometimes to the exclusion of more traditional (and commercial) approaches. Nevertheless, the instruction you will read about in this book is based on research, informed opinion, and/or actual instructional practice with students. Underlying our approach to word recognition and fluency is the following set of instructional principles, aimed primarily at phonics, recently outlined by Steven Stahl and his colleagues (Stahl, Duffy-Hester and Stahl 1998) Exemplary word recognition instruction:

- helps students understand the alphabetic principle—that letters in English represent sounds.
- develops students' phonemic or phonological awareness—the awareness of sounds in spoken words, an essential precursor to employment of the alphabetic principle and success in phonics instruction.
- provides students with a thorough grounding in letter recognition. Exploiting the alphabetic principle and successful phonics instruction demands that students develop the ability to overlay spoken sounds onto written letters. Recognition of letters is necessary for this to happen.
- does not require the teaching of rules, the use of worksheets and workbooks, and absolutely does not have to be boring or tedious. Word recognition instruction that is successful depends on direct teacher instruction followed closely by student use in authentic reading of connected texts, e.g., stories.
- provides practice in reading words. This is done through: (1) reading words in stories and other connected texts; (2) reading words in isolation through word bank activities, word games, and other word-oriented activities; and (3) writing words, through dictation and through invented or phonemic spelling. In dictated writing activities, students learn groups of words that have a common phonic or other pattern. In invented or phonemic spelling, students apply their emerging knowledge of sound-symbol relationships in their writing for their own purposes.
- leads to automatic word recognition. Automatic word recognition refers to the ability to recognize words quickly and with minimal analysis—by sight. This is an important part of fluent reading and is achieved through extensive reading—reading stories, reading words, and practicing words in writing.
- is only one part of reading instruction. We're sure you realize by now that we have mentioned this several times in this chapter. This is an absolutely critical point. Even though this book exclusively focuses on word recognition and reading fluency, these are only two aspects of the total picture. Word recognition and reading fluency are absolutely important in reading, but by themselves they do not provide students with a complete or sufficient reading or literacy program. As Spiegel (1998) has noted, in a balanced reading curriculum "reading is not just word identification, but word identification is a part of reading" (p. 117). Instruction in word identification and reading fluency needs to be balanced with and integrated into authentic reading experiences.

One of the best examples of a balanced approach to literacy instruction in the elementary grades is known as the Four Blocks approach (Cunningham, Hall and Defee 1991, 1998). The approach is simple, yet powerful and effective. In the Four Blocks approach the reading and writing curriculum are combined and divided into four equal blocks of time. Normally, this means about thirty minutes for each block. Each of the Four Blocks focuses on some aspect of literacy. One block is used for self-selected reading, better known as sustained silent reading or SSR. Students spend this time block reading material of their own choosing and talk about it with each other and their teacher.

A second block focuses on guided reading. Here groups of students read common books or other reading material chosen by the teacher. Younger students, as a group, orally read, reread, and perform predictable and big books with the support of the teacher. Older students read stories independently then gather to discuss their reading. These can be stories from basal readers, trade books that are required for the reading curriculum, and/or texts that make connections to other areas of the curriculum. Groups of readers read and gather together to talk about what they have read, their perceptions and understandings, important points, and questions they may have about the reading. This type of reading may be guided by the authentic literature circles, book clubs, or discussion groups (Raphael and McMahon 1994).

The third block is a writing block in which students spend the majority of time writing. Short mini-lessons are followed by student writing—journal writing, writing versions of favorite stories, writing their own original stories, writing essays, making lists, writing letters to friends, etc. In many classrooms, this block is sometimes known as the writing workshop period.

The final block is called word study, a period of time that students work on word recognition and reading fluency through a variety of instructional activities (many of which are described in this book). Essentially, this is the time in which students learn to decode words, expand their word knowledge, and apply their word skills to fluent reading.

Cunningham, Hall and Defee (1991, 1998) have applied this balanced format at the primary grades for several years. They have achieved extraordinary results in students' literacy development as a result of this balanced curriculum. For example, six years of implementation have demonstrated that ninety-one to ninety-nine percent of students who participate in the Four Blocks curriculum during first and second grade read at or above their assigned grade level (Cunningham, Hall and Defee 1998). Moreover, a majority of students maintain their excellent progress in reading through grade five. Few Four Blocks students experience significant difficulty in early reading.

We like the Four Blocks approach, especially for beginning reading teachers. It provides teachers with a clear, workable, and effective framework for literacy instruction. And, while Cunningham, Hall and Defee have used the program in the primary grades, we have worked with upper elementary and middle school teachers who have successfully adapted the Four Blocks framework for their own classrooms. We are convinced that balance is one of the reasons for the success of the Four Blocks Model; children have consistent opportunities to learn to be skilled and strategic readers and writers.

Certainly, other balanced approaches can be developed and employed at any grade level. Whatever approach you devise, remember that, especially in the elementary grades, word study, word recognition, and reading fluency are absolutely essential to the program's success. But equally important, word recognition and reading fluency should be balanced with instruction and practice in the other essential areas of reading.

In Conclusion

This book is aimed at helping teachers develop critical competencies in teaching word recognition and reading fluency. Word recognition and reading fluency are necessary but not sufficient competencies for proficient reading. Teachers of reading must teach other competencies, and they should provide time for students to engage in authentic reading and writing. A balanced approach, one that provides instructional emphasis to all important areas of reading, is required and one that we subscribe to in this book.

This book, then, deals with only one important part of a larger literacy framework. Please keep this in mind as you read. Our hope is that, through reading and applying these ideas, you will be able to provide your students with the very best, state of the art, instruction in decoding words and reading with exceptional fluency. And that proficiency in word recognition and fluency will provide for your students one important step toward successful, life-long, and meaningful reading.

References

Chall, J. S. 1967. *Learning to Read: The Great Debate*. New York: McGraw-Hill.

Cunningham, P. M., D. P. Hall, and M. Defee, 1991. Non-Ability Grouped, Multilevel Instruction: A Year in a First Grade Classroom. *The Reading Teacher*, 44: 566–571.

Cunningham, P. M., D. P. Hall, and M. Defee, 1998. Nonability-Grouped, Multilevel Instruction: Eight Years Later. *The Reading Teacher*, 51: 652–664.

Raphael, T. E., and S. I. McMahon, 1994. Book Club: An Alternative Framework for Reading Instruction. *The Reading Teacher*, 48: 102–116.

Spiegel, D. L. 1998. Silver Bullets, Babies, and Bath Water: Literature Response Groups in a Balanced Literacy Program. *The Reading Teacher*, 52: 114–124.

Stahl, S. A., A. M. Duffy-Hester, and K. A. M. Stahl, 1998. Theory and Research Into Practice: Everything You Wanted to Know About Phonics (but were afraid to ask). *Reading Research Quarterly*, 33: 338–355.

2 BASIC CONCEPTS AND TERMINOLOGY

"I have to admit, sometimes I get mixed up about all the jargon and terms surrounding reading and I know my fellow teachers do also," says Julia, a reading specialist in an elementary school. "Occasionally I will get into a conversation with some other teachers and the discussion will turn to some reading skill or element such as digraphs. Although digraphs is the topic, diphthongs and blends are provided as examples of digraphs. Boy! It's confusing. I don't think students need to know all the special vocabulary we use for reading instruction, but I think I should. How else can we talk about these things unless we agree on what they are and what they mean?"

Our colleague Julia is absolutely correct. Any discussion of issues related to phonics, word recognition, and reading fluency needs to begin with a presentation and understanding of the basic concepts and terminology that frame the phonics, word recognition, and reading fluency. Although these concepts may not be well known by those outside of literacy education, it is imperative for reading teachers and reading specialists to have a language that will allow productive interchange of ideas about issues related to phonics, word recognition, and reading fluency. With this in mind, we will lay a foundation for our presentation by identifying and defining some concepts that are essential to any detailed understanding of phonics, word recognition, and reading fluency. In developing our definitions, we relied heavily on Harris and Hodges' *The Literacy Dictionary*, (1995), as well as our own instructional experience and the experience of our colleagues involved in teaching children to read.

Affix A meaningful combination of letters that can be added to a base word in order to alter the meaning or grammatical function. Prefixes and suffixes are types of affixes.

Prefix An affix that is added in front of a base word to change the meaning (e.g., *predetermine*, *disallow*).

Suffix An affix that is added to the end of a base word to change the meaning or grammatical category of a word (e.g., *reading*, *instrumental*, *actor*).

Balanced Literacy Instruction Literacy instruction that is marked by an equal emphasis on the nurturing of reading through authentic reading experiences with authentic reading materials and more direct instruction in strategies and skills needed for successful reading. It is a "decision-making approach through which the teacher makes thoughtful choices each day about the best way to help each child become a better reader and writer. A balanced approach is not constrained by or reactive to a particular philosophy. It is responsive to new issues while maintaining what research has already shown to be effective" (Spiegel, 1998, p. 116).

Consonants Refers to both letters and sounds. Consonant sounds represent all the letters of the alphabet except the vowels, *a, e, i, o, u* and sometimes *y* and *w*. The letters and letter combinations (blends and digraphs) that represent consonants do so with fairly good correspondence, especially at the beginning of words and syllables.

Consonant Blends Two or three consonants grouped together in which the sound of each of the consonants is retained (e.g., *bl, cl, pr, tr, sm, st, scr, str*).

Consonant Digraphs Two or more consonants grouped together produce one sound. That sound can be a new sound not represented by any other letter or letter combination (*that*), a sound represented by one of the grouped letters (*gnu*), or a sound represented by a letter not present in the group (*phone*).

Context The linguistic environment. For word recognition, context refers to the meaning that precedes and follows words that are analyzed. Readers can use the context or meaning of a passage to help decode unknown words.

Decode To analyze graphic symbols (letters in the form of written words and sentences) into their oral representation and meaning. Synonymous with word identification and word recognition.

Fluency To read expressively, meaningfully, in appropriate syntactic units (phrases, clauses), at appropriate rates, and without word recognition difficulty.

Morpheme The smallest unit of meaning in oral and written language (e.g., The word *cars* contains two morphemes—*car*, an automobile, and *s*, meaning more than one.)

Onset The part of a syllable that contains any consonants that precede the vowel (e.g., *b* in bat, *sl* in slack, *t* and *p* in temper, *c* and *t* in carton). The sound-symbol relationship between onset letters and sounds is quite reliable.

Orthography Symbols or letters in a writing system. Spelling is part of orthography.

Phoneme The smallest unit of speech that affects meaning of words (e.g., *b* in book vs. *k* in cook).

Phonics A method of teaching that emphasizes the sound-symbol (letter) relationships that exist in a language. Phonics is usually employed in the beginning stages of reading instruction.

Phonogram Also known as a *rime* or *word family*. See rime.

Rime Also known as a *phonogram* or *word family*. The part of a syllable that contains the vowel and any consonants that follow the vowel. Letter rimes are easily recognized and are consistent in the sound or sound combination they represent.

Schwa The sound "uh" made by the unaccented syllables in a multisyllabic word (e.g., the vowel sound in the second syllable of *secret*, the vowel sound in the first syllable of *about*). As with many technical elements of language and reading, knowledge of the schwa is not essential to reading success.

Semantics The study of meaning in language. Semantic knowledge can aid readers in decoding unknown words in context.

Sight Word A word that is recognized immediately as a whole and without detailed analysis. Sight words are recognized at sight or automatically.

Syllable A group of letters that are produced as a unit and contain one and only one vowel sound. Some basic syllable patterns are described below.

CVC (also known as closed syllable)	Short vowel sound	cat, sit, shot back, myth
CV (also know as open syllable)	Long vowel sound	be, because, she, try, total, label
CVVC	Often long vowel sound	beak, sail, coat
VCe	Long vowel sound	late, bite, tote
Cle		maple, babble, stable

In addition to the information listed above, there are several patterns that guide readers in dividing longer words into individual syllables. These patterns include:

base word – base word (compound words)	cowboy	cow/boy
prefix – base word – suffix	unfit	un/fit
	retool	re/tool
	basement	base/ment
V/CV	bacon	ba/con
	open	o/pen
	baby	ba/by
VC/CV	temper	tem/per
	carton	car/ton
	ginger	gin/ger

Syntax The pattern of word order in sentences, clauses, and phrases and its effect on meaning. Syntactic knowledge can aid readers in decoding unknown words in context.

Vowels Refers to sounds and letters. The sounds represented by the letters *a, e, i, o, u*. The letter *y* can serve as vowel when it is not in the initial position of a word (e.g., *why*). The *w* can function as a vowel when it follows a vowel (e.g., *cow*). Vowels are the most prominent sound in and defining feature of a syllable. There is not a strong one-to-one correspondence between vowel sounds and letters. Vowel sounds can be represented in a variety of ways with the vowel letters.

Long vowel sounds are associated with the letter name of a vowel. Long vowel sounds are often marked by a macron (-).

make
beak
pie
broke
unit

Short vowel sounds are another group of sounds associated with the vowel letters. The short vowel is marked by a brev (˘), and the sound of each vowel letter is found in the following words:

bad
bed
bid
body
bud

Vowel Digraphs Two vowels grouped together in which one sound, usually the long sound of one of the vowel letters is heard (e.g., *bead, boat, beet, bay, sew, die*).

Vowel Diphthongs Also known as vowel blends. Diphthongs are sounds made up of the blending of two vowel sounds (e.g., *oi* as in boil, *oy* as in boy, *ou* as in ouch, *ow* as in how, *au* as in caught, and *aw* as in flaw).

R Controlled Vowels Occur when a vowel is followed by the letter *r* which alters the sound of the vowel (e.g., *star, her, sir, for, burr*).

L Controlled Vowels Occur when the letter *a* is followed by an *l* producing a particular sound as in *shallow* and *tall*.

Word Family Also known as *phonogram* or *rime*. See rime.

Word Recognition The process of determining the pronunciation and meaning of words in print. Same as *decoding* and *word identification*.

In Conclusion

These definitions are helpful to us because they establish meaning and a common language for terms we use throughout the book. The list is helpful for you because it focuses your thinking in instructionally productive ways. As with so many other areas of education, teachers need to know these terms and their underlying concepts, but students do not. Indeed, many people have probably become excellent readers despite lacking definitions for *macron, dipthong,* or *schwa,* and many other technical terms. Teachers need the labels; readers need to read!

REFERENCES

Harris, T. and R. Hodges (eds.). 1995. *The Literacy Dictionary.* Newark, DE: International Reading Association.

Spiegel, D.L. 1998. Silver Bullets, Babies, and Bath Water: Literature Response Groups in a Balanced Literacy Program. *The Reading Teacher*, 52: 114–124.

3

USING AUTHENTIC TEXTS TO LEARN NEW WORDS AND DEVELOP FLUENCY

It was a rainy vacation day at the beach. Three-year-old Annie took a nap; her mom, aunt Nancy, and uncle each grabbed a book and were engrossed in their reading when Annie awoke. After she rubbed the sleep from her eyes, she began trying to find a playmate. She asked her mom to play Barbies; her mom said, "Sure. Just let me finish this chapter." So she asked Nancy to do watercolors with her; Nancy's reply was the same. Annie looked around at the adults reading, went upstairs to her room, and soon came back with Bill Martin's *Brown Bear, Brown Bear, What Do You See?* (1983). She hopped up on the couch, opened her book, and began reading aloud.

Annie had heard *Brown Bear* many times and had read it along with her mother and others in the family. The story's pattern was easy for her to recall. As a result she could read the words of the story simply by remembering previous readings and by looking at the pictures for clues. For Annie, *Brown Bear* was a supportive and encouraging text—supportive and encouraging of her word recognition as well as her understanding of the story.

Support and *encouragement* are important concepts for readers of all ages, but particularly for those just beginning to learn to read. They describe the instructional environment, the teacher's role, and especially the materials that beginners should read. Effective materials for beginners support and encourage them in their quest for meaning. Authentic texts that are predictable, like *Brown Bear*, work well because they enable the beginning reader to predict, sample, and confirm—in short, do all the things a mature reader does. For our purposes in this book, an added benefit of authentic predictable text is that its familiar, dependable context provides a rich resource for word learning. Moreover, because predictable books are easy for children to read, they often read them repeatedly, which enhances fluency development.

Materials are predictable when children can easily determine what will come next—both what the author is going to say and how it will be said. Language-experience texts (see Chapter 11) are predictable because they reflect children's own experiences and are written in their own words. We de-

14

scribe many other sources of predictable text in this chapter, and we also offer some suggestions for using predictable texts to foster word learning. First, however, we explore some conceptions (and misconceptions) about what makes material easy to read.

WHAT IS EASY TO READ?

Few would quibble with the assertion that young readers need access to texts that they can easily read. The issue of what makes something easy to read, however, is a bit of a problem. For many years, materials used to teach young children to read were highly structured; vocabulary was tightly controlled. These materials were based on the premise that learning would be easy if children encountered the same words again and again in their reading, and if they were exposed to new words and sentence structures gradually and in a predetermined sequence.

At least intuitively, these ideas make a certain amount of sense; some professionals still argue for this type of early reading material. Others, however (and we include ourselves here), see faults with this "go, Spot, go" type of writing. Simple language patterns are usually unfamiliar to children because they do not represent the natural oral language they hear in daily life; moreover, the vocabulary repetition is unnatural (when was the last time you said, "Look. Oh look, look, look" in conversation?). Stories written to fit a formula of certain words and restricted sentence patterns usually lack literary merit. For these reasons, among others, many educators of young children looked for alternatives. Pattern books and other authentic, predictable texts provide one good answer.

Pattern books and other forms of predictable text contain distinct language patterns that make them easy for children to learn to read. Rather than reflecting the assumption that short sentences and frequently repeated vocabulary make materials easy to read, these texts are easy to read because of their naturally repetitive language, cumulating events, use of rhythm or rhyme, or some combination of these factors. Moreover, the repetitive and predictable language patterns are an enjoyable way for children to play with sounds, words, phrases, and sentences.

TYPES OF AUTHENTIC TEXT

In addition to dictated texts (see Chapter 11), several other types of authentic texts provide the support that beginning readers need to learn words, indeed, to learn to read. Below we suggest a variety that we recommend for use with beginning readers.

PATTERN BOOKS

The children's literature market has grown considerably over the last decade or so, due in part to teachers' interests in using authentic literature for instruction. This is good news for teachers who work with beginning readers because many wonderful, new children's pattern books are published each year. These predictable books are easy for children to read because they quickly catch on to the pattern that the author used to write the book. Patterns usually involve repetitive language and/or repeating or cumulative episodes (as in *The House That Jack Built* or *I Know an Old Lady*). Rhyme may also be used. Figure 3.1 provides titles of dozens of pattern books, all of which are appropriate for use with beginning readers and welcome additions to classroom libraries.

Many of these titles are available from children's book clubs in big book format, so teachers might strive to collect sets of children's favorites that include both a big book version and several copies of little books. After the whole group works with the big book version, copies of the little books are eagerly sought for independent reading.

Some teachers also make their own big books. Materials needed for making a big book include chart paper (18" x 20" or larger) for the pages, stiff cardboard such as poster board for covers, a wide felt-tip marker for printing the text, materials for illustrations, and something, such as metal shower rings, to bind the finished product together. Individual pages might be laminated so that they will withstand repeated readings. Print should be large and legible from at least 15 feet.

Children can prepare illustrations for the pages as an independent activity. The first step in this process is for the teacher and students to read the story several times in order to decide where the page breaks should be. Pairs of learners can then read a portion of the text to be illustrated, talk about illustration possibilities, decide, and illustrate. All this activity involves reading and rereading the text—excellent fluency practice and a wonderful opportunity for word learning; children must also comprehend their individual pages in order to create appropriate illustrations. Moreover, children's pride of ownership and accomplishment are a joy to see.

SONGS, FINGER PLAYS, AND OTHER RHYMES

These are already staples in most primary classrooms. To make them into material for reading instruction, the teacher simply needs to make text copies of them, make the copies available for children to see, and use them instructionally. Since children already know the words, they are particularly useful for developing concepts about print (e.g., What is a word?) and for learning sight words.

Some songs are used repeatedly throughout the school year, like "Happy Birthday to You." The teacher can make a copy of this song leaving a blank where the child's name is to be sung: Happy birthday dear _____. Happy birthday to you. The birthday child can create a name card to be affixed at the appropriate spot. After the class sings to the birthday child, the teacher can use the text of the song to help children learn new words.

Because of the repetitive nature of the language and the accompanying actions, children likewise learn finger plays rapidly. These, too, become reading material as soon as the teacher creates a large version of the rhyme for children to read and study. Some finger plays and other childhood rhymes have many stanzas, but they tend to be highly repetitive. A generic chart containing

Adams, Pam. 1974. *This Old Man*. New York: Grosset & Dunlap.

Aliki. 1989. *My Five Senses*. New York: Crowell.

Allenberg, Janet, and Allan Allenberg. 1978. *Each Peach, Pear, Plum*. New York: Viking Press.

Astley, Judy. 1990. *When One Cat Woke Up*. New York: Dial.

Baer, Gene. 1989. *Thump, Thump, Rat-A-Tat-Tat*. New York: Harper & Row.

Barton, Byron. 1989. *Dinosaurs, Dinosaurs*. New York: Crowell.

Becker, John. 1973. *Seven Little Rabbits*. New York: Scholastic.

Brandenberg, Franz. 1989. *Aunt Nina, Good Night*. New York: Greenwillow.

Bridwell, Norman. 1983. *Clifford's ABC*. New York: Scholastic.

Brown, Margaret Wise. 1947. *Goodnight Moon*. New York: Harper & Row.

Brown, Margaret Wise. 1949/1999. *The Important Book*. New York: HarperCollins.

Brown, Ruth. 1981. *A Dark, Dark Tale*. New York: Dial.

Campbell, Rod. 1983. *Dear Zoo*. New York: Four Winds.

Carle, Eric. 1969. *The Very Hungry Caterpillar*. New York: Philomel.

Carlstrom, Nancy White. 1994. *What Would You Do if You Lived at the Zoo?* New York: Scholastic.

Carle, Eric. 1977. *The Grouchy Ladybug*. New York: Crowell.

Cowley, Joy. 1987a. *The Jigaree*. Bothell, WA: Wright Group.

Cowley, Joy. 1987b. *Mrs. Wishy-Washy*. Bothell, WA: Wright Group.

Emberley, Ed. 1974. *Klippity Klop*. Boston: Little, Brown.

Ets, Marie Hall. 1972. *Elephant in a Well*. New York: Viking.

Fox, Mem. 1992. *Hattie and the Fox*. New York: Bradbury.

Galdone, Paul. 1971. *Three Aesop Fox Fables*. New York: Seabury.

Galdone, Paul. 1973. *The Little Red Hen*. New York: Scholastic.

Galdone, Paul. 1984. *The Teeny Tiny Woman*. New York: Clarion.

Guarino, Deborah. 1989. *Is Your Mama a Llama?* New York: Scholastic.

Hennessy, B. G. 1990. *Jake Baked the Cake*. New York: Viking.

Hutchins, Pat. 1968. *Rosie's Walk*. New York: Macmillan.

Hutchins, Pat. 1971. *Titch*. New York: Collier.

Hutchins, Pat. 1972. *Good-Night Owl*. New York: Macmillan.

Hutchins, Pat. 1982. *1 Hunter*. New York: Greenwillow.

Hutchins, Pat. 1986. *The Doorbell Rang*. New York: Greenwillow.

Jonas, Ann. 1989. *Color Dance*. New York: Greenwillow.

Keats, Ezra Jack. 1971. *Over in the Meadow*. New York: Scholastic.

Kovalski, Maryann. 1987. *The Wheels on the Bus*. Boston: Little, Brown.

Kraus, Robert. 1970. *Whose Mouse Are You?* New York: Macmillan.

Langstaff, John. 1974. *Oh, A-Hunting We Will Go*. New York: Atheneum.

Martin, Bill. 1983. *Brown Bear, Brown Bear*. New York: Holt.

Martin, Bill. 1991. *Polar Bear, Polar Bear*. New York: Holt.

Figure 3.1
Predictable Pattern Books

McKissack, Patricia. 1986. *Who is Coming?* Chicago: Children's Press.

McKissack, Patricia, and Fredrick McKissack, 1988. *Constance Stumbles*. Chicago: Children's Press.

Numeroff, Laura Joffe. 1985. *If You Give a Mouse a Cookie*. New York: Harper & Row.

Numeroff, Laura Joffe. 1991. *If You Give a Moose a Muffin*. New York: HarperCollins.

Peek, Merle. 1985. *Mary Wore Her Red Dress*. New York: Clarion.

Raffi. 1987. *Down By the Bay*. New York: Crown.

Roffey, Maureen. 1988. *I Spy At the Zoo*. New York: Macmillan.

Rounds, Blen. 1989. *Old MacDonald Had a Farm*. Holiday.

Sendak, Maurice. 1962. *Chicken Soup and Rice*. New York: Williams.

Seuss, Dr. 1957. *The Cat in the Hat*. New York: Random House.

Seuss, Dr. 1965. *Green Eggs and Ham*. New York: Random House.

Shaw, Nancy. 1989a. *Sheep in a Jeep*. Boston: Houghton Mifflin.

Shaw, Nancy. 1989b. *Sheep on a Ship*. Boston: Houghton Mifflin.

Wager, J. 1971. *The Bus Ride*. New York: Scott, Foresman.

Wescott, Nadine Bernard. 1980. *I Know An Old Lady Who Swallowed a Fly*. Boston: Houghton Mifflin.

Wildsmith, Brian. 1982. *The Cat On the Mat*. Oxford, NY: Oxford University Press.

Williams, Sue. 1992. *I Went Walking*. Orlando, FL: Harcourt Brace Jovanovich.

Wood, Audrey. 1984. *The Napping House*. New York: Harcourt Brace Jovanovich.

Wondriska, William. 1970. *All the Animals Were Angry*. New York: Holt, Rinehart and Winston.

Zemach, Margot. 1965. *The Teeny Tiny Woman*. New York: Scholastic.

Zemach, Margot. 1976. *Hush, Little Baby*. New York: Dutton.

Figure 3.1 (*continued*)
Predictable Pattern Books

most of the stanza can be prepared, and word cards can be used to differentiate the stanzas. In the rhyme below, for example, the beginning blank is completed with word cards containing the numbers ten through one:

_____ little monkeys jumping on the bed.
One fell off and bumped its head.
Mama called the doctor, and the doctor said,
"No more monkeys jumping on the bed!"

As children chant the verse, they need to read the number cards to decide which goes next. So, they learn the number words by sight.

Jump rope rhymes and other childhood chants are likewise helpful for word learning. Teachers should keep their ears open while children are on the playground; opportunities for reading material will abound!

NURSERY RHYMES AND POEMS

Many Mother Goose rhymes and other childhood poems are excellent choices for authentic, predictable texts. These short poems with strong rhythms and clear rhymes are easy for children to learn. As noted in Chapter 14, these texts are also quite useful for fluency activities. Teachers should have ready access to poetry anthologies. Poetry reading should be a daily routine in classrooms.

ENVIRONMENTAL PRINT

Children learn a great deal from their surroundings. Print in the environment, both outside of school and in the classroom, is a great source for incidental word learning. Children begin to recognize print in real-life contexts, such as road signs, fast food logos, and the packaging on their favorite toys, at a very early age, as anyone who lives with a preschooler knows. To recognize environmental print, children appear to attend to shapes, colors, and logos, as well as print. Recognition of decontextualized print comes later, usually when children enter school (Lomax and McGee 1987). Nevertheless, children's strong interest in environmental print makes it a good choice for instructional focus.

Although simply seeing environmental print and other predictable texts may be too indirect to foster precise word learning (Stahl and Murray 1993), teachers can focus children's attention on the words in environmental print messages fairly easily. For example, children can look through old newspapers, magazines, and junk mail to find material to put into theme books about environmental print (Christie, Enz, and Vukelich 1997). Theme books can be created for soft drinks, sneakers, pizza, fast food, cereal, cookies, professional sports teams, and many other common objects. To encourage focus on the words and not just the logos, teachers can insert pages into the theme books that contain the words alone in standard print or type format. Many children enjoy guessing which words belong with which logos.

Labels, lists, schedules, directions, messages, and other forms of environmental print inside the classroom can also foster word learning. In general, we recommend using as much functional print as possible in the classroom. Children see and often must use these words daily, so they naturally learn them. Moreover, such a print-rich classroom shows children rather directly about the functions of writing and the value of the written word.

USING AUTHENTIC TEXT

Probably the best way to introduce authentic, predictable texts to children is through what Holdaway (1979) calls the "shared book experience." This idea was inspired by what happens when parents and children read bedtime stories; stories and pictures are shared in a comfortable, relaxed manner. Translating this experience into classroom practice involves preparing an enlarged version of the story, song, poem, or other text to be read, since it is critical for the children to see the words as the teacher reads them. Teachers may use chart paper to make these enlarged texts. We recommend making two large copies of texts to be used, so that one can be kept fresh for reading at another time and the other can be used for the word study activities described below. We also recommend that teachers prepare smaller versions of the texts so that each child can have an individual copy. Many teachers try to leave room for children's illustrations on these individual sheets.

In general, pattern books or other types of authentic text should be read to children several times to allow children to learn them thoroughly. The next stage is to read the text with children in choral or antiphonal fashion (see Chapter 14). Many teachers pause before reading repetitive portions of the text; the children chime in, usually with gusto, to say the parts that they know. Finally children are invited to read the text alone. (See Chapter 14 for other ideas for repeated readings.) All this can be done over several days, if desired.

After children have learned the text, the teacher can begin to direct their attention to individual sentences, phrases, words, letters, and letter combinations. This natural progression from whole to part, which we have also described in other chapters, allows children to discover how smaller units of language work without distorting or disrupting the process of reading and enjoying the entire text. Moreover, it's easy to help children see the value of what they learn about words and sounds because the new knowledge can be easily related back to the text. Thus, transfer, a critical element in word recognition instruction, is facilitated.

GUESSING GAMES

Texts can be used for instruction that focuses on the conventions of print and other aspects of word learning in a guessing game format. For example, the teacher can ask questions like these:

- Where's the title? How many words are in the title? Where's the first word in the title? Where's the last word? Who can circle all the words in the title?
- Where's the first word in the story? Where's the last word? Where's the first word in line ___? How many words are in the first sentence? How many words are in the last line?
- Where does the first sentence begin? Where does it end? How can we tell where a sentence begins and where one ends? How many sentences are in our text? How many lines?
- Who can find a [letter] in the text? Are there more [letter]s? Who can find a capital [letter]? A lower case [letter]?
- Who can find the word [a word with a featured word family]? How many words that contain the ___ family are there in our text? What are they?
- Who can find a word that has a [phonic element]? How many words that contain [phonic element] are there in our text? What are they?
- Who can find a two-syllable word? How many two-syllable words are there in our text?

Lessons like this focus children's attention on the parts of written language—lines, sentences, words, letters, and phonic elements. Note too the variation in difficulty of the guessing-game questions. Some focus on very beginning print concepts (e.g., Who can circle all the words in the title? Who can find a lower case [letter]?), and others are more advanced (e.g., How many words that contain [phonic element] are there in our text? Who can find a two-syllable word?) Children enjoy this sort of guessing game; it's also an easy way to differentiate instruction to accommodate different ability levels among individual children.

Children can use markers to circle or underline their responses to these questions on the second copy of the text. They can point with their fingers or use a pointer. Some teachers use *word whoppers,* which are fly swatters with rectangles cut in them. Words of interest to children (or the teacher) can also be added to students' word banks (see Chapter 9). However children respond, working with familiar and meaningful text provides support and allows them to discover relationships between the parts and the whole. And the multiple readings that occur naturally support both word learning and fluency development.

WORD SORTS

Word sort activities (see Chapter 9) can also be used to direct children's attention to the language of the texts. Consider, for example, the Mother Goose rhyme:

Jelly on a plate, jelly on a plate
Wibble, wobble, wibble, wobble
Jelly on a plate.

Sausage in a pan, sausage in a pan
Frizzle, frazzle, frizzle, frazzle
Sausage in a pan.

Baby on the floor, baby on the floor
Pick him up, pick him up
Baby on the floor.

After the poem is enjoyed for its own sake, its words can be used to focus children's attention on the sounds of long and short A. The teacher can ask children to identify and perhaps circle or underline all the words containing the letter A in the poem. Next, in pairs or groups of three, they can complete a closed word sort in which they put each A word into a category, as shown below:

Long A	Short A	Other Sounds of A
plate	pan	sausage
baby	frazzle	

After children become accustomed to these word sort activities, they can be challenged to make their own versions of word sorts for classmates to play. The *Jelly* poem could also be used to sort for short *I*, for example.

COPY CHANGE

Individuals or small groups can make their own versions of authentic, predictable texts, especially pattern books or poems. This writing activity is often called *copy change* because children use the author's copy as a framework but change it to reflect their own ideas. Simple pattern books, like *Brown Bear*, work well for introducing children to copy change. The teacher can simply read the book several times to children, eventually asking them to identify what the author "does over and over." Some teachers write children's ideas on the chalkboard so that they can refer to them later. Others prepare sheets with some of the text provided for children. Using the *Brown Bear* example, such a sheet might say:

_____, _____ what do you see?
I see a _____ looking at me.

Then, using the author's framework, individuals or groups create their own versions of the original text. Children may make individual books or class books of their copy changes. In one first grade class, for example, children wrote about a variety of topics using the *Brown Bear* format:

Little mouse, little mouse, what do you see?
I see a hungry cat looking at me.

Pitcher, pitcher, what do you see?
I see the batter looking at me.

Noisy kid, noisy kid, what do you see?
I see the lunch lady looking at me.

Students thought about rhyming words and syllables as they wrote their own books. They also practiced writing sight words. Most important, they enjoyed the entire lesson and celebrated their authorship.

Copy change activities encourage careful reading and listening so that children can discover, appreciate, and use the author's word choice and language patterns. They are also particularly helpful practice for words and word parts because as they think about what to write, children must analyze the structure of the original text as well as the features of the words, phrases, and sentences used by the original author (Leu and Kinzer 1999). For example, when Jenny reads and transforms *Alexander and the Terrible, Horrible, No Good, Very Bad Day* (Viorst 1972) into *Jenny and Her Awful, Miserable, Junky, Absolutely Rotten Day*, she has to think about and spell more words descriptive of bad days. Best of all, students find it fun and satisfying to write stories or poems that are similar to those they have read and to share these new stories or poems with their classmates and families. Practiced reading and presentation of their rewritten stories from the Author's Chair promote fluent, expressive reading.

OTHER INDEPENDENT ACTIVITIES

Copy change texts can be illustrated as an independent activity. Children might also rewrite or type their texts, cut them apart into sentence strips, paste sentences on separate pieces of paper, and make their own books. As an intermediate activity, students can be asked to read and sequence their sentence strips. Figure 3.2 shows an example of an individual book Kevin made of the Mother Goose rhyme, *One, two, three, four, five.* Cloze exercises (see Chapter 10) are also effective.

All authentic texts that are read and studied should be available for children to reread during independent reading or sustained silent reading time. Because of the support they received during the repeated reading and study of the texts, children can usually read them independently. They take great pride

One, two, three, four, five

Once I caught a fish alive.

Figure 3.2
Individual Page from Mother Goose Rhyme

in this accomplishment and are generally interested in reading the texts again and again. This success fosters positive attitudes toward reading and helps children develop good concepts of themselves as readers. Children also learn about the conventions of print, acquire sight vocabulary, practice word recognition strategies, and develop fluency as they practice with the texts.

JUST GOOD BOOKS

Finally, we recommend good stories and lots of reading for students. Not only do good stories prove students with great opportunities for practicing their phonics and word study skills and strategies, they also make reading satisfying and exciting for students—they help to get students hooked on reading and hooked on books. We know that students who are voracious readers tend to be our best readers. A recent large scale international study of reading, for example, found that the amount of reading students did at home and the amount of reading students did in school were two of the three most powerful predictors of reading achievement for primary and middle school students (Postlethwaite and Ross 1992). Reading teachers who work with students on phonics and word study need to know the very best reading materials available for students.

How do you find the very best books for your students? With the thousands of books that are published every year, it's difficult for teachers to become experts in instruction and experts in children's literature at the same time. Fortunately, teachers can use several resources to help find great books for students to read. The primary resources, we think, are media specialists or librarians and other veteran teachers. These professionals are filled with knowledge about the very best books for students, books that they have found through their own experience turn kids on to reading. Media specialists and librarians, in particular, are trained to find books that students will enjoy. They read the professional materials that review, rate, and recommend books for children. If you are a new or young teacher be sure to ask your school librarian and teacher colleagues to recommend books and other reading material for the students you are teaching. You will find them most accommodating.

Book awards are another good resource for finding good books for children. The Caldecott (for illustrations in books) and Newbery (for best story) are two of the most prestigious awards in the United States for children's literature. Most school librarians or children's librarians in public libraries should have a list of books that have won these awards. But don't limit yourself only to the Caldecott and Newbery winners. Caldecott and Newbery Honor Books are books that didn't win the award but still were of exceptional merit. Every year there are several books that achieve Honor status. Again, the local librarian should have access to these books. We have found that some of our (and our children's) favorite books are the Honor books. Many states, also, have book awards. Children love reading books that have been recognized by state groups for their excellence.

Professional journals often provide valuable information for teachers in search of good books. *The Reading Teacher*, published by the International Reading Association (IRA) (1-800-336-READ, www.reading.org), is one of the best. Many elementary and middle schools receive it (if your school doesn't receive *RT* ask your principal to get a subscription or two for your school). Published monthly during the school year, *RT* always features a review column, written by children's literature and reading experts, on recently published books for students. In addition to the regular column, *RT* also publishes *Children's Choices* (October issue) and *Teachers' Choices* (November issue). *Children's Choices* reports on recently published books that children across the country rated as their favorites. *Teachers' Choices* reports on favorite books of recent vintage from the teachers' point of view. More recently, the March issue of *RT* includes *Notable Books for a Global Society,* the best books of the previous year as selected by the IRA Special Interest Group on Literature and Reading.

The World Wide Web is another outstanding resource for learning about children's books. On-line bookstores such as <u>amazon.com</u>, <u>barnesandnoble.com</u>, or <u>borders.com</u> offer synopses and sometimes book reviews of selected titles. In fact, children write and publish reviews of books they have read on these web sites. Another handy feature of these sites is their search capability. At <u>amazon.com</u>, for example, a teacher can select topics and age ranges to search available titles.

General sites for children's literature, such as Ask the Author <u>http://www.ipl.org/Youth/AskAuthor</u> and the Book Nook <u>http://I-Site.on.ca/booknook/html</u> abound, as do more focused resources, such as the Laura Ingalls Wilder Home Page <u>http://webpages.marshall.edu/ irby1/laura.html</u> or a collection of Grimm Brothers fairy tales <u>ftp://ftp.std.com/obi/Fairy.Tales/Grimm/</u>. The searchable Recommended Trade Books site at the Ohio Literacy Resource Center <u>http://literacy.kent.edu</u> offers summaries and teaching ideas for hundreds of picture books that have been approved for use with older readers. Whether used for book selection, teaching ideas, or direct access by children, the Web contains an extraordinary wealth of information.

Texts and Phonics

Our main reason for selecting or recommending books for children should be their literary quality. Is the book a good read? Will the reader find the text engaging? Will the material lead students to want to read more? The strategies we listed in the preceding section of this chapter are some superb ways to find books and reading material of exceptional merit for students. As they read this type of material, students will be exercising their phonics and word study strategies in real life and satisfying contexts.

However, since this book deals specifically with the issue of phonics and word study, it is important and relevant for us to mention that there are good books that also do a good job of focusing on some phonics element or pattern. Listed in Figure 3.3 (adapted from Trachtenburg 1990) are books that highlight particular vowel sounds, long and short. After having received instruction in a particular vowel sound, introducing students to books associated with the relevant vowel would provide students with immediate practice in using their new found knowledge in real reading.

Short *a*

Flack, M. *Angus and the Cat.* Doubleday, 1931.

Griffith, H. *Alex and the Cat.* Greenwillow, 1982.

Kent, J. *The Fat Cat.* Scholastic, 1971.

Most, B. *There's an Ant in Anthony.* William Morrow, 1980.

Robins, J. *Addie Meets Max.* Harper & Row, 1985.

Schmidt, K. *The Gingerbread Man.* Scholastic, 1985.

Seuss, Dr. *The Cat in the Hat.* Random House, 1957.

Long *a*

Aaredema, V. *Bringing the Rain to Kapiti Plain.* Dial, 1981.

Bang, M. *The Paper Crane.* Greenwillow, 1985.

Blume, J. *The Pain and the Great One.* Bradbury, 1974.

Byars, B. *The Lace Snail.* Viking, 1975.

Henkes, K. *Sheila Rae, the Brave.* Greenwillow, 1987.

Hines, A. *Taste the Raindrops.* Greenwillow, 1983.

Short *e*

Aliki. *Hello! Good-bye.* Greenwillow, 1996.

Ets, M. *Elephant in a Well.* Viking, 1972.

Galdone, P. *The Little Red Hen.* Scholastic, 1973.

Ness, E. *Yeck Eck.* E.P. Dutton, 1974.

Shecter, B. *Hester the Jester,* Harper & Row. 1977.

Thayer, J. *I Don't Believe in Elves.* William Morrow, 1975.

Long *e*

Brown, M. W. *Four Fur Feet.* Dell, 1990.

Keller, H. *Ten Sleepy Sheep.* Greenwillow, 1983.

Martin, B. *Brown Bear, Brown Bear, What Do You See?* Henry Holt, 1967.

Oppenheim, J. *Have You Seen Trees?* Young Scott Books, 1967.

Reiser, L. *Beachfeet.* Greenwillow, 1996.

Shaw, N. *Sheep in a Jeep.* Houghton Mifflin, 1986.

Shaw, N. *Sheep Out to Eat.* Houghton Mifflin, 1995.

Thomas, P. *"Stand Back," said the Elephant, "I'm Going to Sneeze!"* Lothrop, Lee & Shepard, 1971.

Short *i*

Browne, A. *Willy the Wimp.* Alfred A Knopf. 1984.

Hutchins, P. *Titch.* Macmillan, 1971.

Kessler, C. *Konte Chameleon: Fine, Fine, Fine.* Boyds Mills, 1987.

Lewis T. *Call for Mr. Sniff.* Harper & Row, 1981.

Lobel, A. *Small Pig.* Harper & Row, 1969.

McPhail, D. *Fix-It.* E.P. Dutton, 1984.

Patrick, G. *This Is* . . . Carolrhoda, 1970.

Robins, J. *My Brother, Will.* Greenwillow, 1986.

Figure 3.3
Trade Books That Repeat Phonic Elements

Long *i*

Cameron, J. *If Mice Could Fly.* Atheneum, 1979.
Cole, S. *When the Tide Is Low.* Lothrop, Lee & Shepard, 1985.
Gelman, R. *Why Can't I Fly?* Scholastic, 1976.
Hazen, B. *Tight Times.* Viking, 1979.

Short *o*

Dunrea, O. *Mogwogs on the March!* Holiday House, 1985.
Emberley, B. *Drummer Hoff.* Prentice-Hall, 1967.
McKissack, P. *Flossie & the Fox.* Dial, 1986.
Rice, E. "The Frog and the Ox" from *Once in a Wood.* Greenwillow, 1979.
Seuss, Dr. *Fox in Socks.* Random House, 1965.

Long *o*

Cole, B. *The Giant's Toe.* Farrar, Straus, & Giroux, 1986.
Gerstein, M. *Roll Over!* Crown, 1984.
Johnston, T. *The Adventures of Mole and Troll.* G.P. Putnam's Sons, 1972.
Johnston, T. *Night Noises and Other Mole and Troll Stories.* G. P. Putnam's Sons, 1977.
Hamanaka, S. *The Hokey Pokey.* Simon Schuster, 1997.
Pinczes, E. *One Hundred Hungry Ants.* Houghton Mifflin, 1993.
Shulevitz, U. *One Monday Morning.* Charles Scribner's Sons, 1967.

Short *u*

Cooney, N. *Donald Says Thumbs Down.* G.P. Putnam's Sons, 1987.
Lorenz, L. *Big Gus and Little Gus.* Prentice-Hall, 1982.
Marshall, J. *The Cut-Ups.* Viking Kestrel, 1984.
Udry, J. *Thump and Plunk.* Harper & Row, 1981.

Long *u*

Lobel, A. *The Troll Music.* Harper & Row, 1966.
Medearis, A. *Rum-a-Tum-Tum.* Holiday House, 1997.
Segal, L. *Tell Me a Trudy.* Farrar Straus, & Giroux, 1977.

Books and Poetry Anthologies that Feature Several Vowel and Consonant Sounds

Carle, E. *Eric Carle's Animals Animals.* New York, Philomel, 1992.
de Regniers, B.S. et al. *Sing a Song of Popcorn: Every Child's Book of Poems.* Scholastic, 1988.
Lansky, B. *Poetry Party.* Meadowbrook, 1996.
Lansky, B. *The New Adventures of Mother Goose: Gentle Rhymes for Happy Times.* Atheneum, 1999.
Lobel, A. (ed). *The Arnold Lobel Book of Mother Goose.* Knopf, 1997.
Moss, L. *Zin! Zin! Zin! A Violin.* Simon and Schuster, 1995.

Figure 3.3 (*continued*)
Trade Books That Repeat Phonic Elements

Prelutsky, J. *The Random House Book of Poetry for Children.* Random House, 1983.

Slier, D. (ed). *Make a Joyful Sound: Poems for Children by African-American Poets.* Checkerboard Press, 1990.

Adapted from Trachtenburg, P. (1990). Using Children's Literature to Enhance Phonics Instruction. *The Reading Teacher, 43:* 648–654.

Figure 3.3 *(continued)*
Trade Books that Repeat Phonic Elements

DICTATED TEXTS

We are great believers in the potential of language experience activities for nurturing students' reading development. Language experience for young readers begins with an experience, individual or shared (see Chapter 11). That experience is discussed with classmates and teacher, and followed with the child or children dictating a story about the experience to the teacher, who immediately transcribes the oral text onto paper that can be seen by all participants, or onto a computer screen using large fonts that enable easy viewing.

That dictated and written text then becomes the material for instruction. Students can read such texts because they are based upon students' own experience and taken from students' own language. Children see themselves as writers as well as readers.

In addition, dictated texts contain a variety of phonic and structural word patterns because they are derived from natural language. It is not difficult, then, for teachers to use these dictated texts to provide focused instruction and practice in decoding skills and strategies being studied. If, for example, teacher and students are studying a particular beginning letter (onset), students can search their dictated texts for examples of words that contain that element. Similarly, students can examine dictated texts for other phonic elements or patterns that may be under study at a particular time. Students can read these texts, and the additional and repeated readings that occur when students read their dictated stories for targeted elements or patterns will also build their sight vocabulary and proficiency in reading fluency.

TEXTS AND READING FLUENCY

Fluency is that bridge between word recognition and comprehension. It is marked by quick, accurate, and expressive oral reading that is well understood by the reader. Fluency is a relative concept—all readers are more or less fluent depending upon the nature and difficulty of the text being read. Although you are probably a fairly good reader, we could easily make you a disfluent reader by asking you to read something highly technical for which you have little background, perhaps an essay on nuclear physics or a legal contract.

Thus, when teaching reading fluency, we recommend that the texts that teachers employ not be overly difficult. Predictable stories and texts, stories drawn out of a series (e.g. Cynthia Rylant's *Henry and Mudge* series or Marc Brown's *Arthur* series), stories around a given theme, stories with a minimum of difficult words or grammar, and stories that are not too long are among those that we recommend for building reading fluency. Once students become familiar with a book that is part of series, for example, their familiarity with the author's style, the book's characters and setting, and the general plot of the story will enable them to read succeeding books in the series with greater fluency and understanding. Passages that are clearly difficult for students may require support from the teacher as in the teacher reading the beginning of the text to the students, reading the text more than once, or reading with a partner.

Among the instructional strategies we have advocated for fluency development is repeated readings. Because repeated readings, by its very nature, requires students to read a passage more than once, texts used in repeated readings should be relatively short (50–250 words in length). Where do you find such texts? One way is to break a story into 250 word segments. Another and preferred approach is to use poetry for students. By its very nature, poetry is short. It is also highly patterned, and predictable and contains letter patterns that can be adapted to phonics instruction. Perhaps most importantly, poetry is meant to be performed, to be read aloud to an audience. If a text is meant to be performed orally, the reader has a real reason to want to practice that text— to read it several times through so that reading to the audience will be without flaw and with meaningful expression. Thus, poetry, the same poetry that we mentioned earlier in this chapter for phonics and word study instruction, is ideal for building students' fluency.

With current reading programs' emphasis on prose reading, poetry is sometimes ignored in the reading curriculum (Perfect 1999). Using poetry for fluency instruction will certainly improve students' fluency. Of equal or greater importance, integrating poetry and poetry performance into the classroom will add variety and help students develop greater appreciation for this most aesthetic of reading texts.

IN CONCLUSION

Predictable materials offer beginning readers the support and encouragement they need to grow as readers, and to grow in their belief in themselves as readers. They also help children acquire sight vocabulary, develop decoding strategies, and practice during a meaningful and enjoyable encounter with print. One study that compared children's learning with predictable literature to their learning with basal reading instruction concluded that "using predictable materials with beginning readers spurs their acquisition of sight vocabulary, encourages them to use context clues when encountering unfamiliar words, and creates more positive feelings about reading aloud" (Bridge, Winograd and Haley 1983, p. 890). This conclusion is a strong endorsement for using authentic, predictable materials with beginners, and one with which we concur.

REFERENCES

Bridge, C., P. Winograd and D. Haley. 1983. Using Predictable Materials Versus Preprimers to Teach Beginning Sight Words. *The Reading Teacher*, 36: 884–891.

Christie, J., B. Enz and C. Vukelich 1997. *Teaching Language and Literacy*. New York: Longman.

Holdaway, D. 1979. *The Foundations of Literacy*. Sydney: Ashton Scholastic.

Leu, D. and C. Kinzer. 1999. *Effective Literacy Instruction* (4th ed). Upper Saddle River, NJ: Prentice Hall.

Lomax, R. and L. McGee. 1987. Young Children's Concepts About Print and Reading: Toward a Model of Word Reading Acquisition. *Reading Research Quarterly*, 22: 237–256.

Perfect, K. 1999. Rhyme and Reason: Poetry for the Heart and Head. *The Reading Teacher*, 52: 728–737.

Postlethwaite, T.N. and K.N. Ross. 1992. *Effective Schools in Reading: Implications for Educational Planners*. The Hague: International Association for the Evaluation of Educational Achievement.

Stahl, S. and B. Murray. 1993. Environmental Print, Phonemic Awareness, Letter Recognition, and Word Recognition. In D. Leu and C. Kinzer (eds.), *Examining Central Issues in Literacy Research, Theory, and Practice* (pp. 227–233). Chicago: National Reading Conference.

Trachtenburg, A. 1990. Using Children's Literature to Enhance Phonics Instruction. *The Reading Teacher*, 43: 648–654.

CHILDREN'S LITERATURE CITED

Martin, B. 1983. *Brown Bear, Brown bear*. New York: Holt.

Viorst, J. 1972. *Alexander and The Terrible, Horrible, No Good, Very Bad Day*. New York: Macmillan.

4
TEACHING PHONEMIC AWARENESS

Walk into Juanita's kindergarten classroom at the beginning of any school day and you are likely to find a lot of singing and choral reading going on. Children are singing favorite childhood songs and re-reading familiar and favorite rhyming poems that they have read throughout the year. Sometimes Juanita will have children change the refrain of some songs to emphasize different sounds. For example, in *Row, Row, Row Your Boat*, the refrain "Merrily, merrily, merrily, merrily" becomes "verrily . . . ," "cher-rily . . . ," or some other variation of "merrily." After reading the poems, Juanita asks children to name words that rhyme from the poem and then to think of other rhyming words not found in the poem. She also provides students with individual sounds from a significant word from the poem and asks them to name the word—"what is this word—*j, a, k*?"

Juanita loves songs and poetry. Her enthusiasm for songs and poetry makes them an integral part of her classroom experience. She also under-stands that in order to be successful in phonics and reading, children need to learn how sounds work so she extends her music and poetry activities into natural opportunities for her children to play with and manipulate sounds. "It's no problem," Juanita says, "to move from the singing of a lyric into draw-ing students' attention to the sounds in the lyrics. In fact, I think it's kind of fun, and I know the children enjoy it too. When I first start doing this with my children at the beginning of the school year, I am amazed by the number of children who have trouble with sounds. But as we make playing with songs, rhymes, and sounds a part of our day, it's not long before they all begin to hear the individual sounds in words. Kindergarten is a place for children to be-come ready for school and ready to learn to read. I think our work with sounds is really helping prepare them by showing them that words have sounds and that those sounds can be moved and changed."

Phonemic awareness, phonological awareness, or what Juanita calls sound knowledge and sound play, refers to a person's awareness of speech sounds smaller than a syllable and the ability to manipulate those sounds through such tasks as blending and segmenting sounds in words. Phonemic awareness is an absolutely key element in learning word recognition through phonics and overall reading. Literacy scholar Keith Stanovich calls phonemic awareness a superb predictor of early reading acquisition, "better than anything else that we know of, including IQ" (1994, p. 284).

This book is about the teaching of phonics, word recognition, and reading fluency. Phonics refers to the knowledge of letter-sound correspondence. Readers use phonics when they visually examine letters or letter combinations in words, and produce a sound or sound combination that corresponds to the visual stimulus. Blending the separate sounds in a word should result in the pronunciation of the word.

Phonics is dependent upon the reader's ability to visually examine words and to recognize, segment, and blend the sounds that are represented by letters. This latter ability is phonemic awareness. Recent research suggests that phonemic awareness is a very important precondition for learning phonics as well as reading (Adams 1990, Ball and Blachman 1991, Bradley and Bryant 1983, 1985, Fielding-Barnsley 1997, Lundberg, et al. 1988, Perfetti, et al. 1987, Stanovich 1986, Yopp 1992, 1995). Students who lack phonemic awareness are most at risk to experience difficulty in learning phonics and learning to read (Catts 1991, Maclean et al. 1987). Thus, success in phonics requires students to have some degree of phonemic awareness. Indeed, the report of the prestigious Committee on the Prevention of Reading Difficulties in Young Children recommends that, among other instructional activities, "Beginning readers need explicit instruction and practice that lead to an appreciation that spoken words are made up of small units of sound . . ." (Snow, Burns and Griffin 1998, p. 7).

Most students appear to develop phonemic awareness naturally through everyday early childhood experiences. Young children have many opportunities to play with language sounds, from reciting nursery rhymes and childhood poems with parents, family members, and friends, to chanting and creating jump rope cadences and chants, to singing childhood songs (e.g., "I've been working on the railroad; fee, fi, fiddly, I, oh"), to simply talking with family members and friends. Through these and other opportunities to make and manipulate the sounds of language, children gradually develop phonemic awareness. By the time children enter kindergarten, they have developed sufficient awareness of language sounds that they can begin to connect specific sounds with individual letters and letter patterns (i.e., phonics).

That is the way phonemic awareness develops for most children. Some children, however, enter school with insufficient awareness of the language sounds. Some children may have been plagued with chronic ear infections, fluid in the middle ear, excessive wax or other ear obstructions that make sound perception and manipulation difficult. Indeed ear infections have increased more than 200% over the past two decades. Other children may have had few opportunities to play with language through childhood rhymes and songs. We have noticed that many kindergarten and first-graders enter school with a restricted knowledge of common poems, rhymes, and songs. Other researchers suggest that some children have inherently less developed abilities to perceive, segment, and blend language sounds. For whatever reason, a fairly significant minority of young children entering school may not have sufficiently developed phonemic awareness to find success in phonics instruction. If certain children have difficulty perceiving the sounds, even before teachers begin to connect them with letters, the process of learning letter-sound correspondence and blending sounds into words may be overwhelming. For many of these young children, phonics will become one of the first of perhaps many frustrations in learning to read.

ASSESSING PHONEMIC AWARENESS

If phonemic awareness is so important to reading success, then it is critical that teachers have methods for assessing this ability among students. Fortunately an easy to use phonemic awareness assessment for young children as well as older students is available. The Yopp-Singer Test of Phonemic Segmentation (Yopp 1995) is a set of twenty-two words in which individual students are asked to segment each word into its constituent sounds (see Figure 4.1 for our variation of the Yopp-Singer Test). For example, the word *back* is presented orally to the student and the appropriate response from the student would be to say the three separate sounds that make up *back: b, a, k.*

The assessment takes only minutes to administer, yet the child's performance can provide an indication of his or her later success in reading as well as providing important instructional information. Yopp (1995b) has followed children to whom she administered the Yopp-Singer test in kindergarten through their later years in school. She has found that phonemic awareness is significantly correlated with students' reading and spelling achievement through grade six. Clearly, this and related research (Stanovich 1994) suggest that phonemic awareness must be considered when assessing young children and students who experience difficulty in reading, and when designing instructional programs for students who do not appear to have developed sufficient awareness of sounds.

Yopp reported that second semester kindergarten students obtained a mean score of twelve on the test. Kindergartners who fall significantly below this threshold, say a score of five or below, should be provided additional opportunities to develop phonemic awareness. As we shall discuss later in this chapter, many children who appear deficient in the area of phonemic awareness can be taught successfully with methods that easily fit well within a normal kindergarten classroom.

The Yopp-Singer Test has implications beyond kindergarten as well. We routinely administer the Yopp-Singer Test in our reading center to students ranging from second grade through high school. Although not all students who are struggling in reading perform poorly on the test, many do. By the beginning of second grade, students should be able to complete the Yopp-Singer Test with little trouble. We expect any students at second grade or beyond to score twenty or better. And yet, it is not unusual to find fifth and sixth grade students, frustrated in reading, score between ten and fifteen.

We wonder if these older students' struggles in reading didn't begin early in their school career when they were asked to master phonics before they were developmentally ready to do so. Moreover, for many of these older

Test of Phonemic Segmentation
(Adapted from Yopp, 1995)

Student's name _____   Date _____

Student's age _____

Score (number correct) _____   Examiner _____

Directions: I'd like to play a sound game with you. I will say a word and I want you to break the word apart into its sounds. You need to tell me each sound in the word. For example, if I say "old," you should say "/o/-/l/-/d/." *(Administrator: Be sure to say the sounds in the word distinctly. Do not say the letters.)* Let's try a few practice words.

Practice items: *(Assist the child in segmenting these items as necessary. You may wish to use blocks to help demonstrate the segmentation of sounds.)* kite, so, fat

Test items: *(Circle those items that the student correctly segments; incorrect responses may be recorded on the blank line following the item.)*

1. to _____   1. dock _____

2. me _____   2. lace _____

3. fight _____   3. mop _____

4. low _____   4. this _____

5. he _____   5. jot _____

6. vain _____   6. grow _____

7. is _____   7. nice _____

8. am _____   8. cat _____

9. be _____   9. shoe _____

10. meet _____   10. bed _____

11. jack _____   11. stay _____

Figure 4.1
Test for Assessing Phonemic Awareness

students, failure to learn to read through phonics early on simply meant more phonics, slower and more intensive phonics. Rather than being provided an alternative route to reading or the chance to develop phonemic awareness, many of these students were simply forced down a road that they were unable to negotiate to begin with. It is easy to imagine how these students became turned off to reading. While their classmates moved on to reading for pleasure and information, these students were stuck reading less and drilling more (Allington 1977, 1984, 1994), which in turn led to even less self-selected reading and further frustration in reading.

The Yopp-Singer Test of Phoneme Segmentation (and our variation published here) offer classroom and clinical reading teachers tools of enormous value. Identifying students at risk as early as possible may save many children from years of frustration in reading. Moreover, gaining deeper insight into the problems of some older readers may allow us to overcome difficulties in phonemic awareness through instruction or design an alternative instructional program that bypasses phonics.

TEACHING AND NURTURING PHONEMIC AWARENESS THROUGH TEXT PLAY AND WRITING

For most students phonemic awareness is nurtured more than it is taught. Children learn the nature of language sounds through their daily play by themselves and with others. That same playfulness about language and the sounds of language can easily be extended into the school. Informed teachers can nurture phonemic awareness in ways that are enjoyable and engaging for all students. Perhaps one of the most useful is simply to bring the rhymes, chants, and songs that feature play with language sounds into the classroom or clinic. For younger children this may mean the reading and rereading of nursery rhymes, jump rope chants, and children's poetry, and songs. Playing with nursery rhyme lines such as:

> Dickery dickery dare, the pig flew up in the air . . .
> Hey diddle diddle, the cat and the fiddle . . .
> Diddle diddle dumpling, my son John . . .

are certain to help children grasp the concept of the sound of *d*. And, the tongue-twisting rhyme, *Peter Piper picked a peck of pickled peppers . . .* , will help children develop an awareness of *p*.

Jump rope chants, poems, and song lyrics can serve the same purpose as nursery rhymes. Griffith and Olson (1992) recommend that teachers read rhyming texts and other texts that play with sounds to students daily and help develop students' sensitivity to sounds (see Figure 4.2 for a list of texts for developing phonemic awareness). Moreover, these texts can be altered to feature different language sounds (Yopp 1992). For example, the familiar refrain of "Ee-igh, ee-igh, oh" in *Old MacDonald Had a Farm* can be transformed into "Dee-igh, dee-igh, doh" if you are emphasizing *d*. The *Camp Town Races*

Anderson, P. F. 1995. *The Mother Goose Pages*. Dreamhouse Nursery Bookcase. http://pubweb.nwu.edu/~pfa/dreamhouse/nursery/bookcase.html

Baer, G. 1989. *Thump, Thump, Rat-a-Tat-Tat*. New York: Harper and Row.

Base, G. 1989. *Animalia*. New York: Harry Abrams.

Bayor, J. 1984. *A: My Name is Alice*. New York: Dial.

Benjamin, A. 1987. *Rat-a-Tat, Pitter Pat*. New York: Cromwell.

Brown, M. W. 1993. *Four Fur Feet*. New York: Doubleday.

Browne, P. 1996. *A Gaggle of Geese: The Collective Names of the Animal Kingdom*. New York: Atheneum.

Butterworth, N. 1990. *Nick Butterworth's Book of Nursery Rhymes*. New York: Viking.

Cameron, P. 1961. *"I Can't," Said the Ant*. New York: Coward-McCann.

Carter, D. 1990. *More Bugs in Boxes*. New York: Simon and Schuster.

DePaola, T. 1985. *Tomie DePaola's Mother Goose*. New York: Putnam.

deRegniers, B., et al. 1988. *Sing a Song of Popcorn*. New York: Scholastic.

Galdone, P. 1968. *Henny Penny*. New York: Scholastic.

Geisel, T. S. (Dr. Seuss). 1957. *The Cat in the Hat*. New York: Random House.

Geisel, T. S. (Dr. Seuss). 1960. *Green Eggs and Ham*. New York: Random House.

Geisel, T. S. (Dr. Seuss). 1963. *Dr. Seuss's ABC*. New York: Random House.

Geisel, T. S. (Dr. Seuss). 1965. *Fox in Socks*. New York: Random House.

Geisel, T. S. (Dr. Seuss). 1965. *Hop on Pop*. New York: Random House.

Geisel, T. S. (Dr. Seuss). 1972. *Marvin K. Mooney, Will You Please Go Now!* New York: Random House.

Geisel, T. S. (Dr. Seuss). 1974. *There's a Wocket in My Pocket*. New York: Random House.

Gordon, J. 1991. *Six Sleepy Sheep*. New York: Puffin.

Hawkins, C., and J. Hawkins. 1986. *Top the Dog*. New York: Putnam.

Hoberman, M. A. 1982. *A House is a House for Me*. New York: Penguin.

Hymes. L., and J. Hymes, 1964. *Oodles of Noodles*. New York: Young Scott Books.

Kellogg, S. 1985. *Chicken Little*. New York: Mulberry Books.

Krauss. R. 1985. *I Can Fly*. New York: Golden Press.

Kuskin, K. 1990. *Roar and More*. New York: Harper Trophy.

Lee, D. 1983. *Jelly Belly*. Toronto, ON: Macmillan.

Lansky, B. 1993. *The New Adventures of Mother Goose*. Deerhaven, MN: Meadowbrook.

Leedy, L. 1989. *Pingo the Plaid Panda*. New York: Holiday House.

Lewison, W. 1992. *Buzz Said the Bee*. New York: Scholastic.

Figure 4.2
Texts for Developing Phonemic Awareness *(continued)*

Martin, B., Jr., and J. Archambault. 1989. *Chicka Chicka Boom Boom*. New York: Simon and Schuster.

Marzollo, J. 1989. *The Teddy Bear Book*. New York: Dial.

O'Connor, J. 1986. *The Teeny Tiny Woman*. New York: Random House.

Obligado, L. 1983. *Faint Frogs Feeling Feverish and Other Terrifically Tantalizing Tongue Twisters*. New York: Viking.

Ochs, C. P. 1991. *Moose on the Loose*. Minneapolis, MN: Carolrhoda Books.

Patz, N. 1983. *Moses Supposes his Toeses are Roses*. San Diego, CA: Harcourt Brace Jovanovich.

Pomerantz, C. 1974. *The Piggy in the Puddle*. New York: Macmillan.

Pomerantz, C. 1987. *How Many Trucks can a Tow Truck Tow?* New York: Random House.

Prelutsky, J. 1986. *Read-Aloud Rhymes for the Very Young*. New York: Knopf.

Provenson, A., and M. Provenson. 1977. *Old Mother Hubbard*. New York: Random House.

Raffi. 1987. *Down by the Bay*. New York: Crown.

Scarry, R. 1970. *Richard Scarry's Best Mother Goose Ever*. New York: Western.

Sendak, M. 1962. *Chicken Soup With Rice*. New York: HarperCollins.

Serfozo, M. K. 1988. *Who Said Red?* New York: Macmillan.

Shaw, N. 1986. *Sheep in a Jeep*. Boston: Houghton Mifflin.

Shaw, N. 1986. *Sheep on a Ship*. Boston: Houghton Mifflin.

Showers, P. 1991. *The Listening Walk*. New York: Harper Trophy.

Wadsworth, O. A. 1985. *Over in the Meadow*. New York: Penguin.

Winthrop, E. 1986. *Shoes*. New York: Harper Trophy.

Yektai, N. 1987. *Bears in Pairs*. New York: Macmillan.

Zemach, M. 1976. *Hush, Little Baby*. New York: E. P. Dutton.

For other texts for developing phonemic awareness see Griffith and Olson 1992, Ericson and Juliebo 1998 and Yopp 1995a.

Figure 4.2
Texts for Developing Phonemic Awareness *(continued)*

exclamation can be changed from "dooh dah" to "booh bah" or "sooh sah," depending on the sound being emphasized.

For older students, the same task can be accomplished with more sophisticated texts. Rhymes for older children, as well as tongue twisters, popular song lyrics, and raps can be learned, altered, rewritten, and ultimately performed to emphasize language sounds.

Hinky Pinkies are another game-like activity for developing sound awareness in a playful way. Hinky Pinkies are simply riddles for which the answer is two or more rhyming words. When making Hinky Pinkies, one should begin with the rhyming word pair answer and then think of a riddle that describes the answer. For example, *duck's truck* could be the answer to the riddle, *what is a vehicle that is driven by a quacker?* Students love making and figuring out Hinky Pinkies. The Hinky Pinky idea could also be altered so that the answers are two or more words with the same initial sounds (alliterations). A wet pup, then, is a *soggy doggy* when the answer rhymes, but becomes a *drenched dog* when the game is changed to alliterations.

In all of these textual activities, students are required to attend to the sounds of language in order to perform the song or rap or provide the correct response to the riddle. Inviting students to examine and play with language in this way will develop their sensitivity to sounds. In addition to songs and poems, many books feature sounds (see Figure 4.2). Although the texts in the list are most appropriate for younger children, older students needing help in phonemic awareness could be paired up with younger students and learn to read such books to their younger buddies, thus developing their own phonemic awareness as well as that of their younger partner. Students can also write their own versions of the books simply by changing the sounds that are being emphasized.

Literacy scholars argue that writing in which students use their knowledge of sound-symbol correspondence, also known as invented or phonemic spelling, is a powerful way to help students develop their phonemic awareness as well as their basic phonics knowledge (Clay 1985, Griffith and Klesius 1990, Morris 1998). When students attempt to write words using their knowledge of language sounds and knowledge of corresponding letters, they are segmenting sounds in words and ordering and blending the sounds in order to make real words. Even if the words are not spelled conventionally, this type of writing provides students with unequaled practice in employing their understanding of sounds.

The research behind invented spelling, incidentally, makes it clear that invented spelling is not an end state in learning to write. Just as children move from babbling and incorrect pronunciation to full and correct pronunciation when learning to talk, children move rapidly from the invented spelling to correct or conventional spelling. By the late primary grades there is little if any difference in spelling errors of children taught to spell in a highly rigid and disciplined system and other children who are given the encouragement and support to play with their knowledge of sounds and letters through invented spelling. In fact, one study of first-graders showed that children encouraged to invent spellings were more fluent writers and better word recognizers than children who experienced a traditional spelling curriculum (Clarke 1988). Considering all the sound-symbol thinking that occurs when children invent their spelling, such results are to be expected.

TEACHING AND NURTURING PHONEMIC AWARENESS THROUGH MORE FOCUSED ACTIVITIES

Many children need only playful reading, reciting, and performance of sound-oriented texts to develop appropriate sound awareness for reading in kindergarten and primary grades (Ericson and Juliebo 1998). For other children who have not yet developed sufficient phonemic awareness skills to benefit from phonics instruction, more specific instruction is needed. Yopp (1992) has identified these conceptual levels of activity to develop phonemic awareness:

- Sound matching
- Sound isolation
- Sound blending
- Sound substitution
- Sound segmentation

These levels provide a conceptual framework for planning and designing instruction that treats phonemic awareness instruction comprehensively, in an easy-to-more-complex order that eventually leads to learning phonics.

SOUND MATCHING

Sound matching simply requires students to match a word or words to a particular sound. When a teacher asks students to think of words that begin with *p*, students are challenged to find words that match that sound. Having students think of the way they form their mouths to articulate individual sounds may further help them match other words and form a more lasting concept of the sound. Sound matching can be extended to middle (vowel sounds), ending sounds, rhyming words, and syllables. As students become familiar with the written form of words, the words can be placed on a word wall (see Chapter 7) according to their beginning, middle, ending, or word family sounds.

Another sound matching activity involves presenting students with three words, two of which have the same beginning sound, for example, *bat, back, rack*. Students must determine which two words have the same initial sound. Again, this same sort of activity can be played with middle and ending sounds , rhyming words, and words with differing number of syllables.

SOUND ISOLATION

Sound isolation activities require students to determine the beginning, middle, or ending sounds in a word or set of words. For example, the teacher may provide three words that begin with the same sound, *pig, pot, pet,* and ask students to tell what sound the words begin with (Yopp 1992). The same procedure can be done for middle and ending sounds, as well as for word families or rimes. After students develop proficiency in determining individual sounds from similar words, they can be asked to analyze individual sounds from different words. For example, the teacher may ask, what is the beginning sound you hear in these words: *bake, swim, dog, pin, that*. Using the same set of words, students can be asked to determine (isolate) the middle and ending sounds.

SOUND BLENDING

In sound blending activities, students synthesize sounds in order to make a word—this is required when decoding words using phonics. Using a game-like or sing-song format, the teacher simply presents students with individual sounds and asks them to blend the sounds together to form a word. The teacher might, for example, say to the class "I am thinking of a kind of bird and here are the sounds in its name *d, u, k*" (Yopp 1992). Of course, the children should say *duck*. If this sort of task is too difficult, teachers can make it easier by presenting three pictures of birds and asking students to pick the one that represents the sounds. The teacher may allow those students who are more adept at the activity to come up with their own questions and present their own sounds and riddles to classmates.

Sound Substitution

Sound substitution requires students to subtract, add, and substitute sounds from existing words. A question such as "What word do you get when you take the *w* off *win?*" requires students to segment sounds from words and then re-blend the sounds using the remaining sounds. Similarly, sounds can be added to existing words to make up new words, "Add *b* to the beginning of *us* and what do you get?"

After adding and subtracting sounds from given words, students can try substituting sounds. Ask students to think what the names of their classmates might be if all their names began with a particular sound (Yopp 1992). If *t* were used as the new sound, Billy's name would become Tilly, and Mary and Gary would have the same name—Tary. Substituting individual sounds can lead to substituting middle and ending sounds.

Sound Segmentation

Sound segmentation requires students to go beyond isolating one sound in a word to determining all the constituent sounds. This may begin with simply segmenting words into onsets (the sounds that precede the vowel in a syllable) and rimes (the vowel and consonants beyond the vowel in a syllable; another name for word family). So *stack* would be segmented into *st* and *ak*. Later, students can segment words into their specific sounds. This time *stack* would be segmented into *s, t, a, k*. Be sure to begin with short, two-sound words at first (e.g., *us, in, at*).

The generic activities we describe here can easily be transformed into a variety of games, performances, and playful activities for students. Teachers should try to make these activities engaging and enjoyable for students. We've found that several short game-like sessions throughout the day keep children's interest better than longer, more involved sessions. The activities can be shared with parents, even parents of preschoolers, so that they too may participate in their children's development of phonemic awareness.

Add a Degree of Concreteness

Playing with sounds may be abstract for many students. Not only are sounds invisible, they can't be held or made to stay. For children who learn things best when they are presented in concrete ways, sound awareness can be quite difficult and abstract. One way to make the task more concrete is to use some sort of physical object to represent the sounds, for example, colored blocks. Each block of a different color can represent a different sound. A blue block can represent *s,* the red block can be the *t,* the black block can be *a,* and the yellow block can represent *i.* Using these blocks, teachers can work with individuals and groups of students in learning to blend, substitute, and segment sounds in words.

For example, the teacher can put the blue, yellow, and red blocks in a row and ask students to blend the sounds into the word *sit.* Then the teacher can remove the blue block to make the word *it.* If the red block is moved from the end of the word to the beginning, the sound produced becomes *sih.* Four or five blocks, each representing a sound, can provide many opportunities for students to make sense of how sounds work. For older students already familiar with the alphabet, magnetic letters on a cake pan can substitute for blocks, and the same manipulations can be made with the added important feature of having the letters that represent the sounds in words.

Also, Griffith and Olson (1992) advocate the use of Elkonin boxes to add a dimension of concreteness in hearing and segmenting sounds. An Elkonin box is simply a series of boxes drawn on a sheet of paper, one for each phoneme in a given word. As students listen to words read by the teacher and hear discrete sounds, they push markers into the boxes, one marker for each sound. Later, as children become more familiar with written letters, they can write individual letters or letter combinations that represent individual sounds in the words (See Figures 4.3 and 4.4).

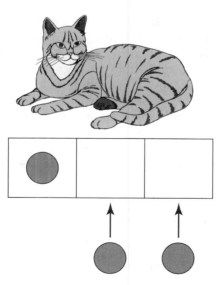

Figure 4.3
Example of Boxes Used for Hearing Sounds in Words

Figure 4.4
Example of Boxes Used for Hearing Sounds and Writing Letters

In Conclusion

There is more to phonics and reading than phonemic awareness. There are many other things that teachers and children can do to develop students' literacy skills. For example, younger children need to be read to daily from the best children's literature available. They need to explore word meanings with their teacher every day, and daily language experience stories should be part and parcel of every primary classroom. Children should be making daily entries into their personal journals. Predictable books, big books, poems, and stories should be read chorally, individually, and repeatedly in a supportive environment.

Nevertheless, we feel that phonemic awareness is essential for phonics and reading success. Children benefit from phonics when they understand what speech sounds are and how they can be manipulated to form words. Informed teachers can find creative and authentic ways to help students develop the critical awareness of speech sounds and employ this awareness in learning to read. Teachers of young children and older students who struggle in phonics and word recognition should develop curricula that are varied, stimulating, and authentic for teaching and developing phonemic awareness in students.

References

Adams, M. J. 1990. *Beginning to Read: Thinking and Learning About Print.* Cambridge, MA: Massachusetts Institute of Technology Press.

Allington, R. L. 1977. If They Don't Read Much, How They Ever Gonna Get Good? *Journal of Reading*, 21: 57–61.

Allington, R. L. 1984. Content Coverage and Contextual Reading in Reading Groups. *Journal of Reading Behavior*, 26: 85–96.

Allington, R. L. 1994. The Schools We Have. The Schools We Need. *The Reading Teacher*, 48: 14–29.

Ball, E., and B. A. Blachman. 1991. Does Phoneme Awareness Training in Kindergarten Make a Difference in Early Word Recognition and Developmental Spelling? *Reading Research Quarterly*, 26: 49–66.

Bradley, L., and P. Bryant. 1983. Categorizing Sounds and Learning to Read: A Causal Connection. *Nature*, 271: 746–747.

Bradley, L., and P. Bryant. 1985. *Rhyme and Reason in Reading and Spelling*. Ann Arbor, MI: University of Michigan Press.

Catts, H. W. 1991. Facilitating Phonological Awareness: Role of Speech-Language Pathologists. *Language, Speech, and Hearing Services in Schools*, 22: 196–203.

Clay, M. M. 1985. *The Early Detection of Reading Difficulties* (3rd ed.) Portsmouth, NH: Heinemann.

Clarke, L. K. 1988. Invented Versus Traditional Spelling in First Graders' Writings: Effects on Learning to Spell and Read. *Research in the Teaching of English*, 22: 281–309.

Ericson, L., and M. F. Juliebo. 1998. *The Phonological Awareness Handbook for Kindergarten and Primary Teachers*. Newark, DE: International Reading Association.

Fielding-Barnsley, R. 1997. Explicit Instruction in Decoding Benefits Children High in Phonemic Awareness and Alphabet Knowledge. *Scientific Studies in Reading*, 1: 85–98.

Griffith, P., and J. P. Klesius. 1990. *The Effect of Phonemic Awareness Ability and Reading Instructional Approach on First Grade Children's Acquisition of Spelling and Decoding Skills*. Paper presented at the annual meeting of the National Reading Conference, Miami, FL.

Griffith, P., and M. Olson. 1992. Phonemic Awareness Helps Beginning Readers Break the Code. *The Reading Teacher*, 45: 516–523.

Lundberg, I., J. Frost and O. Peterson. 1988. Effects of an Extensive Program for Stimulating Phonological Awareness in Preschool Children. *Reading Research Quarterly*, 23: 263–285.

Maclean, M., P. Bryant and L. Bradley. 1987. Rhymes, Nursery Rhymes, and Reading in Early Childhood. *Merrill-Palmer Quarterly*, 33: 255–281.

Morris, D. 1998. *Preventing Reading Failure in the Primary Grades*. Paper Presented at the Annual Meeting of the National Reading Conference, Austin, TX.

Perfetti, C., et al. 1987. Phonemic Knowledge and Learning to Read are Reciprocal: A Longitudinal Study of First Grade Children. *Merrill-Palmer Quarterly*, 33: 283–319.

Snow, C. E., M. S. Burns and P. Griffin. (eds). 1998. *Preventing Reading Difficulties in Young Children*. Washington, DC: National Academy Press.

Stanovich, K. E. 1994. Romance and Reason. *The Reading Teacher*, 49: 280–291.

Stanovich, K. E. 1986. Matthew Effects in Reading: Some Consequences of Individual Differences in the Acquisition of Literacy. *Reading Research Quarterly*, 21: 360–407.

Yopp, H. K. 1995a. Read-Aloud Books for Developing Phonemic Awareness: An Annotated Bibliography. *The Reading Teacher*, 48: 538–542.

Yopp, H. K. 1995b. A Test for Assessing Phonemic Awareness in Young Children. *The Reading Teacher*, 49: 20–29.

Yopp, H. K. 1992. Developing Phonemic Awareness in Young Children. *The Reading Teacher*, 45: 696–703.

5

ONSETS, RIMES, AND BASIC PHONIC PATTERNS

"I use word families because I know they work." So says Ellen, a first grade teacher. If you were to walk into Ellen's classroom about halfway through the school year, you would be struck by all the print hung up and displayed around her room—students' stories, chart stories that students dictated and Ellen wrote, and lots and lots of word family charts. "We try to introduce and cover one or two word families a week. One of the things we do with our word families after each is introduced is to write down all the words we know that belong to a family." Ellen points to one of her word family charts displayed on a side wall. "Look at the *-an* chart. At first we brainstormed words like *Dan, man, tan, ran,* and *can.* But later we added longer words that students thought of at home, either with their parents' help, or through their own reading—words like *Annie, Anthony, candle,* and *tanning salon* began to be added to the chart. Students learn that what they know about word families can help them figure out longer words as well the short one-syllable words. They are intrigued by the word families and use them all the time in their decoding and spelling."

Phonics is defined as a "way of teaching, reading, and spelling that stresses symbol-sound relationships . . ." (Harris and Hodges 1995, p. 186). Essentially, this definition suggests a consistent relationship between the written symbols that make up words and the sound manifestation of the words. Since the relationships in many cases are fairly consistent, it makes good sense to inform beginning readers about them. Traditionally this has meant teaching children how individual sounds or blends of consonant sounds are represented by their corresponding letters. For example, teaching children that the short *a* sound is represented by the letter *a* as in *bat,* that the sound of *b* is represented by the letter *b,* that the long *e* sound is sometimes represented by the letter combination *ee,* that the blended consonant sound is represented by the letters *bl,* or that the *k* sound is represented sometimes by the letter combination *ck,* is a way of teaching phonics that has been around for years. For the most part, this approach to phonics has helped many young readers develop a strategy for decoding words.

However, with the renewed emphasis on phonics approaches to word recognition and reading, it is important that whatever phonics approach is chosen should be the most effective way of teaching children sound-symbol associations. Research by Theodore Clymer (1963, 1996) casts doubt on the notion that teaching children letter associations for individual sounds is a very effective approach for word recognition instruction. Clymer and his associates gathered phonics generalizations that were taught in various reading programs of the time. Then they found those words, taught in the elementary grades, that contained letters related to the generalizations, and examined the extent to which the letter (or letter combination) actually yielded the appropriate sound, or fit the rule. In other words, the researchers asked, "Would this rule help a reader decode this word?" Clymer found that a significant number of the generalizations did not result in the appropriate word with much consistency. So, he questioned the wisdom of actually teaching some of these generalizations. For example, one of the most renowned of all phonics generalizations states that "when two vowels go walking, the first one does the talking"; when a word has two adjacent vowels, the long sound of the first vowel is heard and the sound of the second is not heard. Upon close examination of words children encountered in their elementary reading, and in which there were two adjacent vowels, Clymer (1963, 1996) found that over half of words with this vowel construction did not yield the intended sound. A large number of other generalizations also were suspect according to Clymer's research. Clymer also found that some rules, although highly reliable, applied to so few words that learning the rule hardly seemed worth the effort.

Does this mean that phonics should be thrown out of the school curriculum? Clearly not. Even the novice reader can see the connection between sounds and letters in words. The questions are how much, and what kind of focus on sounds and letters should be presented to beginning readers. Clymer's work suggests that phonics generalizations, especially those beyond the beginning of words or syllables, may be troublesome for readers. Moreover, the notion of going from sound to symbol may also be troublesome. When readers read, they begin with the written word. The written form of the word is then converted into its sound representation. Perhaps the appropriate direction for phonics teaching is to begin with the written symbols, whatever they may be, and then move to the sounds.

BEGINNING LETTER-SOUND (ONSETS) RELATIONSHIPS

What written symbols should we teach children in phonics instruction? Let's begin with letters that begin words and syllables. For the most part, the sounds associated with letters and letter combinations that begin words are fairly consistent. To be more precise, the written consonants that precede the vowel in syllables (remember that every syllable has one and only one vowel sound, except when a dipthong or vowel blend is present) are fairly consistent in the sounds they represent. When a *t* begins a word or syllable and is followed immediately by the vowel, that *t* almost universally produces the *t* sound. When the letters *bl* begin a word or a syllable, it can be fairly well predicted that those letters will yield the sound *bl*. And, when the letters *sh* are found at the beginning of a word or syllable, a reader can be confident that those letters represent the *sh* sound.

So, one area of great consistency for phonics instruction is the consonants that precede the vowel in words and syllables. A more precise name for the those consonants is onsets. Onsets are reasonably consistent and thus can be taught to beginning readers with confidence. Readers can use them. Moreover, initial word onsets tend to be much more useful in recognizing words. As readers our eyes are drawn to the beginning positions of words.

For the most part then, traditional phonics instruction for onsets works well. Usually, beginning consonants are taught by associating them with concepts that begin with those letters and the sounds normally associated with the letters. For example, it is not uncommon for teachers to see these letters taught by associating them with pictures of things that begin with these letters and their corresponding sounds:

b: bat, ball, barn
c: cap, cat, cup
d: dog, duck
f: fire, fish
g: girl, gold

In this approach students are taught the sound-symbol relationship by associating the visual form of the letter with the beginning sound of appropriate words. Students may read texts in which most of the words begin with a targeted letter and sound.

Other similar approaches exist. In the Letter People program, for example, students are taught initial sound-symbol correspondence through cartoon-like characters that have bodily features (e.g., Munching Mouth) that correspond with the visual form of the letter which is also displayed on the body of the character. As with most traditional approaches, students engage in a variety of worksheet-like activities to solidify their knowledge of these beginning letter-sound relationships.

A similar yet novel approach to beginning letter-sound phonics, called Action Phonics (Cunningham 1987), teaches the beginning letter- and letter combination-sound associations through physical actions or movements that begin with the targeted sound. The actions for the Action Phonics (adapted from Cunningham 1987) are listed in Figure 5.1.

Teaching beginning letter-sound relationships using Action Phonics requires students to move their bodies, which tends to reinforce students' memories of the letters and sounds. Students connect the graphic letter with the physical action they engage in and subsequently with the associated sound. The physical movement acts like a conceptual glue that holds the sound and the symbol together until they are thoroughly learned.

One or two initial consonants and their sounds can be taught each week. Teachers begin by reviewing with the students all the previously learned

b	bounce	t	talk	fl	fly
c	catch	v	vacuum	fr	frown
d	dance	w	walk, wiggle	gl	glare, glue
f	fall	y	yawn, yell	gr	grab
g	gallop	z	zip	pl	plant
h	hop, hum	ch	cheer	pr	pray
j	jump	sh	shiver, shout	sw	swallow
k	kick	th	think	sk	skate, skip
l	lick	wh	whistle	sl	sleep, slide
m	march	br	breathe	sm	smile
n	nod	bl	blow, blink	sp	spin
p	paint, pat	cr	crawl, cry	st	stand still, stop
q	quiet	cl	climb	tr	track, trip
r	run, rip	dr	drive	tw	twist
s	sit, sip				

Figure 5.1
Action Phonics—Actions to Accompany Letters and Their Sounds (Adapted from Cunningham 1987)

consonants, actions, and sounds, then the new initial consonant is introduced with its accompanying movement and sound. Initial consonants and sounds can be reviewed by assigning each student a consonant. One student at a time comes to the front of the class and displays the movement associated with the consonant. Students are challenged to guess the letter and sound. In another variation, students are gathered in a circle, with one child or the teacher acting as the leader. The leader has all the letters printed on individual cards. The leader picks one letter, displays it to the group, and the entire group displays the accompanying action. The activity moves from one action to another as the leader moves from one letter card to another. This activity is a great way to integrate physical education into phonics and can easily be employed by the physical education teacher to reinforce students' phonics learning.

Teachers who teach beginning letter-sound relationships often find students making the action at their seats when they try to read or spell words on their own. Cunningham quotes one teacher who uses action phonics with her students, "They are always in motion anyway. They cannot sit quietly and listen. They just naturally move some part of their bodies. Now they all move together purposefully" (Cunningham 1987, p. 249). Action phonics is a great way to continue teaching phonics and reading, even at those times when students' bodies are ready to get out of their seats and move about. Two key letters and sounds to teach early on are *s (sit)* and *q (quiet)*. These two letters are a natural way to bring the activity to an end.

MOVING ON TO PATTERNS (RIMES) BEYOND INITIAL LETTERS

After beginning letters are introduced, students need to explore how to construct the remainder of words. Traditionally this has meant introducing students to short vowel sounds and words containing them, followed by long vowel sounds and the letters that represent them; however, generalizations based on the vowel portions of words are what Clymer (1963, 1996) found so problematic in his analysis of phonics generalizations. Most vowels can represent more than a dozen sounds in English.

Some experts suggest that vowel sounds be taught, not independently, but in the context of the consonants that follow them in syllables. The combination of a vowel and the consonants that follow it in a syllable is often called a rime, phonogram, or word family. Rimes are a productive approach to phonics for several reasons. First, rimes consist of several letters, allowing a reader to analyze a word several letters at a time, rather than analyzing individual letters one at a time. Second, rimes have a high degree of consistency. When the rime *ack* appears in a word, it nearly always makes *ak*; and when *it* appears at the end of a syllable, it almost invariably makes *it*. In addition, by their very nature, words containing the same rime, do rhyme. Thus, it is not difficult to compose poems that feature targeted rimes for children, providing superb practice in learning those rimes. Moreover, it is easy for students to write and celebrate their own rhyming poetry as they begin to understand the connection between the written rimes and their corresponding sounds. Marilyn Adams writes this about the use of onsets and rimes as a core element in phonics instruction:

> . . . the onset and rime are relatively easy to remember and to splice back together. Yet another advantage of exploiting phonograms in decoding instruction is that they provide a means of introducing and exercising many primer words with relative efficiency and this, as we have seen, is in

marked contrast to the slowness with which words can be developed through individual letter-sound correspondences. Again, this advantage has long been recognized in many instructional programs. (1990, p. 321)

As soon as students have some beginning letter-sound relationships established, teachers can begin concurrently teaching longer letter-sound patterns beyond the beginning letters of words and syllables. This is where rimes come in.

There is, by definition, one rime for each and every syllable. Fry (1998) found that 353 rimes can generate at least two fairly common one-syllable words. Given that many rimes exist in English, which ones should be taught first to young students? One approach is to use those rimes that are most productive, those rimes that can be used to decode the greatest number of words. Edward Fry (1998) has identified 38 rimes that can be used to make 654 one-syllable words (see Figure 5.2). That's pretty phenomenal. Further-more, those 38 rimes can be used to decode several thousand longer, multisyllabic words. Teaching one or two rimes per week, the entire list of 38 can be taught in one school year or less.

Now that we have a beginning list of rimes to teach (a more extensive list is provided in Appendix A), the question becomes, how do we teach them to students? Many teachers, who have intuitively pursued rimes as a key element of phonics, often brainstorm with students words that contain targeted rimes. These words and their rimes are listed on a sheet of chart paper and put on display for students to read and use at their convenience.

While this is a good start, we do not feel it goes far enough in encouraging students to learn rimes. Word recognition requires deep learning of word patterns. This means seeing the patterns in isolation, in words and in texts, and reading plenty of words and text that contain those patterns. What follows is a week-long sequence of activities for teaching two rimes per week:

DAY 1

1. Introduce a rime, for example *ack*. Print the rime on the chalkboard and say the sound it represents several times. Ask students to do the same.
2. Brainstorm and list on chart paper words that contain the *ack* rime. Words should be mostly one-syllable words, though a few multisyllabic words can be included.
3. Read the words with students several times. Have groups and individual students read the words. Encourage students to read the words on their own throughout the day. Eventually the words on the chart can be added to the class word wall (see Chapter 7).
4. Challenge students with a hinky pinky, written on the board or chart paper, that uses some of the words just brainstormed. A hinky pinky is a riddle for which the answer is two or more rhyming words. For example, "What do you get when you make a tall pile of students' book bags?" Students will know to think of words that contain *ack* for the answer and it won't take long for a student to come up with *a stack of packs* or *a stack of back packs*.

ay	say, day	ing	sing, ring	est	best, rest
ill	hill, fill	ap	rap, cap	ink	rink, sink
ip	ship, dip	unk	hunk, bunk	ow	low, slow
at	hat, cat	ail	pail, sail	ew	few, dew
am	ham, jam	ain	pain, rain	ore	sore, more
ag	rag, sag	im	him, rim	ed	sled, Ted
ack	rack, sack	uck	truck, luck	ab	crab, lab
ank	bank, Hank	um	hum, drum	ob	rob, lob
ake	rake, make	eed	deed, reed	ock	clock, rock
ine	spine, mine	y	try, my	op	hop, stop
ight	sight, might	out	shout, pout	in	pin, win
ick	sick, lick	ug	hug, slug	an	man, can
ell	bell, tell				
ot	hot, spot				

Figure 5.2
The Most Common Rimes

5. Introduce two or three poems featuring the targeted rime, written by the teacher or some other poet, and displayed for all to see on chart paper. Slowly at first, read each poem to students several times, pointing to the words as you read and asking students to join in as they feel comfortable. After a few readings the entire group should be reading the poem chorally. Divide the students up into smaller groups and continue to read the poems in parts. Ask a few individual students to read each poem on their own. Individual students can continue reading the poems at their leisure throughout the day. These authentic reading activities promote reading fluency and sight word acquisition as well as focusing children's attention on the targeted rime.

Written below are two poems featuring *ack* and written by Ellen, the first grade teacher we introduced to you at the beginning of this chapter:

When a Thousand Ducks Quack

When a thousand ducks go quack
And a set of ear plugs I lack
I find my trusty old jacket.
Placed over my head,
It softens that awful racket.

When the Ducks Return

The ducks are back,
They quack and quack.
What a noisy noise they make.
They return every year
And fill my ears
With quacking that makes me quake!

The poems can come from existing poetry that can be found in the many collections and anthologies available to teachers and children (see Figure 5.3). A second source for poems is the teacher. If you, the teacher, cannot find poems that contain *ack* written by others, surely you can write a couple four- to six-line poems, like Ellen, that present students with real texts featuring the targeted rime. Not only does writing your own poems provide students with a rich source of reading material for practicing their knowledge of rimes, it shows students that their teacher is also a writer.

Once the poem has been read, reread, and read again, students are asked to find individual words and word parts in the poems. This can mean pointing to, underlining, and circling significant words and word parts on a second copy of each poem (the initial copy is kept clean for future use). At this point we want to draw students' attention to individual words in the poem, particularly those words that contain the targeted rimes. One of our colleagues, Belinda, a first grade teacher, uses fly swatters as *word whoppers.* She cuts rectangular holes of various sizes out of several fly swatters (see illustration, page 54.) She "whops" one of the words from the poem and ask students to identify it. The word whopper isolates the word so that it must be read on its own, without the aid of the general context of the poem. Later Belinda will give each child a word whopper and ask individuals to come to the poem and whop words and word parts from the poem that she will pronounce.

Bagert, B. 1992. *Let Me Be the Boss: Poems for Kids to Perform*. Honesdale, PA: Boyds Mills.

Carle, E. 1992. *Eric Carle's Animals Animals*. New York: Philomel.

de Paola, T. 1988. *Tomie de Paola's Book of Poems*. New York: Putnam.

de Regniers, B.S. et al. 1988. *Sing a Song of Popcorn: Every child's book of poems*. New York: Scholastic.

Hopkins, L. B. 1993. *Extra Innings: Baseball Poems*. New York: Harcourt Brace.

Hopkins, L. B. 1995. *Been to Yesterdays: Poems of a Life*. Honesdale, PA: Boyds Mill.

Hopkins, L. B. (ed). 1995. *Small Talk: A Book of Short Poems*. New York: Harcourt Brace.

Hudson, W. (eds). 1993. *Pass It On: African-American Poetry for Children*. New York: Scholastic.

Hudson, W., and C. Hudson (eds). 1995. *How Sweet the Sound: African-American Songs for Children*. New York: Scholastic.

Krull, K. 1992. *Gonna Sing my Head Off: American Folk Songs for Children*. New York: Knopf.

Lansky, B. (ed). 1991. *Kids Pick the Funniest Poems*. New York: Meadowbrook.

Lansky, B. 1996. *Poetry Party*. New York: Meadowbrook.

Larrick, N. (ed). 1990. *Mice are Nice*. New York: Philomel.

Lobel, A. 1983. *The Book of Pigericks*. New York: Harper & Row.

Moss, J. 1989. *The Butterfly Jar*. New York: Bantam.

Moss, J. 1991. *The Other Side of the Door*. New York: Bantam.

Opie, I., and P. Opie (eds). 1992. *I Saw Esau: The Schoolchild's Pocket Book*. Cambridge, MA: Candlewick.

Prelutsky, J. (ed). 1983. *The Random House Book of Poetry for Children*. New York: Random House.

Prelutsky, J. 1984. *The New Kid on the Block*. New York: Random House.

Prelutsky, J. 1990. *Something Big Has Been Here*. New York: Greenwillow.

Silverstein, S. 1974. *Where the Sidewalk Ends*. New York: Harper & Row.

Silverstein, S. 1981. *A Light in the Attic*. New York: Harper & Row.

Slier, D. (ed). 1990. *Make a Joyful Sound: Poems for Children by African-American Poets*. New York: Checkerboard Press.

Figure 5.3
Poetry Collections and Song Books for Celebrating Poetry and Lyrics and for Teaching Word Patterns

6. The lesson ends with these two assignments:
   a. Students are given a sheet of words containing the rimes brainstormed earlier. They are to practice reading and spelling the rimes at home. The sheet also contains the poems practiced during the day so that students can practice reading the poems at home with the assistance of a family member.

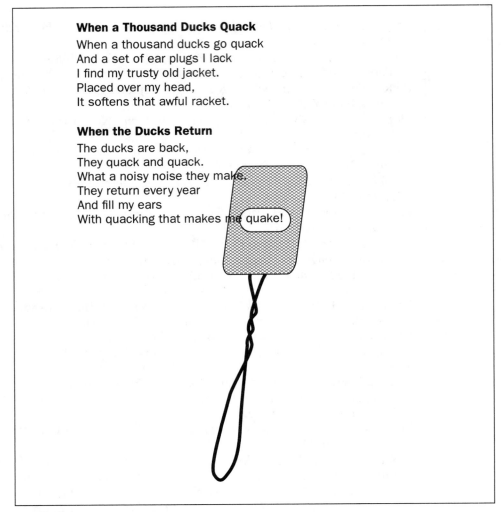

When a Thousand Ducks Quack

When a thousand ducks go quack
And a set of ear plugs I lack
I find my trusty old jacket.
Placed over my head,
It softens that awful racket.

When the Ducks Return

The ducks are back,
They quack and quack.
What a noisy noise they make.
They return every year
And fill my ears
With quacking that makes me quake!

Word Whopper

b. Students are asked to make up their own poetry that features the targeted rime. Students can write their two to six line poems on their own, with a family member, with a classmate, or with a buddy from an upper grade.

This focus on poetry also allows teachers and students to celebrate a wonderful genre that is often neglected and under-used in the language arts curriculum and viewed by many teachers as difficult and unfruitful (Benton 1992, Cullinan et al. 1995, Denman 1988, Lockward 1994, Perfect 1999, Rogers 1985). Even the simple poems that teachers

and children may write say something very important to students–
"poetry is valued and celebrated in our classroom. We are poets!"

DAY 2

1. Day 2 begins with students copying their poems on chart paper supplied by the teacher. These are then hung around the room for later use.
2. Next, students read the words and poems from the previous day.
3. Finally, the lesson turns into a poetry festival as students go around the room reading and celebrating each new poem written by a classmate. Stopping at each posted poem, the author first reads the poem to his or her classmates, pointing out key words. Then, the group reads the poem several times, chorally, antiphonally, and finally in pairs and as individuals. Not only does this activity promote practice of key rimes in real context, it also gives children another reason to celebrate language and themselves as authors.

   If a classroom aide is available, the poems can be quickly transcribed to a word processor, printed and copied for each student to read again at home several times through. Eventually, students may make their own individual or classroom poetry anthologies.

DAY 3

Day 3 is a repeat of Day 1 with a second, contrasting rime. If the rime *ack* was targeted in the first part of the week, the rime for the second half of the week should either include the short *a* sound (*at, ap*) or *ck* ending (*ick, ock*). Before beginning the lesson, students and teacher may want to once again read some of the poems and words practiced over the first two days of the lesson.

DAY 4

The Day 4 lesson is a repeat of the Day 2 lesson with students practicing and making poems using the targeted rime.

DAY 5

Day 5 provides students a chance to review the rimes of the week as well as the opportunity to analyze the differences between the rimes when they occur in the same context.

1. The teacher provides students with a short list of words that contain both rimes that were studied during the week. Students can be asked to read the words, spell them, or both. This activity requires students to discriminate the sounds and spelling of the week's rimes in determining the correct word or spelling.
2. Students read a couple poems or other texts that contain both rimes studied during the week. Again, this provides students with opportunities to examine both rimes within a common context. If the teacher cannot find poems or other texts, she may write her own text or take a dictated text from students, once they understand the lesson routine and the type of text that is desired.

Week Long Routine for Teaching Rimes (Phonograms or Word Families)

DAY 1

Introduce targeted rime

Brainstorm words containing rime; list them on chart paper

Read and reread poems, hinky pinkies, and other texts that feature the rime

Identify individual words from the poems and texts

Assign students to practice reading and spelling the brainstormed rimes

Assign students to write their own poems that feature the targeted rime

DAY 2

Students copy their poems on to chart paper and hang them around the room

Practice reading words and texts from previous day

Read and reread each of the poems written by students as an assignment

Identify individual words from the poems

DAY 3

Repeat Day 1 targeting a contrasting rime (e.g., *ap, at; ack, eck*)

DAY 4

Repeat Day 2 with the contrasting rime

DAY 5

Read and spell words from both rime sets

Students read poems or texts from both rime sets or poems that contain both rimes

Students take home copies of poems read throughout the week to read and practice for possible performance on the next school day

3. Students can take home copies of the poems and texts listed above and be asked to read and reread the texts over the weekend for possible performance on Monday.

This sort of lesson routine provides students with the deep analysis and massed practice that allows them to learn the targeted rimes; however, word recognition instruction on these rimes need not be limited to this routine. Children's books provide the impetus for one activity that first and second grade teacher Jeannine uses with her students (Rajewski 1994). During a study of ants, Jeannine introduces her students to the book *Antics* by Cathi Hepworth, an ABC book in which every word contains the rime *ant* and the accompanying illustration features an ant. For example, the *b* word is *brilliant* and the illustration depicts an Einstein-like ant working in a scientific laboratory. After examining the book, students begin to look on their own for words that have *ant* within them.

Students can also emulate Hepworth's book by writing their own alphabet books with other rimes. This is possible because rimes can be used to generate an enormous number of words. A rime or phonogram ABC book can become an exciting class project as each student is assigned one or two letters and has to think of several words that contain the targeted rime. An illustration reflecting the found words is also done. Students then compile their work into a whole-class ABC book. Students will want to read and reread their phonogram-ABC books for days.

Teachers can simply encourage students to use the targeted words in their talk and writing. A weekly word bank can be developed with some of the words used during the week (or during the following week for additional practice). Moreover, with the two rimes under study, students can sort the word bank by rime or other structural or semantic feature (see Chapter 11 for more information on using word banks). Word bank words can be used for individual or paired word practice. Students can play games such as Word War, Concentration, or Go Fish with the word bank cards. Teachers can introduce other hinky pinkies that feature targeted rimes (e.g. What's another name for John's book bag? Jack's Pack). Cloze passages, in which students use the context of a passage along with the rime knowledge to determine unknown words, can be developed and used (see Chapter 10). Words featuring the targeted rimes may also be used for at least some of the spelling words for the given week. Other word games such as hangman and Wordo (see Chapter 12) can also be played.

In Conclusion

Onsets and rimes are certainly not the only elements of an effective phonics and word recognition program; however, given their efficiency in teaching multiple-letter patterns (rimes and some onsets) as well as their generalizability and consistency, it is clear that they offer students a wonderful entree into the world of phonics, word recognition, and spelling. They can be used to decode one-syllable words in their entirety, and they are very useful in helping readers at least partially figure out longer, more difficult words. Onsets and rimes can be used in ways that allow students to be creative and constructive in their own learning. Onsets and rimes may not be all there is to a good phonics and word recognition program, but they are certainly an important part.

REFERENCES

Adams, M. J. 1990. *Beginning to Read*. Cambridge MA: Massachusetts Institute of Technology Press.

Benton, M. 1992. Poetry, Response and Education. In P. Hunt (ed.), *Literature for Children: Contemporary Criticism*, 127–134. London: Routledge.

Clymer, T. 1996. The Utility of Phonic Generalizations in the Primary Grades. *The Reading Teacher*, 50: 182–187. Originally published in *The Reading Teacher*, 1963, 16.

Cullinan, B., M. C. Scala, and V. C. Schroder. 1995. *Three Voices: An Invitation to Poetry Across the Curriculum*. York, ME: Stenhouse.

Cunningham, P. M. 1987. Action Phonics. *The Reading Teacher*, 41: 247–249.

Denman, G. A. 1988. *When You've Made it Your Own . . . : Teaching Poetry to Young People*. Portsmouth, NH: Heinemann.

Fry, E. 1998. The Most Common Phonograms. *The Reading Teacher*, 51: 620–622.

Hepworth, C. 1992. *Antics*. New York: Putnam & Grosset.

Harris, T., and R. Hodges (eds.). 1995. *The Literacy Dictionary*. Newark, DE: International Reading Association.

Lockward, D. 1994. Poets on Teaching Poetry. *English Journal*, 83: 65–70.

Perfect, K. A. 1999. Rhyme and Reason: Poetry for the Heart and Head. *The Reading Teacher*, 52: 728–737.

Rajewski, J. P. 1994. Anticipating Antipasto in Antarctica? *The Reading Teacher*, 47: 678–679.

Rogers, W.C. 1985. Teaching Poetic Thought. *The Reading Teacher*, 39: 296–300.

6
TEACHING ADVANCED
WORD PATTERNS

Justin teaches fourth grade, and he still considers himself a phonics teacher.
"Sure, I teach phonics, but it's not the b buh, t tuh phonics that people think of when they hear the word phonics. I think that phonics means helping students see the connection between letters and groups of letters and the sounds that they represent. That is just what I do with my students, except the groups of letters we work with are the root words and prefixes that come from Latin and Greek. This week we are studying the prefix anti and the root word phobia. I introduce one or two roots or prefixes a week and we spend about ten minutes each day exploring the meaning, pronunciation, and real words that contain those roots. I ask students to look for the roots we have studied in their reading and I challenge them to use the roots in their school talk. This is the first year I've tried looking at words in this way with my students, but I can really see that it's turning some of the kids on to words and how they get their meaning. I get a lot more predictions about words when we come across unknown words in reading, especially in the different content areas."

Onsets and rimes provide teachers with a powerful tool for helping students discover how words work. With knowledge of only the 41 onsets that are taught in Action Phonics (Cunningham 1987), and the 38 most common rimes (Fry 1998), students are able to decode thousands of single and multi-syllabic words; however, onsets and rimes are not the only patterns that we can teach students as part of a word recognition program. As Justin has found, other patterns exist that have the added feature of containing meaning, which can help a reader learn not only to decode a word, but also provide some information about its meaning. These types of patterns are generally taught after students have developed some basic reading skills and are beginning to read independently to learn on their own.

In general, meaning bearing patterns fall under two categories. The first is affixes, patterned word parts that are attached to existing words to alter their basic meaning. Prefixes and suffixes are both affixes; prefixes come at the beginning of words and suffixes come at the end of words.

The second category of meaningful word patterns are called derivational patterns or roots. These are word parts derived from other languages, notably

Greek and Latin, that have found their way into many English words. Derivational word patterns are important for understanding and decoding unfamiliar words and often appear in new words in English (e.g., *microchip*) as well.

By teaching affixes and derivational patterns to students, teachers will not only expand students' strategies for decoding unknown words, they will also expand their vocabularies and provide students with strategies for determining the meanings of unknown words. Given this enormous potential of meaningful word patterns, it is reasonable to assume that a good word recognition program should provide ongoing instruction in their recognition and use.

TEACHING AFFIXES

A fairly comprehensive list of prefixes and suffixes that are worth teaching students is provided in Appendices C and D. It is not necessary to teach each and every affix listed in these appendices; however, these lists provide teachers with the raw material for exploring affixes with students.

Teaching affixes can begin in the first grade with suffixes that denote number (*-s* ending) and tense (*-ed* ending). As students begin to develop their basic word recognition skills, teachers can introduce them to prefixes and suffixes that have more elaborate meanings. Exactly how many affixes should be taught in a year is a judgment call that depends on the students' affix needs, affixes related to particular content areas, and students' and teachers' interest in words and affixes. As a rule of thumb, teaching approximately fifty affixes per year in grades two through eight would cover the entire list in Appendices C and D. We recommend that teachers in these grades confer to determine which grade levels will be responsible for teaching students particular affixes.

Some affixes should be taught and revisited throughout the elementary grades. These are the affixes that appear most frequently in words. According to Carroll, Davies and Richman (1971) the following seven prefix groups represent sixty-six percent of all words that contain prefixes:

un-
re-
in-, im-, il-, ir- (not)
dis-
en-, em-
non-
in-, im- (in or into)

With suffixes, the frequency analysis yields an even more critical set that should be taught. The following seven suffix groups represent eighty-two percent of all words containing suffixes:

-s, -es
-ed
-ing
-ly
-er, -or (agent as in presenter or actor)

-ion, -tion, -ation, -ition
-able, -ible

How should affixes be taught? As with other areas of word study, no single method has proven more successful than others. We suggest an eclectic approach in which one or two affixes are taught per week. Introduce students to the affix, discuss the meaning, and brainstorm words that contain the affix. List the words on a word wall and encourage students to use the words in their speaking and writing and to be on the lookout for other words to add to the list. Selected words from the brainstormed list can be added to the class's spelling list. Revisit the targeted affixes and words briefly throughout the next several days.

Many of the activities discussed in later chapters can be employed to teach affixes: Making and Writing Words (Chapter 8), word banks and word sort activities (Chapter 9), Cloze activities in which the teacher might compose texts that focus on targeted affixes and words (Chapter 10), and word games (Chapter 12). For the most part, affixes are learned through wide reading and in-depth examination. These activities should provide sufficient opportunities for examination and learning.

TEACHING DERIVATIONAL PATTERNS

As we mentioned previously, derivational patterns or roots refer to those word parts, derived from Greek, Latin, and other languages, that are found in English words. Knowledge of these word parts will help students decode words and discover their meanings. For example, knowing that the root *hem-* or *hemo-* means blood, helps us with some of the pronunciation and meaning of longer words like *hemodialysis, hemoglobin, hemorrhage, hemostat, hemophilia,* and *hematoma.* An extensive list of Greek and Latin derivatives or roots can be found in Appendix E. (You may also want to checkout some of the websites listed in Appendix F for ideas to turn your students on to words and word study.)

Derivational patterns are best taught after students have developed some facility with basic word recognition strategies and affixes. Third or fourth grade is a good time to begin study of derivational patterns, though teachers at any grade level can take advantage of teachable moments to introduce and explore individual patterns.

The same sort of instructional strategies and activities that we suggested for teaching affixes can be used for derivational patterns. Introducing students to one or two roots and their derivations per week should be sufficient to whet students' appetites for learning and exploring derivational patterns. Additional activities such as adding words to spelling lists and word walls, word banks and sorts, Making and Writing Words with Letter Patterns, Cloze activities, and word games should help solidify students' recognition and understanding of these important word parts.

An alternative or complementary approach to teaching derivational patterns is to begin not with the word part or root itself, but to begin with actual words that are derived from the Latin or Greek root. Our list of essential words and derivations is provided in Figure 6.1, and a list of resources for teaching derivations can be found in Figure 6.2. Used as the basis for word of the week, it would take over two years for students to cover all the targeted words. The words on this list contain one or more derivational patterns that can be used to learn the pronunciation and meaning of many other words. The targeted word is really only the starting point for study. Students are exposed to and learn the meaning of other words that contain the derivational root as well as the targeted word itself. Word study expands to a wide variety of longer, more difficult, multisyllabic words.

This list of words provides teachers with a body of words (and derivations) that are worth teaching at the elementary and middle school levels. Knowledge of the words and their meaningful word parts can be generalized to a large number of words and concepts that students will encounter in various content areas.

The words appear alphabetically. We recommend that the words be presented approximately one per week and that teachers across content areas demonstrate the words to students and discuss the words daily.

	Definition/ Comment	Derivative & related words	Derivative & related words
1. Acrophobia	Fear of heights.	acro = high *acropolis* *acrobat* *acronym*	phobia = fear *agoraphobia* *hydrophobia*
2. Ambidextrous	Able to use both hands.	ambi = both, all around *ambiguous* *ambivalence* *ambient*	dexter = skilled *dexterity*
3. Amphitheater	A theater in an oval form with an open center and seats all around and higher.	amphi = both, all around *amphibian* *amphibious*	thea = to see, to view *theater* *theatrics*
4. Anarchy	Lack of government, law, or supreme power.	an = no *anesthetic* *anonymous* *anomaly* *anorexia*	archos = ruler, chief person *archbishop* *archenemy*
5. Antebellum	Before the war (usually meant to be before the Civil War).	ante = before *antecedent* *anteroom* *antemortem*	belli, bellum = war *bellicose* *belligerent*

Figure 6.1
Essential Words and Essential Derivatives for Upper Elementary and Middle Grades

6. Antithesis	A contrast or opposition of ideas or words.	anti, anto = against, in opposition to, before *antidote* *antonym* *antiseptic* *antipasto* *antipathy* *antisocial*	thesis = an assertion or statement to be considered *synthesis*
7. Appendix	Something added that is not essential.	pend = to hang *append* *appendicitis* *pendant* *depends* *pending*	
8. Asterisk	A little star.	ast = star *astronaut* *asteroid* *aster* *astrology* *astronomy*	
9. Auditorium	Large room in which to listen.	aud = hear *auditory* *audition*	orium = room, building *sanitorium*
10. Automobile	A car.	auto = self *autobiography*	mobile = to move, movable *mobile home* *mobilize*
11. Bicameral	A legislature with two houses or chambers.	bi = two *bicycle* *bilingual* *biped*	camera = chamber, house *unicameral* *camera*
12. Captain	One who is at the head, who has authority.	cap = head *capital* *capitol* *cap* *decapitate*	
13. Cartography	The practice of drawing maps.	cart, chart = paper *cartoon* *carton* *carte blanche* *Magna Carta*	graph = write, chart *photograph* *phonograph* *telegraph*

Figure 6.1 *(continued)*
Essential Words and Essential Derivatives for Upper Elementary and Middle Grades

14. Cent	One hundred.	cent = 100 *century* *percent* *centennial* *centigrade* *centipede* *centurion*	
15. Centimeter	One one-hundredth of a meter.	cent = 100 *century* *centurion* *percent*	meter = a unit of or device that measures *thermometer* *barometer* *odometer* *kilometer*
16. Chili con carne	A Mexican food made with red peppers (chili) and chopped meat.	con, cum = with *cum laude* *conspire* *constellation* *contact*	carne = meat *carnivore* *carnage* *carnal* *incarnate*
17. Circumspect	Inspect or examine all sides carefully.	circum = around *circumstantial* *circumnavigate* *circus* *circumvent*	spect = look, view *specter* *spectator* *inspect* *spectacles*
18. Cognition	To come to know, to think.	cognos = to know *recognize* *cognizant*	
19. Contemporary	Existing or occurring at the same time.	con = with *conscious* *congruence* *confluence*	temp = time *temporary* *tempo* *temporal*
20. Contract	An oral or written agreement.	con = with *contrite* *contribute* *convene* *convent*	tract = pull *abstract* *retract* *traction*
21. Contradict	To deny; to say or assert not to be so.	contra = against *contrary* *contraband* *contrast* *contraception*	dict = to say, speak *dictionary* *dictate* *dictator* *dictaphone*

Figure 6.1 (*continued*)
Essential Words and Essential Derivatives for Upper Elementary and Middle Grades

22. Contribute	To give; to assign.	con = with *contrite* *contract* *convene*	tribut = to give, to bestow *tribute* *tributary* *attribute* *retribution*
23. Corpus	The body of a person; the collection of laws or writing of one type.	corp = body *corpse* *corporation* *habeas corpus* *coporal punishment*	
24. Countermand	To revoke an order; to change a command to the opposite or reverse direction.	counter = against *counterintelligence* *counterespionage* *encounter*	mand = order, dictate *command* *mandate* *mandatory* *demand*
25. Demented	Insane, out of one's mind.	de = from, out of *demerit* *demoralize* *deport* *derail*	ment = pertaining to the mind *mental*
26. Democrat	A person who believes in rule by the people.	demo = people *demography*	crat = rule; govern *autocrat* *bureaucrat* *theocracy*
27. Demography	Statistics about groups of people.	demo = people *democracy* *democrat*	graph = to write, to chart *graphite* *graphic* *photograph* *phonograph*
28. Doctrine	A particular principle or belief that is taught.	doc, dogma = that which seems true *dogmatic*	
29. Equilateral	Having all sides equal in length.	equi = equal *equinox* *equilibrium* *equidistant*	lateral = side *unilateral* *bilateral* *quadrilateral*

Figure 6.1 (*continued*)
Essential Words and Essential Derivatives for Upper Elementary and Middle Grades

30. Exhume	Remove a body from its burial place.	ex = from *excommunicate* *exhale*	humus = ground *posthumous*
31. Extraterrestrial	Someone from outside the limits of earth.	extra = beyond, in addition to *extrovert* *extravagant* *extraordinary* *extrapolate*	terra = land *terrace* *terrapin* *Mediterranean*
32. Fidelity	Faithfulness, observance of duty.	fides = faith *confide* *confidential* *infidel*	
33. Forecast	To make a prediction.	fore = preceding in time, place, or order; at the front of *foremost* *forerunner* *forearm* *foredeck* *forebade*	cast = to throw, calculate, plan *recast* *downcast* *castaway*
34. Fragment	A part broken off.	frag, frac = break *fracture* *fraction* *fractious*	
35. Fratercide	To kill one's brother or sister.	frater = brother *fraternal twins* *fraternity* *fraternize*	cide = murder *suicide* *homicide* *regicide*
36. Hydrophobia	Fear of water.	hydro = water *hydrant* *dehydrate* *hydraulic* *hydroplane* *hydroponics*	phobia = fear *acrophobia* *anthophobia* *agoraphobia*
37. Hypodermic	Under the skin as in a hypo-dermic needle.	hypo = under, below *hypoglycemia* *hypochondria* *hypocrite* *hypothesis*	derm = skin *dermatologist* *epidermis*
38. Immortal	Cannot die.	im = not *immobilize* *immature*	mort = death *mortuary* *mortal* *mortician*

Figure 6.1 (*continued*)
Essential Words and Essential Derivatives for Upper Elementary and Middle Grades

39. Innate	Characteristics one is born with.	in = within *inland* *inmost* *inmate*	nat = born *nativity* *nature* *native* *prenatal*
40. Intermission	A temporary pause between two periods of action.	inter = between *intermediate* *interfere* *international* *interrupt* *interval*	mission = a purposeful activity *missionary* *dismiss* *remiss*
41. Intramural	Within the limits of a school, organization, or community.	intra = within *intravenous* *intrastate* *intramolecular*	murus = wall *mural*
42. Journey	A travel. Originally the length traveled in one day on foot (20 miles).	jour = day, daily *soup de jour* *bon jour* *journal* *journalist*	
43. Lackluster	Dull, without brightness or vitality.	lack = without *lackadaisical*	luster = brightness, reflected light *illustrious* *illustrate*
44. Macrocosm	The great world; the universe; the entire complex.	macro = large, great, long *macrostructure* *macron* *macrophage*	cosmos = world or universe or entire complex *cosmopolitan* *cosmology* *cosmography*
45. Mandate	A command or order.	mand = to commit, enjoin, command *command* *mandatory* *remand* *countermand*	
46. Mediterranean	The sea surround-ed by (in the middle of) large land masses.	medi = middle *media* *mediocre* *medium* *median* *intermediate* *mediate*	terra = land *terrarium* *terrapin* *extraterrestrial* *terra cotta*

Figure 6.1 (*continued*)
Essential Words and Essential Derivatives for Upper Elementary and Middle Grades

47. Megalopolis	A large city or combination of cities—main city and its suburbs.	mega = large *megabyte* *megaphone* *megaton*	polis = city, land area under one government *metropolis* *acropolis* *Indianapolis* *political*
48. Memorial	Something to preserve the memory of someone or something.	memor = mindful *remember* *memory* *memorize* *memoir* *memorandum*	
49. Microscope	A scientific instrument that allows very small items to be seen.	micro = extremely small *microbe* *microfilm* *microwave* *microorganism*	scope = to see a target *telescope* *endoscope* *periscope*
50. Misanthropy	A hater of mankind (people).	mis = incorrect, hate, wrong *miscalculate* *misdirect* *misfile* *mislead*	anthro = pertaining to people *anthropology* *anthropomorphic* *philanthropy* *anthropocentric*
51. Navigate	To steer; to travel, especially by ship.	navis = ship *navy* *navigator* *naval* *navigable*	
52. Novel	Something new.	nov = new *novelty* *novice* *novocain* *nouveau riche* *nova* *innovate* *renovate*	
53. Omniscient	Having knowledge of everything (all).	omni = all *omnipotence* *omnivorous* *omnibus*	scient (science) = knowledge *conscience* *reminiscent*

Figure 6.1 (*continued*)
Essential Words and Essential Derivatives for Upper Elementary and Middle Grades

54. Orthodontist	A dentist who specializes in straightening and aligning teeth.	ortho = straight *orthodox*	dont (dent) = pertaining to teeth *dentist* *periodontist*
55. Paralegal	A clerk with some expertise in the law.	para = besides, in addition *paramedic* *paranormal* *parable* *paraphrase*	leg, legis = dealing with the law *legislature* *legal* *legitimate*
56. Parlor	A room for receiving guests; a room for conversation.	parl- (Fr.) = to talk *parliament*	
57. Pathology	The study of the nature of diseases.	pathos = suffering, illness, sorrow *empathy* *sympathy* *pathogen*	logo = discourse, to reason ogy = study of *sociology* *psychology* *logic*
58. Pedestrian	A person in the act of walking. (foot travel).	ped (pod, pied) = pertaining to feet *pedestal* *pedal* *podiatrist* *tripod* *piedmont*	
59. Pentagon	Five-sided geometric shape.	pent = five *pentathlon* *pentagram* *Pentecost*	gon = side *polygon* *octagon*
60. Perimeter	The boundary measurement of a figure having two dimensions.	peri = around, surrounding *periscope* *periphery* *perigee*	meter = to measure *barometer* *odometer* *sphygmometer*
61. Periscope	An instrument that allows one to view around objects that are in the direct line of vision as in a submarine.	peri = round, around *perimeter* *pericardium* *periodontal* *periphery*	scope = to see a target *microscope* *telescope* *endoscope*

Figure 6.1 (*continued*)
Essential Words and Essential Derivatives for Upper Elementary and Middle Grades

62. Philanthropy	Love of humanity shown by practical gifts or kindness.	phil, phile = lover or admirer of *Philadelphia* *philharmonic* *bibliophile* *philosopher*	anthropos = having to do with humankind *anthropology* *anthomorphic* *misanthropy* *anthrophobic*
63. Philosopher	A lover of knowledge or wisdom.	philo = love *philanthropy* *philander* *philharmonic* *Philadelphia*	soph = knowledge or wisdom *sophomore*
64. Plateau	A plain (flat place or plate) on the mountains.	plate, plat, pla = wide and flat *platform* *platter* *platypus* *plaza* *place* *misplace*	
65. Polygraph	A machine that charts several features; i.e., a polygraph (truth detector) measures and charts pulse, respiration, and other body functions.	poly = many *polygon* *polygamous* *polymer* *polysyllabic* *Polynesia* *polytheism*	graph = to write or chart *telegraph* *graphite* *seismograph* *graphic* *cartography* *phonograph*
66. Polytheism	Belief in many gods.	poly = many *polygamy* *polymer* *polygraph* *polyglot* *polynomial*	theo (theism) = pertaining to god *theocracy* *monotheism* *theology*
67. Porter	A person who carries another's luggage, especially on a train.	port = to carry *portage* *transport* *export/import* *report*	
68. Pseudonym	A false name.	pseudo = false *pseudo science*	nym = name *synonym* *antonym*

Figure 6.1 (*continued*)
Essential Words and Essential Derivatives for Upper Elementary and Middle Grades

69. Psychopath	A mentally ill person.	psych = mind *psychology* *psychic* *psychoanalyst* *psychiatry*	path = suffering illness *pathology* *sociopath*
70. Regal	Pertaining to a king (or queen); ruler.	reg = king *regent* *regalia* *regime* *regicide* *regency*	
71. Regicide	The murder/killing of a king or ruler.	regi = king, ruler *regent* *regulation* *regal* *region* *regime*	cide = to kill *suicide* *homicide* *infanticide*
72. Submarine	A boat that is able to travel under the sea.	sub = under *subway* *subterranean* *submerge*	marin = pertaining to the sea *mariner* *marinade* *marina*
73. Synchronize	At the same time.	syn = same *synonym*	chron = time *anachronism* *chronological* *chronic*
74. Theology	The study of God.	theo = God *theosophy* *theocracy*	ology = the study of *sociology* *psychology*
75. Thermometer	A device for measuring temperature.	therm = heat *thermodynamics* *thermophile* *thermostat* *thermograph* *thermal*	meter = measure *centimeter*
76. Transform	To change in form or appearance.	trans = change, across *transcribe* *transfigure* *transfusion* *transfer* *transition*	form = shape, appearance *formal* *uniform* *reform* *deform* *inform* *formula*

Figure 6.1 (*continued*)
Essential Words and Essential Derivatives for Upper Elementary and Middle Grades

77. Unison	To speak with one voice; decide together.	uni = one *uniform* *unicycle*	son = voice, sound *sonic* *supersonic* *sonar* *sonorous* *song* *sonata*
78. Vacuous	Empty; without contents.	vac = empty *evacuate* *vacuum* *vacant* *vacancy* *vacation*	
79. Vagabond	Wandering from place to place; unsettled; worthless.	vag = wander *vagrant* *vagary* *vague* *extravagant*	
80. Variegated	Varied in appearance.	var = to change *varied* *variable* *variance* *variety* *various*	
81. Voracious	Extreme hunger.	vor = eat *carnivore* *herbivore* *omnivore*	

Figure 6.1 (*continued*)
Essential Words and Essential Derivatives for Upper Elementary and Middle Grades

ENCOURAGING CREATIVITY

Behind all this instruction and activity is the idea that students need to learn these important word patterns, but also that students develop an intense fascination with words—to become wordsmiths. One of the greatest wordsmiths of all time was William Shakespeare. Recently, Richard Lederer (1998) reported that Shakespeare invented approximately 8.5% of all the unique words he used in his plays. Words such as *assassination, bedroom, dishearten, frugal, majestic, obscene, premeditated,* and *sanctimonious* have their first known attribution to one of Shakespeare's works. That's pretty remarkable.

Well, if word invention is good enough for Shakespeare, it certainly should be good enough for our students. Once students gain understanding and control of a fair number of affixes and derivational patterns, they can join the teacher in inventing new words to describe particular phenomena. For example,

Ehrlich, I. 1968. *Instant Vocabulary*. New York: Simon & Schuster.
The book highlights 259 derivational patterns, mostly from Greek and Latin, used in English. Each pattern is identified with its meaning. A list of words and definitions that contain the targeted derivational pattern is embedded is also provided

Fry, E. B., D. L. Fountaoukidis, J. K. Polk. 1999. *The New Reading Teacher's Book of Lists* (4th ed.). Englewood Cliffs, NJ: Prentice-Hall.
This book of lists is a treasure trove for reading teachers. Among other resources, it contains lists of homophones, homographs, instant (high frequency, sight) words, spelling demons, word idioms, metaphors, prefixes, suffixes, and Latin and Greek roots.

Lundquist, J. 1989. *English From The Roots Up: Help For Reading, Writing, Spelling, and SAT Scores*. Bellevue, Washington: Literacy Unlimited.
Individual Greek and Latin roots are presented in lesson-like formats. Words derived from each root are presented as well as teaching notes for telling the story behind each root.

Figure 6.2
Valuable Resources for Teaching Affix and Derivation Patterns

in one fifth grade class we recently visited, students who had been studying affixes and derivational patterns came up with the following words and riddles:

What sort of animal might experience *photophobia*?   A mole
In what countries might a person find *paleologs*? Ancient Egypt, Greece, Rome
What is a more common word that girls use
    to describe a boy who has a *graticorps*?   Hunk
Why might dogs be called *brevorous*?   They eat quickly
What is an *autophiliac*?   A person who loves himself

Students enjoy engaging in such creative use of words, especially if it gives them the opportunity to stump their teacher and classmates.

Another creative use of words is found in poetry writing. Myra Cohen Livingston (1997) devised a poetry game to encourage her students to think creatively and play with words when writing poetry. The activity is really quite simple. Provide students with a set of unrelated words, begin with one word and work up to six or more. Challenge students to write a poem (or other text) that uses all the chosen words. It can be a difficult task for many students at first, but, over time and with practice, students can become quite adept at using words in creative and divergent ways to create a coherent poem.

In Livingston's poetry workshop she began by asking students to make a poem that contained the word *rabbit*. Next she gave her students these three words to incorporate into their poem: *ring, drum, blanket*. Finally, students were asked to use six words, *hole, friend, candle, ocean, snake,* and *bucket* or *scarecrow*, in their writing.

Livingston (1997) published her students' remarkable poetry using this game technique in a volume entitled *I Am Writing a Poem About . . . A Game of Poetry*. Here's an excerpt from one poem called "A Summer Hum" by Peggy Levitt:

> Gonna dig a hole,
> crawl right in,
> serenade a mole
> on my violin.
>
> Gonna burn in the sun
> without suntan lotion.
> If I get too hot
> gonna jump in the ocean.

As you can see, giving students license to use words creatively and inventively can result in some dynamic, enjoyable, and publishable texts.

In Conclusion

Word recognition and word study need not end in the primary grades as students develop mastery of their basic phonic skills and strategies; rather, we can nurture a fascination with words, along with a deeper understanding of how words work, by continuing to explore words well beyond the years of fundamental phonics instruction. Affixes and derivational word patterns are wonderful places to continue our study of words beyond initial phonics.

Onsets and rimes are not the only word patterns that are useful for students in decoding words. As Justin, the fourth grade teacher we introduced you to in the beginning of this chapter discovered for himself, sound-symbol patterns and other word characteristics can be explored well beyond the initial school years. In particular, affixes and Greek and Latin derivations are very useful in helping students decode (pronounce) and understand particular words. As students move beyond the initial stages of word recognition, word study should turn toward these more sophisticated word patterns. Students who learn about these word patterns will be more able to pronounce unknown words that contain the patterns, and knowledge of the patterns will help students predict the meanings of many unknown words. The same activities and playful attitude that characterize early word study should also manifest themselves in learning about these more sophisticated patterns. If we approach word study with a sense of playfulness and fascination, it is likely that students will be fascinated by words throughout their lives.

References

Carroll, J. B., P. Davies, and B. Richman. 1971. *The American Heritage Word Frequency Book*. Boston: Houghton Mifflin.

Cunningham, P. 1987. Action Phonics. *The Reading Teacher*, 41: 247–249.

Fry, E. 1998. The Most Common Phonograms. *The Reading Teacher*, 51: 620–622.

Lederer, R. 1998. A Writer of Fire-New Words. *Writers Digest*, 78: (4), 7.

Livingston, M. C. (ed). 1997. *I Am Writing a Poem About . . . A Game of Poetry*. New York: McElderry Books.

7
WORD WALLS

A classroom that fosters word learning looks the part. Words are every-where—labels, children's writing, chart stories. Sometimes children's attention is purposefully drawn to all this print. Other times, class-room print is just a literate backdrop while children engage in other activities. It's been said that interest in words is caught, not taught. We agree, and we think that the physical environment in the classroom can encourage children to catch an interest in words.

Within these word-laden classrooms, several principles drive word recognition instruction (Rasinski and Padak 2000). Word recognition instruc-tion is an inherent part of, rather than separate from, meaningful reading and other reading activities. Indeed, the whole-to-part instructional princi-ple that we mention throughout the book is an example of this kind of think-ing. Instruction that takes on a playful, problem-solving feel encourages children to think about words actively and to take the risks that can lead to a thorough understanding of how words work. Children need lots of opportu-nities to see words and word parts within the context of meaningful activity, a notion that Sandy McCormick (1994) calls "multiple contexts/ multiple ex-posures." Throughout, the teacher's role is to help children see their options for word recognition and to encourage practice of these options in real read-ing situations.

Word Walls are one part of an overall program that achieves these goals. Moreover, Word Walls send significant messages to students and classroom visitors: "Words and reading are important in this room," "We celebrate words here!" Some teachers and students who use Word Walls extensively call their classrooms wordshops! In this chapter, we describe Word Walls and offer lots of examples of Word Wall activities.

WHAT IS A WORD WALL?

Think of a Word Wall as a working bulletin board in which words are the focus. That's essentially what it is—and more. To create a Word Wall, the teacher first places a large sheet of chart paper or butcher paper on the wall.

Either alone or in discussion with students, the teacher decides on the focus of the Word Wall. (Below we offer many possible topics.) From that point on, anything goes. Students may add several words to the Word Wall each day, and the teacher may add words as well. Students may look for and make connections between and among words. The teacher may ask students to read the words on the Word Wall for practice or may use the words as a source of quick guessing games: "Find a word on the Word Wall that _____." And of course, the words are easily visible for other student uses, such as checking on spelling. Elsewhere, we have described Word Walls as "part community word bank, part graffiti wall, a place where students feel free to write their own words and commentaries" (Rasinski and Padak 2000, p. 87).

Depending on their intended uses, the teacher and children may either write directly on the Word Wall or make smaller word cards that can be manipulated. If lots of categorizing activities are anticipated, the latter may be the better choice. Words can be printed on large sticky notes, or cut-up pieces of newsprint and masking tape can be used to make moveable word cards. Most Word Walls are temporary; after a few days or weeks, new Word Walls replace old ones. Moreover, Word Walls are meant to be used not just viewed; so, teachers might experiment with formats to find a means of construction that works well for them and their students. In any event, the words should be large enough for easy viewing from any place in the classroom.

All students should watch and listen when Word Wall words are added. The teacher should say the word and comment briefly on it. These comments may connect to the word's meaning, its relevance to the focus of the Word Wall, or even some aspect of word study, such as "what vowel sound do you hear?" or "how many syllables does this word have?" These quick displays in both developing and using Word Walls provide just the sort of "multiple exposures" essential for successful word learning.

SOURCES OF WORDS

Words for Word Walls can come from any area of the curriculum. One caution though: don't include too many totally unfamiliar words on a Word Wall. Learning new words in isolation is very challenging for most children. New words or concepts should first be encountered in the context of reading or discussion. After they have gained some familiarity with the new word or concept, children will be able to think about it apart from context. This is the time for Word Wall activity.

Beyond this general guideline, teachers will find many uses for Word Walls. In reading, for example, a Word Wall might focus on synonyms, particular word families, or vowel or consonant sounds. As described below, Word Walls are a good choice for vocabulary development activities as well. In writing, Word Walls may be used to collect powerful verbs, similes, metaphors, or even contractions. A math Word Wall might offer synonyms for addition or subtraction, or examples of geometric figures (perhaps accompanied by sketches). In science, social studies, or health, new concepts can be listed on Word Walls along with related concepts with which students are more familiar.

We hope this list of possibilities helps you see that Word Walls are very adaptable. In essence, teachers may use them in any way that supports students' learning, either about words and word parts or about new concepts. The versatility of Word Walls is one of their instructional strengths. Students quickly become accustomed to what Word Walls are and how they work, so teachers have a useful routine for addressing lots of curricular goals.

USING WORD WALLS

In this section, we offer many ways to construct and use Word Walls. By no means is this an exhaustive list. Our intent is to help teachers think about possibilities.

NAME WALLS

An early activity in most kindergarten and early primary classes is to focus on children's names. This enables children to get to know one another and provides an immediately meaningful reading activity. Teachers who create Word Walls of students' names have a handy instructional tool. Children can read the names each day, with teacher assistance initially. Names can be sorted into categories like *boys or girls, present or absent,* or *school lunch or brought lunch.* As the school year progresses, the name wall can be a source for introducing alphabetical order or drawing children's attention to letters within words. The latter could involve simply counting letters within each person's name, grouping names by numbers of letters, or arranging the entire list from least to most letters (or vice versa). Even quick guessing games, such as "Who has more letters? [Student A or Student B]?" or "How many of us have a B in our names?" provide quick, game-like practice thinking about letters as parts of words. "Who has more letters" is also a way to teach the mathematical concepts *more* and *less.*

Hall and Cunningham (1997) describe an activity called "ABC and You" that is easily adapted to Word Wall format. First, children's names are listed in alphabetical order; next, each child selects at least one word that begins with the same letter as his or her name. These are added to the alphabetical list:

A . . . Adorable Annie
E . . . Energetic Emily
M . . . Merry Matt
. . . . Mysterious Mike

Children are so fond of this version of a name wall that they sometimes wish to find new words to go along with their names. If moveable word cards are used, "Adorable Annie" can easily become "Active, adorable Annie" and so forth. Children enjoy reciting the chart and sometimes may be heard mentioning possible additions for themselves or others. "Hey!" one child said to Mike. "You could add *munching* to yours."

Student of the Week is another feature of many kindergarten and early primary classrooms. Why not create a Word Wall about the featured student? It might contain words that are special to and descriptive of the student, such as names of family members, pets, favorite foods, personal characteristics, or it might be a sort of name poem that includes words other children think are related to the featured child. Figure 7.1 shows an example of this kind of Word Wall. At the end of the week, the featured student can take the Word Wall home for further celebration.

ENVIRONMENTAL PRINT WALLS

Attention to environmental print is a staple in many early literacy classrooms because of children's interest and familiarity in the words that surround them outside of school. An environmental print wall is a Word Wall focused on some type of environmental print. One way to accomplish this is to make the wall general, for example, "Words We See." Another option is to select some category of environmental print, for instance, cereal or sneakers,

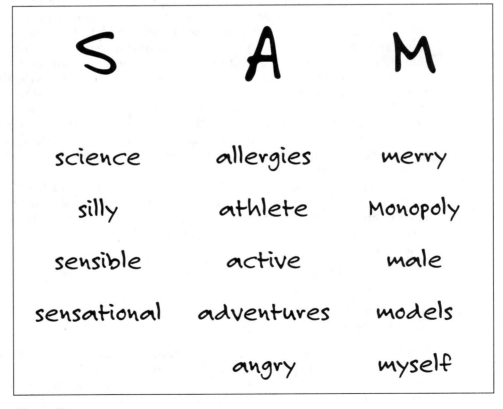

Figure 7.1
Sam's Name Wall

and challenge children to find as many examples in the category as possible. They may even want to bring in logos from empty boxes or look through old newspapers and magazines for homework, to find additions to the wall. We know that for beginning readers the logos are often more salient than the print; therefore teachers should add logos to the Word Wall and should also print the words separately, apart from the logos, to provide children with a context-free look at the words.

The resulting wall can be used for practicing words and developing many other early literacy notions, such as letter recognition. Depending on the focus of the wall, children's concepts of print can also be addressed. Think of fast food restaurants, for example, which have one-word names? Two? And math activity is possible as well. Again, with fast food restaurants as an example, children might select their favorites and create a class chart (e.g., bar graph) entitled "where we like to eat."

WORD WEBS

Word webs (Fox 1996) is a small group instructional activity that focuses students' attention on particular word parts. To engage students in word webbing, the teacher selects a meaningful word part for focus, such as a prefix or Greek or Latin root, and assembles dictionaries, paper, pencils, chart paper, and markers. To begin the activity, the teacher introduces the word part, for example, *port,* and invites students to brainstorm words that contain the word part. (See Chapter 6 for more on derivations.) These are written on the chalkboard; after a few have been suggested, the teacher asks students to speculate on the meaning of the word part.

Next, small groups assemble. One person in each group, acting as the recorder or secretary, writes the word part in the center of a sheet of paper and circles it. Now group members search their memories and the dictionary for other words containing the word part. The goal is to find as many words as possible. They list these, talk about word meanings, and ultimately group related words in ways that make sense to them. These word groups are added to the word web as clusters or mini-webs (see Figure 7.2). When all groups have completed their webs, a whole-class discussion provides each group the opportunity to share its word web with the rest of the class.

After the whole-class discussion, small groups reconvene, make changes in their initial word webs if they desire, and prepare a final copy of their webs using chart paper and markers or the computer. Final copies of the word webs are combined on a *word web wall,* which is a large sheet of chart paper labeled with the word part that children studied. The word web wall may be replaced every week or two with another that reflects children's understanding about a different word part. Another alternative, perhaps a bit more challenging, is to ask different groups to create webs for different word parts. The resulting word web wall, then, would be a compilation of students' individual webs.

As described by Fox (1996), word webbing is probably most appropriate for intermediate-level students, but the same idea could be used in primary

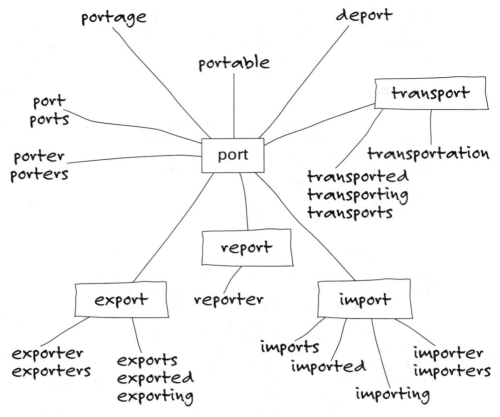

Figure 7.2
A Word Web

classrooms to create *word family walls*. Here students would brainstorm about words that contain a given word family, for example, *ant*, then proceed as described above. Reading a book like Cathi Hepworth's (1992) *Antics!* to children beforehand may spark their imaginations.

CONTENT AREA WALLS

One obvious use of Word Walls in content area study is to record words that students believe to be important to some unit of study. As a new unit begins, the teacher can ask students to brainstorm words associated with the topic of the unit: "We're going to study electricity. What words do you think of when I say the word *electricity*?" This brief activity serves two important purposes. First, of course, it gets students thinking about the topic of the unit. In this respect, beginning to develop the content area wall is a quick and effective prereading activity. An additional benefit is the diagnostic value of the resulting list, since teachers can learn about students' prior topical knowledge by examining the quantity and variety of words.

Every now and then throughout the unit, the teacher can invite children to add more words to the content area wall. For example, Word Walls can provide content area cohesion for teachers who use trade books to augment conceptual learning. Here's how Bonnie, an intermediate-grade teacher, explains it:

"Our textbooks are pretty boring and much too difficult for some of my students, so I try to supplement with a few library books. When we started studying electricity last fall, I read *Nikola Tesla: Spark of Genius* (Dommermuth-Costa 1994) to the children, one chapter each day. In addition to learning about this fascinating man's life, the students jotted down words related to electricity as I read, then they talked in small groups to decide which words to add to our electrifying word wall. Sometimes these were interesting and lively discussions—I remember quite a chat about *gigantic streaks of light*, which ended up on the word wall, and *nature's secrets*, which didn't."

Finding important words to add to the wall is an interesting comprehension activity—students must understand the content and select words that are important to the topic under study. The content area wall provides a good record of what children have learned, especially if new additions are written with different colors of markers. A semantic web (like a word web) of all the words is an effective culminating activity.

SIGHT WORD WALLS

Sight words are words that students recognize instantly and effortlessly. Common, high-frequency words, such as the words on the Dolch list or the Fry Instant Word List (see Appendix B), are good candidates for learning by sight. Sight words are best learned by lots of contextual reading because students will encounter these high-frequency words often. Teachers can reinforce this learning by developing a sight word wall. Five words can be added to the word wall every week and practiced occasionally during spare moments in the classroom. In one year over one hundred words can be added to a classroom sight word wall. Although one hundred words may not seem like much, the first one hundred words in Fry's Instant Word List represent fifty percent of all the words elementary students encounter in their reading! Learning those words can be quite an advantage for readers.

Fluency games can keep children's practice with the words fresh. For example, children can say the first five words in soft voices, the next five in loud voices, and so on. Or one student might read the first word, two the second, three the third—a sort of word symphony! Children also enjoy reading in different voices, e.g., grumpy or happy, or as different characters, e.g., Donald Duck or Superman.

WRITING WORD WALLS

Teachers often wish to draw children's attention to effective aspects of the writing they read to help them see their own options as writers. Word Walls can help here, too (Ziebicki and Grice 1997). For example, the teacher might ask children to collect especially descriptive words, good character descriptions, powerful sentences, or some other longer-than-a-word aspect of their independent reading. As they find these features, children can write them on a writing word wall. When the wall is complete, the examples that children have selected can be used instructionally. Discussions can focus on drawing conclusions based on the examples: what can we learn about effective character descriptions? What makes a powerful sentence?

The notion that students can choose and add words to such walls challenges and empowers them to be on the lookout for good writing—whether words, phrases, or sentences. Students are more likely to be fully engaged in an activity when we give them choice and ownership.

SPELLING WORD WALLS

Certain words—*because*, *of*, and *they*, to name three—seem to cause universal problems for young spellers. At least part of a child's spelling ability depends on visual memory. In fact, we teach children to inspect their writing to see if the words look right. A spelling word wall consisting of a few of these troublesome words may provide additional spelling support for children (Cunningham and Hall 1998). Children's unaided writing can help the teacher decide which words to feature. Common words misspelled by a number of children would be good candidates. After these words are posted on the spelling word wall, the teacher can remind children to look at the wall if they are unsure of the spelling of the words. In fact, many teachers have a classroom rule that word wall words must be spelled properly. In time, when most children have mastered the first group of troublesome words, a new spelling word wall can be created.

Spelling lessons sometimes focus on common rules, such as when to double a consonant before adding a suffix. A spelling word wall is a useful instructional prop for this kind of instruction as well. Children and the teacher can collect words, decide about whether the consonant should be doubled before adding the ending, and put both the base word and its inflected forms in one of two columns on the spelling word wall: double or do not double. In addition to providing visual reinforcement of the rule, children often enjoy creating this type of spelling word wall because they search for words to include. Moreover, the decisions about where to place the words involve problem solving aimed at the spelling rule of interest.

IN CONCLUSION

One of our goals in word recognition instruction is to create a physical environment that invites exploration and play with words. The many possible Word Wall formats described in this chapter can help to achieve this goal. No matter the variation selected, all these activities meet the criteria we established at the beginning of the chapter for effective instruction about words. Students are free to explore and play with words; thinking and sharing are featured. Developing a Word Wall is a meaningful way for children to work with words, and using the Word Wall becomes a joint venture that interests all children. As such, Word Walls are an easy and effective addition to the classroom.

REFERENCES

Cunningham, P., and D. Hall. 1998. *Month-by-Month Phonics for Upper Grades.* Greensboro, NC: Carson-Dellosa.

Fox, B. 1996. *Strategies for Word Identification.* Englewood Cliffs, NJ: Merrill.

Hall, D., and P. Cunningham. 1997. *Month-by-Month Reading and Writing for Kindergarten.* Greensboro, NC: Carson-Dellosa.

McCormick, S. 1994. A Nonreader Becomes a Reader: A Case Study of Literacy Acquisition by a Severely Disabled Reader. *Reading Research Quarterly,* 29: 156–176.

Rasinski, T., and N. Padak. 2000. *Effective Reading Strategies: Teaching Children Who Find Reading Difficult.* Columbus, OH: Prentice Hall.

Ziebicki, S., and K. Grice. 1997. Building Walls and Opening Doors. *Primary English,* 16: 7–9.

CHILDREN'S LITERATURE CITED

Dommermuth-Costa, C. 1994. *Nikola Tesla: Spark of Genius.* Minneapolis, MN: Lerner.

Hepworth, C. 1992. *Antics!* New York: Putnam.

8
MAKING AND WRITING WORDS

Beth has just finished "Making Words" with her first grade students. As she and her students were picking up the letter cards students had used to make their words, other students were still buzzing about the challenge word that required the students to use their entire complement of letters for that day. Clearly, these kids were engaged in the process of manipulating letter cards to make and spell words dictated by their teacher.

Making Words (Cunningham and Cunningham 1992) is a word making-word play activity in which students are guided through the process of using a limited number of letters (individual letters are written on letter cards) to make a series of words, beginning with short words and ending with longer words. As one part of a more comprehensive reading curriculum for elementary students, Making Words has become a very popular and effective approach for teaching students about words (Cunningham, Hall and Defee 1998, Snow, Burns and Griffin 1998). Stahl, Duffy-Hester, and Stahl claim that Making Words appears "to be effective as part of an overall approach to teaching reading" (1998, p. 347).

As originally described by Pat and Jim Cunningham, in Making Words individual students manipulate a limited set of letter squares or cards (one letter per card, letter card sizes can range from 1" x 1" to 3" x 5" cards) in order to form a set of words under the guidance of the teacher. It is much like the age-old activity that has been widely used in many classrooms in which the teacher provides students with one word and challenges students to make up as many words as they can using the letters from the word. The major differences between Making Words and that traditional activity are that the letters in Making Words are not initially provided in the context of any one word—they are simply listed for the children, the words that are made from the letters are predetermined by the teacher, and the teacher guides students in making the words. Also, the Making Words activity moves on to making new words that are not fully represented by the original set of letters, and students study and sort the words they make into various categorical schemes.

Here's an example of a Making Words lesson that Beth does with her students toward the end of grade one. She plans the lesson in advance and arranges for each student to have letter cards for the vowels *e* and *i*, and the consonants *c, d, h, l, n,* and *r.* The vowels are usually written in a different color than the consonants in order to differentiate them from the consonants. Beth also has a larger set of the same letters in a pocket chart at the front of the room in which she (or an assigned student) will make the same words she asks students to make.

Once all the letter cards are distributed to her children, Beth begins the lesson by saying individual words, beginning with short words and moving on to longer ones. By this time of the year students are familiar with the routine and know that their job is to make the words as Beth calls them out. Beth has determined the words earlier and now she dictates them—*Ed, in, red, hid, lid, rid, chin, ice, rice, nice, hide, ride, chide, child.* The final word is one that uses all the letters (the word that Beth started with in planning her lesson). Students are challenged to figure out the word without any clues except that the word uses all the letters. Of course, the word is *children* and most of Beth's students are able to figure it out in a minute or two. As suggested by Cunningham and Cunningham (1992), Beth picks her challenge word from a story her children will be reading, a topic under study in a content area, or a particular holiday that is nearby. The challenge word can make for a nice transition into the story or content area.

Once the challenge word is determined, Beth directs her students' attention to her pocket chart and she demonstrates how new words can be formed from some of the patterns just written. For example, she shows students how the words *slid* and *slide* can be made from the *id* and *ide* patterns. Students also see what changes need to be made to go from *chin* to *chip, chirp, chick,* and *chicken.* On the following day Beth has students write these words on word cards, practice them with a partner, and sort them various ways—by word family, by beginning sound, or by presence or absence of a consonant blend or digraph.

Beth becomes quite animated when she talks about Making Words. "I think it's a fabulous activity! My kids never seem to get tired of it. In fact, they often ask me when we are going to do it again. I've even taught some of my parents how to do it at home with their children. . . . I've seen my students make progress in learning to decode and spell words through this activity that I hadn't seen before."

MAKING AND WRITING WORDS

Although very effective in its originally described form, Tim has developed a variant of Making Words he has called Making and Writing Words (MWW) (Rasinski 1999a). Rather than use letter cards or squares, which can be cumbersome for some teachers and students (Beth hasn't mentioned to us that it is a concern, but we have noticed that it does take her a few minutes to distribute and collect the letter cards from her students with every lesson), Making and Writing Words uses a form sheet on which the words are written by students as they are made. Because the form sheet is generic and can be used for any Making and Writing Words lesson, the sheet alleviates problems associated with creating letter squares, sorting them before and after lessons, and keeping track of letter squares during the lesson. In short, the Making and Writing Words sheet makes the activity logistically less complex and permits all students to respond in writing to all aspects of the lesson. The one drawback to MWW is that it requires students to have some facility in writing. Students in the first half of first grade or below may better be suited for the Making Words using the letter squares.

As in Making Words, MWW begins with the specification of letters (vowels and consonants) to be used in the lesson. These are listed at the top of the MWW sheet in the appropriate box (see Figure 8.1). Beneath this listing of letters are empty boxes in which students will write words under the guidance and direction of their teacher. The teacher reminds students that for any one box, they may use only those letters that are listed at the top of the page, and only one use per letter for any word unless more than one of the same letter is listed at the top.

The first part of the activity begins with the teacher pronouncing words or providing clues for words to be written in each of the boxes. The teacher should have a transparent blank form so that he or she may do the activity on an overhead projector with the students. Below is a typical scenario of how Making and Writing Words might be used (see Figure 8.2).

Each student has a blank Making and Writing Words sheet. The teacher instructs the students to write the following letters in the appropriate boxes:

Vowels a, a, e, i ; Consonants c, m, r

For Part 1, the teacher begins to either pronounce words or give clues to the words and asks students to write them in the appropriate boxes, beginning with short words and moving onto longer words.

OK, in box number 1 write a three-letter word that is another name for an automobile.

(Students write the word *car* in box 1)

Good, now write *car* again in box 2 and add one letter to make the word *care*.

(Students write the *care* in box 2.)

Now in box 3, write the word *ram*. Does anyone know what *ram* means?

(Students write *ram* in box 3)

In box 4 use the same letters as in *ram* to make a word that is a part of your body; your hand is attached to it.

(Students write *arm* in box 4)

In box 5 please write the word *rim*.

(Students write the word *rim* in box 5)

Vowels	Consonants

1	6	11
2	7	12
3	8	13
4	9	14
5	10	15

Transfer

T-1	T-2	T-3

Figure 8.1
Making and Writing Words

Vowels	Consonants
a, a, e, i	c, m, r

1 car	6 race	11
2 tin	7 cram	12
3 ram	8 cream	13
4 arm	9 crime	14
5 rim	10 America	15

Transfer

T-1	T-2	T-3
crust	carpet	hammer

Figure 8.2
Making and Writing Words

The teacher may lead the students in a discussion of other words that have the *am* and *im* phonograms or rimes. These could be listed on the board.

The teacher continues with the class through other three- and four-letter words such as *race, cram, cream,* and *crime.* The MWW activity sheet has room for 15 words, but a teacher can stop at any word. The last word in any MWW activity is a secret word that is made up of all the letters used in the activity. Students are challenged to use all the letters without any further clues to determine and spell the final word. In this case the secret word goes in box 10 and the word is *America.* The final word could be a connection to something that is under study in another part of the curriculum, an introduction to a story about to be read, or a word related to a current event or time of year.

As in Making Words, after all the words have been written, the teacher guides the students to transfer words they used in Part 1 to new words that follow some of the patterns or principles found in the words just written (Part 2).

In the boxes marked T1, T2, and T3 the teacher directs students to write words related to those in boxes 1–10. In this example the teacher asks students to look over the words they have just written and write the words *crust* in T1, *carpet* in T2, and *hammer* in T3. Students give it a go and then talk about the information they used in Part 1 to figure out the transfer words. Given the informal nature of MWW, the teacher may wish to challenge students with other transfer words beyond the three boxes on the given MWW sheet.

Part 3 of Making and Writing Words involves students sorting the words they have just written. Students cut out each word written on the MWW sheet into individual word cards, which can be kept in an envelope as students work with them over the next several days. In the word sorts the teacher provides students with categories and the students sort their word cards into the appropriate piles. Here are some of the sorts the teacher may pose with the 13 words from the MWW activity described above:

- Sort 1: Words that belong to the *am* family, and those that don't.
- Sort 2: Words that have 1 syllable, 2 syllables, and 3 or more syllables.
- Sort 3: Words that contain consonant blends, and those that don't.
- Sort 4: Words that contain long vowels sounds, and those that don't.
- Sort 5: Words that end in *m,* and those that don't.

Not all the sorts have to be letter-sound related. Teachers can also have students sort words into semantic or meaningful categories, such as:

- Sort 6: Words that are things, and words that aren't things.
- Sort 7: Words that describe things you shouldn't do inside a home and other words.

As students become more familiar with Making and Writing Words, they can assume more responsibility, including leading the word sorts. Many students will demonstrate a lot of creativity in leading this part of MWW. Additionally, older students may wish to write the categories on a blank sheet of paper and write the words in the appropriate categories, rather than cutting the words into word bank cards and sorting them manually.

PLANNING FOR MWW

As in Making Words, planning for Making and Writing Words begins with the final or challenge word. Once the challenge word is determined, teachers simply brainstorm words that can be written from the letters, going from short words to longer words, and developing clues that can be used to help students figure out the words. As students develop facility in Making and Writing Words, you will want to choose longer final or challenge words so that students can make longer words and be more challenged by the secret word.

The challenge word and sequence of words used in Making and Writing Words should be guided by the ability of the students. Beginning readers may benefit most from 5–6 letter challenge words containing one vowel. Students in late grade 1 through 3 may find words with 6–8 letters and two vowels appropriate. And, older students in grades 4 through 6 will be appropriately challenged by secret words longer than 8 letters and containing 3 or more vowels. Beth has found that challenge words in the 7–8 letter range work very well with her first graders in April.

MAKING AND WRITING WORDS USING LETTER PATTERNS

As we noted earlier in this book, readers use letter patterns to help them decode words they don't know (Adams 1990). The basic patterns readers use are the parts of syllables known as onsets (initial consonant in a syllable) and rimes (the vowel and succeeding consonants in a syllable). Other common patterns exist in English and are useful to readers in decoding and understanding words. These include prefixes, suffixes, inflected endings, and derivations primarily from Greek and Latin.

Making Words and its variation Making and Writing Words are powerful activities in and of themselves. Students use individual letters to think about and make words that conform to their teachers' pronunciation and other cues. Furthermore, this instruction may be made even more powerful, especially for older students if, instead of individual letters, students engage in the activity using onsets, rimes and other patterns. Such an activity helps students develop a greater sensitivity to onsets, rimes, and other patterns in unknown words they will encounter in their contextual reading. Since onsets and rimes are more complex forms of written language than individual letters, letter pattern knowledge helps older students deal with the longer and more elaborated words they encounter in advanced reading. Thus, Making and Writing Words with Letter Patterns (MWW-LP) (Rasinski 1999b) is a somewhat more complex activity to promote word knowledge among older students.

As in MWW a form is used to simplify the MWW-LP process (see Figure 8.3). Prior to engaging in the activity with students, the teacher should identify the onsets, rimes, and other patterns to be used. One of the best and easiest ways to plan such an activity is to begin with a long word that contains several onsets and rimes. These are then listed in the appropriate boxes. From here the teacher adds other onsets, rimes, and patterns, creating a wide range of one, two, and three or more syllable words. In Appendix A are a number of letter patterns and words that can be used for a MWW-LP lesson.

Once the patterns and the words to be used are found and planned in appropriate order and students have a copy of the form on their desks, the fun can begin. In the example presented in Figure 8.4, the onsets *b, c, l, r, t*, the rimes *ace, ake, et, ice, ink, ise, y* and the other prefix pattern *pre* are used. To come up with this set of letters and patterns we began with a multisyllabic word, in this case the word *bracelet*. Using these onsets and rimes we brainstormed several single and multi-syllable words. Next, we determined other onsets, rimes, and patterns that would be needed to use with the original set in order to make more words.

Now, given this set of patterns we would guide students in making the words listed below. The words are listed with some semantic clues, although in many cases the teacher may want the students to make the words after simply hearing them. Students write the words in the appropriate boxes on the blank form as they are pronounced, given a semantic (definitional) clue, or provided with some other clue to help students figure out the words.

1. prerace
2. trace
3. Tracey   a girl's name that uses the word in box 2.
4. rice   a grain food that is used often in Asian and Mexican dishes.
5. rise
6. baker
7. bakery   a place where a baker works.
8. blink   when your eyes shut and open quickly.
9. brink   on the edge.
10. brake
11. brace
12. ice rink   a place to go skating in the winter (two words).
13. trinket
14. try
15. bracelet

After students complete writing about and discussing their words, the teacher proceeds to the transfer section of the MWW-LP form. In this section the teacher challenges students to use their new found and/or practiced knowledge of various word parts to make and write new words. The new words contain some of the word parts and patterns used in the initial section of the activity, but not all. Students have to use existing knowledge to make

Onsets	Rimes	Other Patterns

1	6	11
2	7	12
3	8	13
4	9	14
5	10	15

Transfer

T-1	T-2	T-3
T-4	T-5	T-6

Figure 8.3
Making and Writing Words—Letter Patterns

Onsets	Rimes	Other Patterns
b, c, l, r, t	ace, ake, et ice, ink, ise, y	pre

1 prerace	6 baker	11 brace
2 trace	7 bakery	12 ice rink
3 Tracey	8 blink	13 trinket
4 rice	9 brink	14 try
5 rise	10 brake	15 bracelet

Transfer

T-1 icy	T-2 crinkle	T-3 practice
T-4 letter	T-5 laced	T-6 spiced cake

Figure 8.4
Making and Writing Words—Letter Patterns (MWW-LP)

and write the words in this transfer section. Here are some words that the teacher may have asked students to write in the transfer section.

T1. icy
T2. crinkle
T3. practice
T4. letter
T5. laced
T6. spiced cake

The third and final part of MWW-LP has the students cutting out each of the 21 words from the blank MWW-LP form. The word cards are kept in an envelope throughout the next several days, students practice the words with a partner, play games with the word cards, and engage in word sort activities. In word sorts students are asked to sort their word cards into two or more piles according to the categories given by the teacher. The categories could include the following:

- By word family: words containing the *ace* rime, words containing *ice*, words containing *ake*, and all other words.
- By number of syllables: one syllable, two syllable, and three or more syllables.
- Words that have more than one meaning, and those that don't.
- Words that have real words within them, or words that have one, two, or three different words within them and words that don't have any words within them.
- Words that describe things (nouns), words that describe actions (verbs), and all other words.
- Words that have positive connotations for you, words that have negative connotations for you, and words that have neither negative nor positive connotations.

The word sorts and word card games and activities can take place over a day or two. At the same time, the words from this activity can be added to a word wall in order to give students additional exposure to the words. Students can be encouraged to use the words in their oral speech as well as in their writing to further enhance their knowledge of the structure and the meaning of the words.

MWW-LP is a good activity for older students who must deal with considerably longer and more complex words than in the previous grades. MWW-LP allows students to examine in detail the structure of more sophisticated words, thus giving them some strategies for decoding these more difficult words often encountered in the elementary curriculum.

In Conclusion

Manipulating a limited set of letters, with the guidance and support of the teacher, in the process of spelling words challenges students to explore the nature of the sound-symbol relationship in a way that allows all students to be successful. We have found that most students thoroughly enjoy Making Words and its variants Making and Writing Words, and Making and Writing Words with Letter Patterns. The fast paced and multi-faceted nature of these activities keeps them lively and enjoyable for students while at the same time giving them practice and opportunities for insight in learning about old and new words in their reading. Done as a regular part of the word study portion of the reading curriculum, students will develop their understanding of how words work and overall facility in spelling and writing.

REFERENCES

Adams, M. J. 1990. *Beginning to Read.* Cambridge, MA: MIT Press.

Cunningham, P. M. and J. W. Cunningham. 1992. Making Words: Enhancing the Invented Spelling-Decoding Connection. *The Reading Teacher*, 46: 106–115.

Cunningham, P. M., D. P. Hall, and M. Defee. 1998. Nonability-Grouped, Multilevel Instruction: Eight Years Later. *The Reading Teacher*, 51: 652–664.

Rasinski, T. V. 1999a. Making and Writing Words. *Reading Online* (an electronic journal available at http://www.readingonline.org/articles/words/rasinski.html).

Rasinski, T. V. 1999b. Making and Writing Words using Letter Patterns. *Reading Online* (an electronic journal available at http://www.readingonline.org/articles/).

Snow, C. E., M. S. Burns, and P. Griffin (eds.). 1998. *Preventing Reading Difficulties in Young Children.* Washington, DC: National Academy Press.

Stahl, S. A., A. M. Duffy-Hester, and K. A. Stahl. 1998. Theory and Research Into Practice: Everything You Wanted to Know About Phonics (But Were Afraid to Ask). *Reading Research Quarterly*, 33: 338–355.

9
WORD BANKS AND WORD SORTS

W̱e were invited to visit Sam's first grade classroom not long ago. Upon entering, we were struck by the variety of activity—children were reading, working with words, writing—literacy activity was everywhere. Little Jeremy soon approached us. "Hey!" he said, beaming. "I learned 17 words last week! Wanna see?" Of course we did, so Jeremy took us to his desk and proudly extracted several words from his word bank. "Here they are. These came from the poem we have been reading. Did I tell you I can read the poem? And these are from the science story we dictated to Mr. Johnson. Want me to read the words to you?" Jeremy had great pride in his accomplishments. He was so enthusiastic about the words he had learned. He was well on his way to becoming a reader.

Beginning readers like Jeremy need meaningful, familiar text to read and reread. They also need to work with words, particularly to develop and maintain their sight vocabularies and to discover features of the graphophonic cueing system. Word banks are very useful for these purposes (Stauffer 1980). Instruction and practice with word banks will be discussed later in this chapter; here we consider what a word bank is and how one gets assembled.

WHAT IS A WORD BANK?

A word bank is a collection of words that a child knows in isolation and by sight or is in the process of learning. Beginning readers primarily use word banks to reinforce the learning of words and characteristics within words. Beyond the beginning stages of reading, word banks are used as reference for spelling and writing and as a source of words for instruction and practice in phonics or other related reading skills. Hall (1981) outlines several major functions for word banks:

- to serve as a record of individual students' reading vocabularies.
- to serve as a reference for writing and spelling.
- to serve as examples and context for group language study or skills instruction.

• to provide reinforcement through repeated exposure to words.

Throughout this chapter we will provide examples of all these uses of word banks.

Word bank words can come from anywhere. In fact, the child's own name, family members' names, and words related to outside-of-school interests and favorite TV shows often appear in children's word banks. Inside the classroom, dictations, predictable pattern books, rhymes, poems, songs, and copy changes are supportive texts for beginning reading instruction. As children read and reread these texts, they will learn the words within them. These words become candidates for deposit in children's word banks.

As previously noted, word banks consist almost exclusively of words a child already knows, and here's why: "Known words are always used because they make it easier for students to look across words for similarities and differences among words" (Bear, et al. 1996, p. 159). Children may select some words to add to their word banks because of interest. Although they may not know these words at sight, they can usually decode the words. In our summer reading program, we have found that the added incentive of learning "my words" enables successful learning. Working with too many unfamiliar words in isolation is frustrating, however, so most of a child's word bank should be known words. Asking children to underline the words that they know as they read individual copies of their texts is an easy way to find such words. This is a positive approach to word learning because the emphasis is on what students know and what they want to learn (Stauffer 1980).

Word bank cards themselves should be rather small, from 1″ × 2″ to 3″ × 5″, and sturdy, since children use them often. Index cards or pieces of index cards or oaktag work well. Children also need a method for storing their words. Envelopes work well initially, but larger containers, such as plastic recipe boxes or small cardboard boxes, are soon needed. In some classrooms, teachers punch holes at one end of word bank cards, and children use large metal shower rings to keep the cards together.

Students' word banks grow slowly and steadily. At first, cards can be stored in random order. As deposits accumulate though, children need a system for organizing their words so that they can locate needed words quickly. Alphabetical order is a good choice that provides a natural reason for children to learn and practice alphabetizing skills and sound-symbol relationships. Suppose, for example, that a child has envelopes labeled with letters of the alphabet and that the envelopes are stored in alphabetical order. To locate a word a child needs to think about the word's beginning sound, decide what letter of the alphabet to look for, and find the corresponding envelope in alphabetical order. So even the process of finding a word offers many word-learning opportunities!

Over time word banks may become cumbersome due to the number of cards children have accumulated. At this point the teacher may want to suggest that children add only new, special, or more difficult words. Another option is to restrict the number of words that can be selected from any new text.

The sheer volume of accumulated words is important to some students, though, so we urge caution in providing too many restrictions on the size of a child's word bank.

Obviously, students do not carry word banks with them throughout their school years, so when should they be discontinued? When most children in the class have more than 200 words in their word banks, it may be time to discontinue their active use. Another sign for termination, also related to the size of the children's sight vocabulary, is students' ease in reading words in teacher-made sorts. When most children can read nearly all teacher-selected words easily, they may not need word banks anymore (Bear, et al. 1996). Many children keep sets of word cards with them even after the entire class eliminates work with word banks, however. Some keep cards of their individual spelling demons for easy reference, for example. Older students also find word banks useful for learning foreign language vocabulary. We know some high school students who keep packs of vocabulary words for their subject area study.

We also know teachers who develop their own word banks. These are special collections of words, usually drawn from books or poems that the teacher always uses instructionally, often selected to illustrate some aspects of word learning. Simply saving these lists of words after their first use facilitates subsequent instructional planning.

Children learn individual words in the same manner that they learned to read, through repeated exposure in familiar, dependable contexts. Word banks provide potentially useful material for further instruction and reinforcement and a concrete record of progress. We say potentially, because a great deal of their effectiveness depends upon what's done with them. In other words, the teaching-learning activities make a great deal of difference, as does the overall instructional environment. In the next section we describe several ways in which word banks can be used, including activities that foster reading growth.

USING WORD BANKS

Having a large sight vocabulary doesn't guarantee reading success, but it certainly helps. The more words a reader know by sight, the fewer times he or she will need to stop reading to figure out unknown words. Reading interesting, easy, familiar material affords children many opportunities to encounter words over and over again in meaningful contexts, thus increasing the possibility that they will become sight words.

Instruction also helps children acquire sight words. Stauffer (1980) describes the overall instructional approach as cue reduction. Initially, children encounter words in the context of a familiar text. Children listen to and look at the words as the teacher reads them. A gradual cue reduction occurs when children read with the teacher, especially when the teacher allows his or her voice to trail behind the children's voices. Still more cues are reduced when children read chorally without the teacher or take turns reading parts of the text by themselves.

The next stage involves independent practice with whole texts, and children underline the words that they know. Finally, known words are stripped of their context entirely; words a child can pronounce in isolation are sight words and are added to the child's word bank. Such a meaningful and context-rich instructional approach, based on the idea of gradual cue reduction, helps facilitate the acquisition of sight vocabulary.

Beyond the general principle of cue reduction, there's lots that can be done with word bank words. Below, using Hall's (1981) broad categories, we suggest many uses for word banks.

RECORDING INDIVIDUAL READING VOCABULARY

Jeremy, whom we introduced at the beginning of this chapter, was very proud of the 17 words he had learned in the past week. Children often benefit from concrete proof that they are learning. This gives them a sense of pride of course, but it also propels them toward further learning. In many classrooms, children keep simple charts in their reading folders that record the date, perhaps every two weeks or so, and the number of words in their word banks.

Teachers should keep track of students' individual reading vocabularies as well. Word banks are helpful tools because they contain words that students *know* (or want to know), not simply those the children have seen or the teacher has introduced. Evaluating students' reading vocabularies by examining the contents of their word banks, then, provides a safe estimate of what words children are learning and trying to learn. Indeed, it's probably a conservative estimate, since most readers can identify more words in context that they can in isolation. In addition to keeping track of the numbers of words in students' word banks, teachers may also want to look at the rate and quality of word learning over time. These quick calculations can provide indications of a child's ease and progress in learning to read as well as the overall size of the child's sight vocabulary.

Because word banks are individual and no two are alike, teachers sometimes worry that children are not learning important sight words, such as those on high frequency lists. This concern is almost always unfounded. Since a high frequency word is, by definition, used in a great deal of written text, the odds are great that children will encounter it often and eventually learn it. Nevertheless, to set their minds at ease, teachers may wish to keep high frequency word lists in students' reading folders. Periodically students can mark the words on the list that they know by sight, perhaps by using a different symbol each time (a check mark, a plus, and so on) to show growth over the months.

Parents are another audience for information about word banks and reading vocabulary growth. Children can complete simple charts (or better yet, computer-made certificates) to take home each month. The charts or certificates can record the number of new words learned that month and the total number of words in the word bank. In some classrooms children use the computer to create triple-spaced lists of their word bank words. Mary, a first grade teacher, notes that "this is an easy way to introduce elements of word processing. Besides that, children take their lists home, cut the words apart, and play word games with their families." What a positive way for parents to learn about their children's reading progress! And the children get the added benefit of having everyone at home congratulate them for their learning.

SERVING AS A REFERENCE FOR WRITING AND SPELLING

Since children know the words in their word banks, it's fair for teachers to expect the words to be spelled accurately in final drafts of children's writing. For this expectation to be realized, it must be clear to children. Moreover, they should arrange their word bank cards so that they can find needed words quickly.

Word banks can also be used to focus on issues related to language in writing. For example, teachers might ask students to think about possible synonyms for commonly used words (e.g., *good* or *said*) by finding and then sharing alternatives from their word banks. In some classrooms, we have seen charts of alternatives to common words posted on walls for easy reference. These charts, usually titled "Instead of ___, try . . . " contain lists of synonyms from students' word banks. Matt's second graders have a chart about words to use instead of *nice* including *kind, friendly, good, pretty, beautiful,* and *favorite.* Matt says that the list grows steadily during the year and that he frequently sees students looking at the list while writing.

SERVING AS EXAMPLES FOR GROUP LANGUAGE STUDY AND SKILLS INSTRUCTION

In general, it's easier to learn something new using what we already know. Recently, for example, our young friend Lee was trying to tell one of us about her new interest—lacrosse, which she described as "kind of like field hockey but you can't body check and there's a net on the stick." By relating the unknown game to one we already knew, Lee was able to explain her new interest. This same principle applies to one of the most powerful uses for word banks, that is, using words children know to teach them about language or to teach skills and strategies that will help them grow as readers. The examples we provide below illustrate how this instruction can work.

Judy knew her Title 1 students needed to learn about hard and soft C. As she listened to children read, she noted situations where lack of this knowledge was hampering children's decoding ability, so she planned a lesson to introduce these sounds. She prepared by finding pictures of common objects that had the two C sounds—celery, cereal, circle, circus; cat, car, comb, comics, cup, cucumber. She showed the pictures to children and asked them to say the words. Then she showed the pictures again, this time asking children to listen carefully to the beginning sounds of the words. Children quickly discovered that the words began with either the *s* sound or the *k* sound. Together Judy and the children sorted the words into *s* sound or *k* sound categories. Judy used magnets to attach the words to the chalkboard, where she also labeled each picture.

At this point, the children were ready to use their word banks. Judy asked that they find all the words in their word banks that began with C and to make three groups of words—*s sound, k sound,* and *other* (to accommodate words like *chop* and *church*). After individuals had completed this task, they shared with the larger group. Judy made two large charts containing everyone's *s sound* and *k sound* words. When the list was complete, she asked children to look for spelling similarities among the *s sound* words and *k sound* words. Children were quick to hypothesize about the vowels after the C. Judy concluded the lesson by asking children what they had learned and how that new information might help them if they encountered unknown words that began with C. By developing new knowledge, i.e. the two sounds of C, based on words children already knew, Judy focused their attention where she wanted it—on the beginning sounds.

Judy's instruction is an example of a *closed word sort*, an activity in which students sort their word bank cards into categories set by the teacher. Through the designation of categories teachers can provide instruction and reinforcement on important word features that students use to decode words. Here are some examples of categories that teachers can use in different word sorts:

- words with consonant blends
- words with prefixes
- words with suffixes or inflected endings
- words with a certain vowel sound
- words with 1 or two syllables
- words that have other words in them (e.g., *be* and *eagle* in *beagle*)
- words containing a designated word family
- words that are nouns
- words that tell how a person feels
- words you think are interesting

- words without consonant blends
- words without prefixes
- words without suffixes or inflected endings
- words without that vowel sound
- words with 3 or more syllables
- words without other words in them
- words without the designated word family
- words that are not nouns
- words that do not express feelings
- words that aren't so interesting

With every sort, students get practice on each word in their word banks, each time from a different structural, syntactic, or semantic perspective. And, with each sort, students develop deeper knowledge and insights into important word and intra–word characteristics.

Maintaining a sight vocabulary requires practice with the words. Two instructional activities, *open word sorts* and *odd word out*, which is a type of closed word sort, are effective practice techniques. Word sorts are small group activities that invite students to categorize or classify words. Students either use their word bank words or other sight words for word sort activities. If other words are used, the teacher makes small word cards for students to manipulate.

An *open word sort* is a divergent thinking activity. Students may group words however they wish—there's no right answer. Instead, the focus is on the process that students use to arrive at groupings and the reasons for their choices. Students may work individually in an open word sort, but pairs or triads are often more successful because of the talking that occurs as students consider possible groupings. The teacher simply tells students to put word bank words (or other sight words) into categories that make sense and reminds them to be ready to explain their groupings to others. After a few minutes of discussion and grouping, children either explain their categories, or the teacher asks students to share their word groupings with others in the class, who are invited to guess the categories.

As mentioned earlier, the teacher provides categories in a *closed word sort.* Other than this, the activity is completed just like an open word sort. Although closed word sorts tend to yield more convergent responses, the goal is not only to produce "correct" responses. Again, students' thinking processes and their reasoning are of primary importance.

Kay and her kindergarten students worked with blocks and then dictated a language experience story, *The Crazy Monster,* about what their block monster looked like:

The Crazy Monster

The crazy monster has lots of eyes. The crazy monster has two hats. The crazy monster has twelve eyes. The crazy monster has six pairs of eyes. He has two necks and two heads. The crazy monster is scary. The monster is funny. The monster has two eyes on each head.

After reading the text to the children and reading it with them, Kay gave children individual copies of the text to read with partners and on their own. Two days later, to prepare for word study, Kay selected several words from the text and printed each on a 3" x 5" index card:

eyes	heads	funny	necks	twelve
monster	crazy	scary	six	two

She and the children used these word cards for an open word sort and for playing odd word out.

For the open word sort, Kay put the word cards on the carpet so all the children could see and manipulate them. She then invited pairs of students to find words that could go together. Here's what the children decided:

- twelve, two, and six "because they're number words."
- crazy and monster "because the monster's crazy."
- scary and funny "because they both end in *y.*"
- heads, necks, and eyes "because they're parts of the body." (Another child added, "Yeah, but it could also be that they all end with *s.*")
- scary and six "because they're *s* words."

In the diversity of children's responses, we see that they thought about word meanings, word parts, and sounds to arrive at their answers.

In "odd word out," the teacher provides several related words along with one unrelated word, and children guess which word doesn't belong, again providing reasons for their decisions. Kay placed these two groups of words on the chalkboard using magnets: *twelve, two, six,* and *monster* and *eyes, funny, heads,* and *necks.* Children easily found the odd words. Students can also play odd word out with partners using their own word bank words.

Former first grade teacher Francine Johnston (1998) explored three ways to support young children's development of sight vocabulary. Children in three first grade classrooms read three easy books each week. On a rotating basis, they also participated in three types of follow-up activities: repeated readings, in which they simply read and reread the stories at least ten times each; sentence strips, in which they read text-only versions of the books and reassembled the stories from sentence strips; and word banks, in which children read text-only versions of the books, developed word banks, and participated in many of the word study activities we describe in this chapter. Although children learned words with all three methods, she found that children learned the least number of words with repeated readings and the greatest number of words with the word bank activities. This result held for children of different ability levels as well. The word bank activities gave "students in each achievement level a slight edge over the students in the next higher level who simply read and reread the text" (p. 671).

All three of these examples—Judy, Kay, and Francine—demonstrate an important principle of word study with word banks: working from the whole to the parts. In each case, the teacher began with something that was meaningful for students—pictures, a dictated text, or simple story books. Children were familiar and comfortable with these *wholes* before the teacher focused their attention on *parts*—sounds, words, or both. This balance among wholes and parts can be tricky to achieve but is well worth attaining. Too much exclusive attention to whole texts can lead children to memorize or to rely too heavily on picture cues. Too much exclusive attention to words or word parts can be overly abstract and confusing for children. In whole-to-part instruction, children "begin with the full support of the text, but they also work with sentences, words, letters, and sounds in a way that demands close attention to print" (Johnston 1998, p. 668). This balance enables children to maximize their word learning.

PROVIDING REINFORCEMENT THROUGH REPEATED EXPOSURES TO WORDS

Word banks are excellent sources for independent practice activities and word games. Below we list many possibilities. Since some of these activities involve children sharing word bank cards with others, teacher may want to ask children to write their initials on the backs of their own cards. This will facilitate clean-up after the activities.

Although classified as primarily word study or concept development, many of these activities and games engage children in categorizing and sorting known words. This not only anchors the words in children's sight vocabularies, it also helps them discover the parts of the words, also useful in solving the mystery of unknown words. Moreover, a bit of creative thinking on the teacher's part can change a word study activity into a concept development activity, and vice versa. Several authors have described many other word bank activities (Bear, et al. 1996, Fresch and Wheaton 1997, Garton, Schoenfelder and Skriba 1979, Hall 1981).

Word study

- Children can sort word bank cards according to consonant or vowel sounds. The teacher can provide a key word ("Find words with the vowel sound you hear in *box*"), a chart can be used to organize children's sorting ("long *a*, short *a*, other"), or the sorts can be left open for student exploration.
- Children can sort by word families (e.g.,-*it* or -*ate*).
- Students can sort words by function (e.g., naming words, action words, describing words).
- Children can sort words according to the numbers of syllables they contain.
- Learners can find words that contain (or could contain) prefixes or suffixes.
- Students can fold pieces of paper into three columns and select word bank words that begin with different consonants (or contain different vowel sounds) for each column. Then they look through old magazines or junk mail like catalogs to find pictures of objects that match the selected sounds. These are pasted into the appropriate column.
- The teacher can ask children to find all the words in their word banks that could have -*ing* (or other endings) added. These can simply be shared, or children can sort the words according to a spelling rule, such as words that need a doubled consonant (e.g., *hop – hopping, bat – batting*), and words that do not (e.g., *read – reading, rain – raining*).
- Children can play *Go Fish* with beginning sounds, ending sounds, rhyming words, or vowel sounds.
- Students can practice their words with a partner occasionally as a quick warm up.
- Children can play *Concentration* by matching word bank cards that share beginning sounds. Singular and plural forms, synonyms, contracted and uncontracted forms, etc., can also be used.
- A student can select two word bank words to read to a partner and then ask one or more of the following questions: Do they begin the same? Do they end the same? Do they have the same vowel sound? Do they rhyme?

- The teacher can suggest a word. Children find additional words from their word banks based on inflectional or derivational forms (e.g., *rain—rains, raining, rainy, rained, raincoat*).
- Learners can play *Change Over*, which is like Crazy Eights. Words played must match the beginning consonant sound or medial vowel sound from the previous word. A wild card allows the player to change to a new consonant or vowel sound. The winner is the first person to use all his/ her cards.
- Children can play *Word War*. In groups of three or four, one child's word bank cards are distributed equally. One card is played and read per child per turn. The student with the longest word wins the round and all cards played. If there's a tie, students who tied play and read another card, and the longer word wins. Students play for five minutes, after which cards are counted and a winner is named. Most students will want to play for another 5-minute period, perhaps using another child's word bank cards.
- One partner names a word bank word. The other partner finds a word bank word that comes before (or after) in alphabetical order.

Concept development

- Children can sort word bank words into semantic categories, such as people words or color words. They can also look for some of these words in old magazines or in junk mail and create collages.
- Children can find words that have more than one meaning. They can also look for homonyms or opposites.
- Students can make and share sentences using their word bank words.
- Children can use word bank words to make short sentences as long as possible.
- Learners can make compound words using words from their word banks. Children may want to make up and then illustrate their own compound words as well.
- Partners can use both their word banks to write a story.
- The teacher can prepare modified cloze exercises: The dog is _____ the table; I saw a _____ balloon; Tim has a _____. Children find as many words from their word banks as possible to complete the sentences.
- Children can make riddles using their word bank words:
  I am small.
  I am brown.
  I eat carrots.
  I am a _____.
- Students can create picture dictionaries using their word banks as a source.
- Children can find word bank words related to concepts being discussed in science or social studies. Or they can complete *concept sorts*, such as a

seasons sort in which children find and categorize word bank words that belong with spring, summer, etc.

- Class members can play word bingo. Each child lays out nine, sixteen, or twenty-five words, face up, in rows like a bingo card. The caller says, "Turn over a word that . . . " and gives a characteristic common to some of the words. For example, a word that begins or ends like [another word]; a word that has an ending; a word that tells something to do; a word that names an animal; a word that has two syllables; your shortest word; your favorite word. The winner is the first child to turn over an entire row, column, or diagonal.

STORY WORD BANKS

An alternative (or complement) to a master, ongoing word bank is a story word bank. This is a temporary word bank with words drawn from a story students have read or listened to. This type of word bank works well in grades two and up.

Before reading a story to students (or asking them to read it), the teacher asks students to write down interesting words they encounter during the reading. After the reading, a group list is written on the board or chart paper. Individual students contribute their own interesting words, and the teacher can add a word or two. (Twelve to twenty-four words is a good number.) Students then write the words on word bank grids, which are simply plain sheets of paper with one vertical line and three horizontal lines resulting in eight rectangles (one word is written in each rectangle). Cut the grids into individual word cards, look over the words, and then put them in envelopes for storage.

Over the next several days, students can do open and closed word sorts, play word games, practice the words, and use them in their talk and writing. Before long, they learn the words, and they also get interesting practice in examining the words for important word features. When most students have learned the words, a new story word bank can be developed.

Story word banks illustrate the versatile nature of word banks. They also provide a nice example of the whole-to-part learning that we mentioned earlier. Students begin with a whole story, choose and study individual words from the story, and finally, through word sorts and other activities, examine the intra-word features of the words. They also demonstrate for students the important notion that good writing contains interesting words.

IN CONCLUSION

Children learn about words and written language as they successfully encounter words and stories. They learn individual words in the same manner that they learn to read, through repeated exposure in familiar, dependable contexts. Word banks show evidence of this word learning while providing fertile ground for additional learning. Word sorting activities reinforce the recognition of the words themselves. Equally important, they offer children the opportunity to generalize about sound-related characteristics of words.

REFERENCES

Bear, D. R., et al. 1996. *Words Their Way.* Englewood Cliffs, NJ: Prentice Hall.

Fresch, M. J., and A. Wheaton. 1997. Sort-Search-Discover: Spelling in the Child-Centered Classroom. *The Reading Teacher,* 51: 20–31.

Garton, S., P. Shoenfelder and P. Skriba. 1979. Activities for Young Word Bankers. *The Reading Teacher,* 32: 453–457.

Hall, M. A. 1981. *Teaching Reading as a Language Experience* (3rd ed.). Columbus, OH: Merrill.

Johnston, F. 1998. The Reader, the Text, and the Task: Word Learning in First Grade. *The Reading Teacher,* 51: 666–675.

Stauffer, R. G. 1980. *The Language-Experience Approach to the Teaching of Reading* (2nd ed.). New York: Harper & Row.

10 Contextual Word Recognition

W hen we asked young Gabe whether he ever encountered difficult words in his reading, he replied, "Oh, sure. Some of them are real tricky." "What do you do with those tricky words?" we asked. Gabe answered, "I say blank," and then told us how he had learned to say "blank" at the difficult spot, read to the end of the sentence, and then try again. "It usually works," he commented, "but you have to look at the word, too. The sounds have to match."

Maria, Gabe's teacher, was pleased that he was able to explain his word recognition strategies. "Most of the children know something about phonics by the time they get to me in second grade. Many know about context, too, but few understand the power of using them simultaneously. I've been working on helping the children see how all these decoding options work together," she said. We believe that Maria has the right idea. Although both phonics and context are helpful alone, they work far more effectively together. In this chapter we explore issues related to context—what it is, why it's important, and how teachers can encourage its use.

What Is Context?

When talking with children, we sometimes describe context as the neighborhood where a word lives. Put more formally, contextual analysis is a word identification strategy; a reader attempts to determine the meaning and/or pronunciation of an unknown word by the way it is used in the text (Johnson and Baumann 1984). To do this, the reader uses one or more cues. Illustrations often provide clues for young readers, as do graphic aids, such as charts, diagrams, and typographical cues. When a reader sees quotation marks, for example, the reader can guess that someone is saying something, a guess that is usually but not always correct.

Pragmatic context refers to the general structure of the text as well as the situation in which the reader is reading. With regard to the former, consider the opening phrase "Once upon a time." What would you expect to find in a text that begins with those words? Your experience with fairy tales provides a rich resource for decoding and understanding such a text.

Sometimes the context in which the reading is done affects understanding. Here's an example:

Both f_____ and m_____ have problems with ch_____ that are not easy to s_____.

How did you fill in the blanks? We use this example in our teaching, and students almost invariably decide that the sentence refers to *fathers, mothers,* and *children.* Makes sense, doesn't it? But if the sentence were used in an agriculture class, students might decide that it referred to *farmers, merchants,* and *chickens.* We even develop and use expectations related to reading that are based on the reading situation.

But the most powerful context clues are the linguistic ones provided by the positional nature of English (syntax) and by the knowledge the reader has of the meanings of other words and ideas (semantics). Below we consider these important clues in a bit more detail.

Syntax refers to the way words go together to form sentences. Even very young speakers of a language understand its syntax and how to form sentences. The linguist Noam Chomsky (1957) offers this example:

Colorless green ideas sleep furiously.

Could this be a sentence of English? Yes, although it makes no semantic sense—something can't be both colorless and green; ideas have no color; ideas don't sleep, and so on—it makes syntactic sense. It expresses a complete thought (bizarre though it is), and the words appear in an allowable order for a sentence of English. Even though few of us would be able to articulate the grammar rules that make this an allowable sentence, as speakers of the language we know that it could be.

This point has important instructional implications: children do not need to be able to say syntactic (grammar) rules in order to use their knowledge of language to guide their reading. Teachers can help children understand syntactic context by offering examples such as:

Sally watched as the wind blew her _____ balloon away.

When children are invited to fill in the blank in the sentence, they will offer adjectives. The teacher can underscore the necessity that what we read must sound like a sentence of English.

Semantics refers to word meanings. In essence, the reader asks, "What would make sense here?" and, using information from the text along with the reader's prior knowledge and experience, makes a guess. Put another way, words represent concepts, which reflect experience. Most linguists argue that individual words have little or no real meaning apart from their use. For example, most of us would say we know what *window* means. But consider these uses:

The eyes are a *window* to the soul.
What is our *window* of opportunity?
You make a better door than *window*.

These windows are semantically related to the panes of glass we ordinarily think about, but they're not exactly the same. Meaning resides not so much in individual words but in the way they're used.

Semantic context is a powerful way to identify a word. Here's a little test: What's this word?

_____

Were you able to get it? No? OK, try this: w_____   Got it? Still not enough? Here's a third clue: You make a better door than a w_____.   There. We bet you have it now.

The power of semantic context is one reason why children need to practice decoding by reading meaningful text. And, as we will suggest later in this chapter, teachers need to help children see how to use semantic context as they read.

WHY IS CONTEXT IMPORTANT?

Context is important because thinking about the various aspects of context helps us make predictions about the text. In a summary of research related to context use, Johnson and Baumann (1984, p. 599) explain how this works: "It has been theorized . . . that a reader uses this tacit knowledge of language by reducing the number of possible alternative candidates for an unfamiliar word and thereby enhances his/her chances of making an accurate identification." Stanovich (1991) calls this the notion of expectancy—when readers use context to develop notions about what they expect to see, the subsequent reading is more fluent and successful. This is probably why most of us read connected text more fluently than lists of words. But good readers are probably not consciously aware of using context. In fact, poor readers appear to rely heavily, perhaps too much, on context (Stanovich 1991). Some researchers see context as a compensation strategy, as a way to figure out an unknown word when no other tools are available for use.

This raises another important issue for teachers to consider: how to help children see that word recognition is essentially a problem-solving activity that works best when they rely upon all cueing systems for information. The problem is the unknown word; the solution involves finding a word that makes contextual sense and bears graphophonic resemblance to the unknown word. Another way to think about word recognition is in terms of prediction and confirmation. A reader predicts what a word is likely to be, i.e., what the reader expects the word to be, based on syntactic and semantic contextual information, and confirms the prediction using graphophonic information and subsequent contextual information. In other words, proficient readers orchestrate context and phonics as an overall word recognition strategy and as a prompt for self-correction, should it be necessary.

Information about the graphophonic cueing system is valuable for word recognition, particularly when readers attend to the beginning portions of words, which generally contain the best and most useful information (Johnson and Baumann 1984). However, phonics works best when the reader knows what a word is likely to be in the first place. "If you know that the word you're looking at is probably *horse, cow,* or *donkey,* phonics will enable you to tell the difference. But here you do not have to run through all 11 alternatives for the first two letters of *horse*—you just have to know that a word beginning with *ho* could not be *cow* or *donkey*" (Smith 1985, p. 54). So all cues—graphophonic and contextual—help readers reduce alternatives, which makes determining the unknown word more efficient and effective.

Although our emphasis in this chapter is primarily on using context to recognize words, most reading authorities agree that context can be a powerful tool for word learning. Most also agree that context is not enough. Consider the following (Leu and Kinzer 1999):

My sister Ginger has blonde hair and a light complexion. She is very slim.
Her best friend Sam, however, is *corpulent.*

Suppose you didn't know the meaning of *corpulent.* From context (specifically the word *however*), you can determine that *corpulent* is something that Ginger is not. Does Sam have some other color of hair? Does he have a dark complexion? Is he chubby? The passage contains some clues but not enough to solve the problem with assurance. Using context clues and reading in context are, however, important aspects of vocabulary learning.

Nagy's (1988) model of vocabulary instruction shows how important they are. To learn new concepts, we must first link them to what we already know. Helping children learn concepts related to different forms of government, for example dictatorship, may begin with a discussion of what they already know about their own form of government. The next stage in Nagy's model is repetition, in which readers need many meaningful encounters with the new concept in context. This leads to automatic access, so that the reader doesn't have to stop and think, "Now what is this again?" when encountering the new word. The final stage, meaningful use, also involves many encounters with the new concept, but this time children use the concept in their own writing and speaking rather than reading someone else's use. As can be seen, both the second and third stage of the model involve contextual reading and using the concept in writing and oral communication.

These are important points to remember when planning how to help children use context as they read. First, when using context to decode, children need to confirm their contextual guesses at unknown words, perhaps using beginning letters and sounds. They should learn to ask, "Does it make sense? Does it look right?" as a means of checking contextual guesses. Second, contextual reading can facilitate word learning or vocabulary acquisition; indeed, it's one of the very best ways to do so, but children will need instruction as well. In fact, most children, especially struggling readers, need instruction in what context is, how using context can help them, and especially how to double-check their contextual guesses (Johnson and Baumann 1984, Stanovich 1991).

TALKING ABOUT CONTEXT

Discussion helps children learn how and why to use context. Teachers can encourage children to talk about how context helped them figure out unknown words (or didn't) by using a strategy called Reader-Selected Miscues (Goodman, Watson and Burke 1996). In this procedure, students keep track of tricky words during any independent reading time, such as SSR. They may make a light pencil mark in the margin next to a line with a difficult word, or they may jot down the word and page number on a separate piece of paper. After the reading time concludes, the teacher asks children to return to their tricky words to see if they can now figure them out. Then a discussion ensues, in which children talk about how they solved word-related problems in their reading. Questions like these can guide the discussion: How did you figure out the tricky word? Did you think about other possibilities? How did you know _____ was right? Teachers often make editorial comments during these discussions to help other students see the benefits of using the strategy one particular student describes.

Teachers can also use reader-selected miscues collected from a group to find productive topics for mini-lessons. To use the strategy in this way, children will need small 3" x 5" slips of paper. When they encounter a tricky word, they insert a slip of paper at that spot in their books and continue reading. After reading, they return to each slip of paper, write the sentence in which the word appears, and underline the word in question. Some teachers ask that children also note the title of the book. When the papers are complete, the teacher collects them for later categorization and analysis. Looking at the types of words that give children difficulty can provide direction for small group or whole-class lessons.

In many classrooms, teachers and students occasionally discuss ways children have identified unknown words. This discussion might simply begin with the teacher asking, "Who has figured out a hard word? How did you do it? How did you know you were correct?" Discussions like these help children see that all readers encounter problems from time to time, which is an important aspect of an accurate concept of reading. Additionally, children's attention is focused on the problem-solving nature of word identification, and they may get new ideas from their peers. Together they may make charts of their successful word identification strategies to post in the classroom.

CLOZE AND MAZE ACTIVITIES

Many instructional activities supporting the use of context rely on some sort of fill-in-the-blank format. This makes sense because to fill in the blanks, children must use context. Reading professionals call these *Cloze exercises,* after a term coined by Wilson Taylor (1953). Cloze takes advantage of the natural human tendency to find closure—if we see almost all of a photograph, for example, our tendency is to fill in the missing detail so that we perceive a complete photo. This happens almost automatically; we are often not even conscious of our thinking. To complete a Cloze activity successfully, the reader does the same thing, and in the process, thinks along with the author.

As described in Chapter 16, Cloze can be used to test whether a child can read a particular text successfully. When used as a testing technique, the rules for developing and scoring Cloze exercises are fairly well set. Teachers have much more latitude in developing Cloze activities for instructional purposes. Figure 10.1, which we have adapted from Tierney, Readence and Dishner (1995), shows the major differences between these two uses of Cloze. Although many children find Cloze tests frustrating, most students enjoy solving the puzzles represented by instructional Cloze activities.

Before children can benefit from instructional activities based on Cloze procedures, they need to understand the concept of closure. Oral Cloze activities can help in this regard (Leu and Kinzer 1999). For example, the teacher might recite a line from a familiar pattern book, leaving a word out and asking children to replace it:

Brown bear, brown bear, what do you _____?
_____ bear, brown bear, what do you see?
(Martin 1983)

Because the language is familiar and the pattern is strong, children will easily fill in the blanks. Doing so will help them see that language users naturally fill in the blanks while listening or reading.

Another way to help children understand the principle of closure is to write a sentence on the chalkboard or chart paper and invite children to complete it:

Feature	Assessment	Instruction
length	150+ words	at least a sentence; length can vary
materials	usually instructional level or higher	usually independent level; easy for child
deletions	1st sentence in tact; then delete every 5th word for a total of at least 25 deletions	varies; teacher decides
evaluation	exact or close to exact replacements only	synonyms acceptable
follow-up	usually none, although teacher may analyze responses for syntax or semantics	teacher and student discuss replacements and how/ why they were made

Figure 10.1
Cloze for Testing and Teaching

I wish I could eat some _____.

As children offer possibilities, the teacher can write and affix word cards with their choices to complete the sentence. This activity also provides opportunities for indirect learning about print conventions, such as left-to-right progression, learning that letters make up words, and developing a concept for word in print.

Oral Cloze is also helpful for showing children how to use context and phonics together. For example, the teacher might change the sentence above:

I wish I could eat some c____.

Children can then offer possibilities that fit the context and begin appropriately. Often this activity presents opportunities for teachers to distinguish possible completions, e.g., *cabbage,* or *celery* in the example above; from likely ones, e.g., *cake,* or *cookies*, which shows children how easy it can be to double-check their guesses as they read.

To make a Cloze activity, the teacher first selects a passage, usually from something children have read. Words chosen for deletion are typically those that can be determined from context and require a variety of strategies to figure out. Instructional modifications include providing initial letters or onsets for the deleted words or cueing the replacement word's length by the length of the space. Here are some examples from Ludwig Bemelmans's (1939) book, *Madeline*:

Cloze
They left the _____ at _____past nine in two straight _____ in rain or _____.

Initial letter/ onset modification
They sm_____ at the g____ and fr_____ at the bad and sometimes th____ were very s_____.

Word length
She was ___ afraid __ mice—she loved _____, snow, and ice.

Interactive Cloze (Ruddell and Ruddell 1995) is a discussion activity that can help children see how context works to aid decoding. To prepare for this activity the teacher develops a Cloze passage with a few deletions that are chosen to spark conversation. Either individually or with a partner, students complete the passage. Then they join with others in small groups to share and discuss their replacement words. Children are sometimes surprised when others select the same words or when someone shares a completely different, yet sensible word. A whole-class conversation can conclude the session.

Indeed, we think that no Cloze or Maze activity is complete until students and the teacher discuss it. Through discussion students can share the strategies they use to determine the deleted words. For example, in the preceding Cloze, the final blank can be completed by reading beyond the deletion, developing a sense for the items enumerated, e.g., _____, *snow*, and *ice*, and using that knowledge to choose a word that fits the sequence. This is a nice demonstration of the strategy of reading on when one meets a difficult or unknown word.

Maze (or multiple choice Cloze) activities are another option for helping children learn to use context. In one version of Maze, the teacher provides words to be replaced; the student's job is to decide which goes where, as in this example from Ezra Jack Keats's *Snowy Day* (1962, p. 7):

> One _____ morning Peter woke _____ and _____ out the _____. Snow had fallen _____ the night.   [during, window, looked, up, winter]

Maze activities can also be developed to draw children's attention to how syntactic and graphophonic information combines with semantic information. To achieve this goal, the Maze activity should offer children options that are graphophonically similar, at least in the beginning portions of words, but syntactically different. Again, from *Snowy Day* (p. 28):

> (Beater, Before, Befuddled) he got into bed, he looked (if, is, in) his pocket.
> His (snowman, sandbox, snowball) wasn't there.

"I put Maze activities on the computer," says Lou, a second grade teacher. "It's pretty easy, actually. I create a master file and then copy it for everyone. The children enjoy cutting and pasting their choices, and they reread the sentences to make sure they make sense. The children save their work on the computer so that later I can look at what they've done. And, I keep all the activities on a master disk so that I'll have them for the next group of students."

Cloze and Maze activities can also be constructed by retyping a passage with underscores for deleted words. An alternative and significantly less time-consuming approach is to photocopy the original text and use a dark marker to line out the words to be deleted. Deletions should be numbered, and students can use a numbered answer sheet to record their word choices.

Cloze and Maze activities are powerful ways to help students strengthen their abilities to use context. The teacher's task in all these activities is to help children become accustomed to looking at and thinking about the surrounding context to guess unknown words. Once children understand the principle of Cloze, teachers will find it an adaptable instructional strategy.

HELPING READERS SEE THEIR OPTIONS

What do children think they're supposed to do when they encounter an unknown word? We routinely ask this question of children who attend our summer reading program, all struggling readers, and their responses are surprisingly similar. Primary-age children think they're supposed to "sound it out." Older students believe that they must "look it up." Although both of these can be effective ways to solve the problem of an unknown word, we strive to help students see that they have other options, which may sometimes be more successful than their old stand-bys. We have found that incidental, but purposeful in-process teaching is a powerful way to help children expand their word recognition repertoires.

Perhaps the best time for this incidental teaching comes when a child encounters a difficult word during occasional read-aloud activities or when reading to the teacher for diagnostic or evaluative purposes. This can be a golden opportunity to help the reader see his or her options, but only if the teacher understands the reader's current strategies and knows how to provide informal instruction in other options. For using context, three options may provide focus for the teacher's talk, depending on what the reader seems to need.

Some readers need encouragement to predict an unknown word. These are the readers who stop when they encounter difficulty, often waiting patiently for someone else to solve the problem (a surprisingly effective strategy in some classrooms!) To help the reader see that making a guess is appropriate, the teacher can:

- say nothing for two or three seconds. This silence sends two important messages to the reader: This is your problem to solve. I believe you can do it. Many teachers find that this strategy alone makes a remarkable difference in their students' willingness and ability to decode unknown words.
- ask, "Why did you stop?" to ensure that a word difficulty is the reason and to learn which word is providing trouble.
- ask, "What would make sense there?" This prompt reminds the reader to make a guess based on contextual clues.
- say, "Read to the end of the sentence. Now try again. Think of a word that makes sense and looks like [point to difficult word]." A similar prompt is "Look at the word, get your mouth ready for the first sound, and think of a word that would also make sense." Both of these prompts show the reader a way to use context and graphophonic cues together. They also remind students that clues can often be found after the unknown word and not just before it.

Other readers need to learn how to confirm their contextual guesses as well. These are the readers who make inappropriate guesses but read on, apparently not thinking at all about the sense (or lack of sense) of what they have just said. To help these readers, teachers can:

- say, "Was that OK? How do you know?" This reminds the child about confirmation, checking that a word is "OK."
- say, "How did you decide what that word was?" or "How do you know that word is _____?" These questions, too, point back at meaning, but they also give the teacher a glimpse into the child's strategies, at least the ones he or she can articulate. Answers to the questions sometimes provide additional valuable diagnostic information, as in the case of Sara, who replied, "I saw the L." Sara knew to look at beginning

letters, a strength, but her teacher could also see that additional work in using context and in confirming guesses might help Sara.

- say, "Does that make sense?" This directs the child's thinking to the author's message and to using context as a confirmation tool.

Children sometimes know they've made mistakes but don't know that they should correct them. These readers typically pause and sometimes look puzzled but read on. To encourage self-correction, the teacher can

- say nothing for two or three seconds to ensure that the reader needs additional support and to signal that the reader is responsible for solving the problem.
- ask the child to read the sentence again. This enables the teacher to see if the mistake was a careless error or if the reader may have corrected it mentally without saying the correction aloud.
- ask the child to tell you the sentence in his or her own words and then ask if the sentence makes sense. An alternative to the child's rendering is to say, "You said _____. Does that make sense?" Both of these strategies should wait until the child has finished reading so that the incidental instruction doesn't interfere with the flow of the child's reading. The teacher can simply make note of the problem sentence and return to it later. Like many of the other teacher comments we have described, these comments guard against the careless error while focusing the reader's attention on contextual meaning.

We suspect that the children in our summer reading program have decided on the worth of "sound it out" and "look it up" based on comments their teachers have made to them. By basing their comments on what children seem to need, rather than using these pat responses, teachers can help children develop a well-rounded word recognition strategy that takes advantage of all available linguistic cues. There's no doubt that the teacher's verbal support can, like all direct instruction, show a reader what a strategy is and how and why to use it.

IN CONCLUSION

Contextual analysis is a very important strategy for recognizing unknown words. Determining a word by scrutinizing its surrounding context is efficient and, most often, effective, especially when double-checked against graphophonic information.

Although filling in the blanks is, to some extent, a natural cognitive activity, some students need help thinking about context clues as a tool for reading. Through activities such as Reader-Selected Miscues, Cloze, and Maze, teachers can show children the power of contextual information. Talking about context-based decision making is particularly critical. Lots of independent reading offers excellent practical application of this knowledge about context. This instructional package can help children see what decoding tools they have and how they can work together.

REFERENCES

Chomsky, N. 1957. *Syntactic Structures*. The Hague, Holland: Mouton.

Goodman, Y., D. Watson and C. Burke. 1996. *Reading Strategies: Focus on Comprehension*. (2nd ed.). Katonah, NY: Richard C. Owen.

Johnson, D., and J. Baumann. 1984. Word Identification. In P.D. Pearson, et al. (eds.)., *Handbook of Reading Research*. pp. 583–608. New York: Longman.

Leu, D., and C. Kinzer. 1999. *Effective Literacy Instruction*. (4th ed.). Upper Saddle River, NJ: Merrill.

Nagy, W. (1988). *Teaching Vocabulary to Improve Reading Comprehension*. Newark, DE: International Reading Association.

Ruddell, R., and M. Ruddell. 1995. *Teaching Children to Read and Write*. Boston: Allyn & Bacon.

Smith, F. (1985). *Reading Without Nonsense*. (2nd ed.). New York: Teachers College Press.

Stanovich, K. (1991). Word Recognition: Changing Perspectives. In R. Barr, et al. (eds). *Handbook of Reading Research*. 2: 418-452. New York, Longman.

Taylor, W. 1953. *The Cloze Procedure: How it Predicts Comprehension and Intelligence of Military Personnel*. Urbana, IL: University of Illinois, Human Resources Research Institute, Division of Communication.

Tierney, R., J. Readence, and E. Dishner. 1995. *Reading Strategies and Practices*. (4th ed.). Boston: Allyn & Bacon.

CHILDREN'S LITERATURE CITED

Bemelmans, L. 1939. *Madeline*. New York: Viking.

Keats, E. J. 1962. *The snowy day*. New York: Viking.

Martin, B. 1983. *Brown bear, brown bear*. New York: Holt.

The Language Experience Approach and Word Learning

To prepare for a math lesson about categorization, Gloria, a first grade teacher, collected dozens of stray buttons from around her house and brought them to school in two small cardboard boxes. After the students were seated around her, but before she opened the boxes, she shook them and then asked the children, "What's in the boxes?" This aroused the children's curiosity, of course, and they began making guesses: shells, rocks, buttons, keys, marbles. While children guessed, Gloria continued shaking the boxes. She said, "Listen again. What do you hear? What do you think?" By the time the boxes were emptied on the table, the children were interested in the lesson to come.

Next, Gloria said, "Look these over. Just use your eyes. Examine them. What can you discover about these buttons?" The children did examine them, and after awhile, Gloria said, "What did you notice about the buttons?" A lively discussion ensued, with some children pointing to interesting buttons and others remarking about the variety of buttons. Finally, Annie said, "They're different," and Kevin agreed: "They're different colors."

This gave Gloria the opening she was looking for. She asked the group, "What did you notice about the different colors?" Molly said, "Some are dark and some are light." So Gloria asked the children to sort the buttons into two piles, dark and light. The children talked informally with one another as they completed this task.

When they were finished making their piles, the discussion continued. Gloria pointed to one pile and asked, "What would you call this group?" She also asked if the children agreed that all buttons in the dark category belonged there, which led to an interesting debate about a dark pink button. When the children were satisfied with their dark category, Gloria repeated her questions, this time with the light category. Then she asked the children, "Now, what did we do?" Jenny replied, "These are dark and these are light." Jose added, "We sorted them into two groups—dark and light."

Next, Gloria put all the buttons back into one big pile and asked the children what else they noticed about them. Eventually, the children sorted the buttons three more times, according to size, luster, and texture. Finally, Gloria invited a lesson summary by asking, "What have we been doing? What did you find out? Let's talk about it. Who can make an observation?"

At this point, the children were ready to talk about what they had done and discovered. They offered their ideas, and Gloria recorded them on chart paper exactly as they were said. She also spoke each word as she wrote it and reread each sentence after it was written, asking the child who offered it, "Is this what you want to say?" Each child contributed to the dictation. When it was finished, Gloria encouraged the children to read the text silently as she read it aloud (again pointing to words as she read them):

Buttons

We put the buttons into piles. Some buttons are rough. Some are smooth and some are lumpy. Some are shiny. Some are different and some are the same. We called the piles categories.

By Annie, Kevin, Molly, Jenny, and Jose

WHAT IS LEA?

Gloria and her students participated in language-experience approach (LEA) activities, such as this button lesson, nearly every day and in all content areas. The language experience approach is a teaching process whereby students' experiences are represented first by their oral language and later re-represented, or converted to written language by the teacher or another scribe. This written text, which is based on students' own experiences and understanding, becomes material used for instruction in reading. LEA activities feature attention to the interrelationships among oral language, written language, and readers' thoughts and experiences. With beginning readers, LEA generally involves some shared experience, discussion, dictation, and subsequent reading and reading instruction. In this chapter we describe LEA and offer practical suggestions for obtaining and using dictations for early reading instruction. (This discussion relates to Chapter 9, which focuses on word banks and their uses.) We also address copy change activities, another good source of early reading material, in this chapter. Both LEA and copy change transform children's oral language into something that can be read.

LEA is not a new idea. In the years following the Civil War, Colonel Francis Parker advocated experience-based learning, as did John Dewey around the turn of the century (Rippa 1984). Descriptions of LEA activities are also found in Edmund Burke Huey's *The Psychology and Pedagogy of Reading* (1908/1968). In her book, *Teacher* (1963), Sylvia Ashton-Warner provides a detailed description of LEA as used with Maori children in New Zealand. At about the same time, U.S. scholars such as Russell G. Stauffer, Roach Van Allen, and Jeanette Veatch advocated LEA and conducted research in LEA classrooms.

Over all these years, scholars have amassed lots of evidence to show us the benefits of LEA-related instruction. For example, the U.S. Office of Education's massive First Grade Studies research project, conducted in the late 1960s, provided "evidence that language experience approaches do result in good achievement" (Hall 1985, p. 7). Another research review, conducted almost two decades later showed

> very convincingly that language experience programmes work. . . . And not only that it works in the attainment of good achievement scores but that it does far more than that. It promotes learning that is pleasurable and that is congruent with how language competence flourishes. (Hall 1985, p. 10)

The LEA philosophy is based on several related theories: how people learn, how people read, and how others can help. At the intersection of these theories are notions about what makes learning easy. Hall (1985, p. 6) notes that LEA is "rooted in the elements of success, relevance, involvement, attitude, interest, and motivation." Relationships among thinking, problem solving, and reading are another aspect of the foundation of LEA. Stauffer (1969, p. 4) describes reading as "a phenomenon of mental activity akin to thinking." To comprehend, he says, readers restructure meaning from experience, they think and reason while they read. So, "reading is never treated as something apart from language and thought" (Allen 1976, p. 10), or, as Stauffer (1969, p. 186) says, "Meaning is the important thing—not saying words. Reading is a thinking process and not a parroting process."

To create a classroom environment that reflects these beliefs, Veatch (1986, p. 32) advises teachers to "utilize some aspect of the internal world of the pupil. There must be some kind of personal choice, some kind of individual input into the task of learning." This sort of environment features student freedom and choice, to be sure, but also student responsibility.

> In sum, teaching and learning . . . is firmly grounded on order, on rigor of knowledge acquisition, on system, and on the high degree of personal commitment that comes from one's own world of thought, ideas, and language. With such activities in our schools, [children] cannot help but feel that the world is [their] oyster. (Veatch 1986, p. 34)

Let's take a closer look at how we can create such a dynamic learning environment.

LEA: THE BASICS

LEA activities are successful with students of all ages. In general, LEA will work well if a learner's oral language (i.e., vocabulary and sentence structure) is more complex than the written language the learner can read successfully. Certainly beginning readers fall into this category. So too do readers of any age who experience significant difficulty with reading. Here, for example, is a text dictated by two parents, both beginning readers, who were making family photo albums as part of a family literacy program.

> Chris said, "We try to take pictures of the important stuff, like birthdays and Christmas. It's fun to look back at them and see how you used to look."

> Helen said, "We take pictures, too. The kids, they change so fast. I forget those times without the pictures."

LEA's flexibility and effectiveness in a variety of instructional settings and with a variety of learner types is one of its strengths. A search of the professional literature (Padak and Rasinski 1996) shows that LEA-related activities are used with beginning readers, to be sure, but also with middle school, high school, college, and adult readers. Many teachers who work with nonnative speakers of English rely heavily on LEA, as do teachers of learners with special needs, especially those who are deaf, hearing impaired, or learning disabled. Teachers who know the basic assumptions and procedures underlying language-experience, then, have a flexible set of instructional procedures that can be implemented in many classrooms with a wide variety of learners.

What are the basic LEA procedures? To obtain dictated texts with groups of students, teachers follow six steps:

- Provide a stimulus for the language-experience activity. Possibilities abound: some event or interesting happening (in or out of the classroom), a field trip, a story read aloud or viewed on videotape. Content area connections are also fruitful sources for dictated texts. In science, students may observe weather patterns or plant growth, for example, and in social studies they may dictate texts about famous people, current events, holidays, elections, and so forth. Family events, stories, and experiences can also be the basis for individual LEA activities. Several additional examples are described in the next section.
- Initiate discussion about the stimuli. Encourage students to share their ideas and to express their thoughts, opinions, or feelings in words. Facilitate the discussion by acknowledging learners' contributions, inviting summarization, and encouraging further exploration.
- When discussion seems complete, begin to take dictation. Encourage children to recapture the discussion so that you can write it for them. The length of dictated texts varies, but for beginners, short texts (perhaps six to eight sentences) work well. Write on chart paper, the chalkboard, an overhead transparency, or the computer if you have access to an LCD panel. Use print that is large enough for the whole group to read. Space words clearly. Say the words as you write them. Use standard spelling and adhere to capitalization and punctuation rules. Don't edit the text in any other way, though. Record students' language exactly as expressed.
- After the dictation is complete, reread it aloud. Encourage learners to read it silently as well. Ask children if they want to make changes, and make those requested. Finally, ask learners to provide a title for their text.
- Read and reread the dictation several times as a group, which also builds fluency.
- Make individual copies of the text for further use. Study individual sentences, lines, phrases, words, and word parts within the text. (See Using Dictations, below.)

The same procedures work for taking individual dictations. Instead of writing on an overhead transparency or on chart paper, though, the child's text can be written on regular paper. Some teachers use the computer to capture dictations. With individuals, it's often helpful for the child to sit at your side (to the left if you are right-handed), so that he or she can watch as you print the words on the page.

OBTAINING DICTATIONS

As noted above, virtually any happening, in or out of the classroom, can serve as a source of dictation. Although children are often interested in speculating about outside-the-classroom events, most teachers also plan classroom experiences that will lead naturally to dictation. These experiences need not be spectacular; in fact, the typical classroom routine offers many opportunities for LEA. What happens during the experience and how the teacher facilitates children's learning, however, are very important.

Look again at the beginning of the chapter for a moment. Think about Gloria's role during the *Buttons* lesson. The lesson was successful, we believe, because of what she did and did not do. She encouraged the children to express their thoughts and to share their ideas with one another, but she did not tell children what to say or what to think. For example, she asked children, "What did you notice?" and let children generate categories, rather than telling them which categories to use. She facilitated language and learning without controlling it. She also encouraged summarizing at appropriate points in the lesson by asking questions such as, "What have we been doing?"

In other words, Gloria's primary function was to keep conversation flowing so that children could continue to discover through their actions and their talk. Gloria chose her words carefully because she knew the importance of her contributions: "If we are to use talk as a means of supporting and extending children's learning then we must select what we say with the same awareness and deliberateness as we would when we select and use other resources" (Tough 1979, p. 80).

At the dictation stage, Gloria encouraged children to summarize their learning. Here she functioned primarily as a scribe. She recorded children's comments verbatim rather than making editorial changes or even suggestions. This, too, was done purposefully. Gloria wanted children to maintain interest in the dictated text so that they would want to reread it, and she knew that children would be more interested in language that was their own. She also knew that maintaining the children's exact language would facilitate their learning about connections between oral and written language and about the conventions of print. As LEA evolves in the classroom, it may be possible to address issues of revising and editing the text that children present orally to demonstrate that written text is often revised and is rarely a direct transcription of talk. But especially at first, be sure to write down exactly what students say.

Dictation can occur in whole group, small group, or individual situations. The overall LEA procedures remain the same. Good LEA activities feature lots of language, sharing, exploration, and problem-solving. The teacher facilitates the learning process and demonstrates the value of the children's thoughts and language by recording the children's words exactly.

Possibilities for motivating dictation are almost limitless. Here, for example, is part of a book dictated by several children who were just beginning a library unit in their special reading class. They had discussed how valuable the library was for finding answers to questions, and Gary, their teacher, asked them what they would like to learn:

> "I would like to learn about dinosaurs. I know almost everything, but how big is T. Rex? I know how big some dinosaurs are."
> By Akio

> "I want to learn what makes the babies grow in the mommy's stomach. Why do they cry a lot? After they cry, why do they fall asleep?"
> By Jancey

> "I would like to learn how the world spins around. I want to learn if it spins on anything or not."
> By Alison

> "I want to learn how the baby dogs are. How do the baby dogs jump?"
> By Eliza

The children didn't just ask questions. With help from Gary and the school librarian, they found answers. These, too, were dictated. Eventually, Gary and the students put the questions and answers into a class book about the library project.

Sometimes LEA activities can promote the use of specific vocabulary. Kay, a kindergarten teacher we introduced in Chapter 9, wanted children to learn color words, number words, and names for parts of the body. So she arranged an activity where children worked together to make a creature out of large, colorful, interlocking blocks. Her hope was that the activity would encourage children to dictate some color words, number words, and words for body parts. Here's the children's text:

The Crazy Monster

The crazy monster has lots of eyes. The crazy monster has two hats. The crazy monster has twelve eyes. The crazy monster has six pairs of eyes. He has two necks and two heads. The crazy monster is scary. The monster is funny. The monster has two eyes on each head.

Kay's plan worked pretty well. The children did, indeed, use number words and names for parts of the body in their dictation. They didn't use color words to describe their monster, though, and Kay didn't force the issue. She knew that the text must reflect the children's ideas, not hers. She also knew she could plan another LEA to invite focus on color words.

Another natural use of LEA is to summarize an entire unit of study. The text shown below, also from Kay's kindergarten classroom, was created at the end of several weeks' study about birds. Children had heard and read stories, poems, and nonfiction texts about birds; listened to recordings of bird sounds; and visited the bird exhibit at the local zoo. The dictation offered them an opportunity to summarize and synthesize what they had learned, and the resulting text became a permanent record for their continued use.

Birds

All birds have feathers. A lot of birds know how to fly. Some birds walk. Some birds swim. Birds are different colors. Some birds are small. Some birds are big. Some birds have crests. All birds have bills. All birds lay eggs. Birds eat different things.

Literature, too, can serve as a stimulus for dictation. After hearing a favorite book, children can dictate their reactions or recount their favorite episodes. They can also create their own versions of a story or poem, a procedure called copy change that is introduced in Chapter 3 and also described later in this chapter. Wayne's students enjoy dictating stories to accompany wordless picture books. He puts copies of the children's texts in large zip-lock bags along with copies of the wordless books. These are available for check out in the classroom library. "Children love these!" he says. "It's not unusual to see a student spend lots of time—sometimes almost an hour—pouring over different versions of a wordless book, comparing them to each other and the pictures. It's amazing."

LEA can also "glue" several aspects of a lesson together. For example, Sue, a Title 1 reading teacher, read the book *Shadow* by Marcia Brown (1986). Then she and her second grade students, all of whom were beginning readers, talked about shadows, what makes them, and where they are found. Next each child stood in the light beam of the overhead projector, and Sue traced the child's shadow using white chalk on a piece of black construction paper that had been taped to the chalkboard. Children cut their silhouettes out and glued them on large pieces of construction paper.

The next day, Sue read some of the sentences from June Behrens' (1968) book *Who Am I?* She selected only sentences beginning with *I* because she wanted to encourage her beginning readers to dictate sentences beginning with *I*. Then she and the students discussed things that were different about each person, such as eye color, length of hair, color of skin, gender. Children dictated riddles about themselves that ended with "Who am I?" They copied their riddles onto the construction paper next to their silhouettes. Each child then made an answer key by putting his or her name on an index card and placing it inside a library pocket card that was pasted onto the construction paper.

Sue found the entire LEA very rewarding. "The children were surprised to see how much their silhouettes resembled them," she commented. "They were fascinated by the shadows. Before we even wrote the riddles, they were trying to guess whose was whose. And then when the riddles were written, they LOVED reading them and guessing. I think each child preferred his or her own riddle, though. I noticed that they read their own riddles again and again."

LEA and Individual Students

Dictations with individuals have the added benefit of bringing the child's unique interests into the classroom. Most children have interests that may not be addressed during instruction in school. Providing texts for students to read that reflect their interests can be a powerful motivator for reading growth.

For example, Nancy's son Matt is a sports fanatic. When he was a little boy, he used to spend hours pouring over the sports pages in the newspapers and magazines about professional sports. He was particularly drawn to charts, such as the ones shown below, which came from a magazine about professional football that reviewed the 1986 season and made predictions about the 1987 season:

1986 RESULTS		
Sept. 7	NEW YORK JETS	24-28
Sept. 14	at Cincinnati	33-36
Sept. 21	ST. LOUIS	17-10
Sept. 26	KANSAS CITY	17-20
Oct. 5	at New York Jets	13-14
Oct.12	at Miami	14-27
Oct.19	INDIANAPOLIS	24-13
Oct. 26	NEW ENGLAND	3-23
Nov. 2	at Tampa Bay	28-34
Nov. 6	PITTSBURGH	16-12
Nov. 16	MIAMI	24-34
Nov. 23	at New England	19-22
Nov. 30	at Kansas City	17-14
Dec. 7	CLEVELAND	17-21
Dec. 14	at Indianapolis	15-24
Dec. 21	at Houston	7-16

1986 RESULTS		
Sept. 7	at Chicago	31-41
Sept. 14	at Houston	23-20
Sept. 18	CINCINNATI (Thurs.)	13-30
Sept. 26	DETROIT	24-21
Oct. 5	at Pittsburgh	27-24
Oct.12	KANSAS CITY	20-7
Oct.19	GREEN BAY	14-17
Oct. 26	at Minnesota	23-30
Nov. 2	at Indianapolis	24-9
Nov. 10	MIAMI (Mon.)	26-16
Nov. 16	at Los Angeles Raiders	14-27
Nov. 23	PITTSBURGH	37-31
Nov. 30	HOUSTON	13-10
Dec. 7	at Buffalo	21-17
Dec. 11	at Cincinnati	34-3
Dec. 21	SAN DIEGO	47-17

	1986 RESULTS	
Sept. 7	CLEVELAND	41-31
Sept. 14	PHILADELPHIA	13-10
Sept. 22	at Green Bay (Mon.)	25-12
Sept. 28	at Cincinnati	44-7
Oct. 5	MINNESOTA	23-0
Oct.12	at Houston	20-7
Oct.19	at Minnesota	7-23
Oct. 26	DETROIT	13-7
Nov. 3	L.A. RAMS (Mon.)	17-20
Nov. 9	at Tampa Bay	23-3
Nov. 16	at Atlanta	13-10
Nov. 23	GREEN BAY	12-10
Nov. 30	PITTSBURGH	13-10
Dec. 7	TAMPA BAY	48-14
Dec. 15	at Detroit (Mon.)	16-13
Dec. 21	at Dallas	24-10

Matt used these three charts, which summarized the 1986 seasons for the Buffalo Bills, the Cleveland Browns, and the Chicago Bears, to dictate the following text to his mom.

What I Like About Football

What I like about football is to watch it on TV because it has a lot of tackling and sacking and stuff like that. Now we go on to the statistics.

OK, I'll tell about the Bills, the Browns, and the Bears. In the Bills' first game they lost to the New York Jets to kick off the football season. The final score was New York 28 and poor Buffalo had 24. In the second game of the season they lost again, a surprising loss for the Bills. Except this time they lost it 33–36. But luck is going to change for the Bills. It finally turns around, 17–10 for the Bills. Bills in front; Cardinals in back.

In the Browns' first game of the 1986 season, they lost to the Bears, 31–41. But luck may change for the Browns, and it does, 23–20. They pick up a win against the patriotic Patriots. Then luck turns around again. This time the Chiefs beat the Browns, believe it or not, 33–13.

I want to tell about the Bears because they're my favorite team. The first game of the season they won against the Browns, but we already know that, 31–41. Then they beat the Steelers, and then they beat the Giants. Then they picked up another win off Kansas City, 44–7.

Why do I like the Bears so much? Because they've had great talent over the years. Another reason is the Bears are just a winning team. Like they won the Super Bowl, 46–10. And the Pats are good, but not too good for the Bears. It was one of the great challenges of my life to see my team win the Super Bowl!

By Matt, age 6

Dictated texts are valuable and effective as reading materials for beginning readers. LEA activities enhance written language awareness and demonstrate the connection between spoken and written language. As children watch their words recorded, they learn that print is meaningful; they also learn about the conventions of printed language. And they learn that writing is valuable for preserving information, ideas, and feelings. Teachers who rely upon LEA also note its flexibility. Any curricular area can provide the stimulus for dictation, and subsequent reading can foster content area learning as well as reading growth.

Later, as children mature in their writing ability, students can write texts based on their own experiences. This is LEA at its zenith and, we contend, the type of experience-based writing that many professional writers do for a living!

USING LEA TEXTS FOR EXTENDED READING AND WORD EXPLORATION

In many respects, dictations can be used like any other reading material. For example, children can read and reread current and previous dictations, either silently or with a partner. Many teachers make dictation notebooks, individual three-ring binders, so that students have easy access to the texts they have helped to prepare.

Sometimes teachers prepare their own versions of students' texts to provide extra practice with texts and words. These teacher-developed texts contain the same content and most of the same words but differ in form from the students' original text. Here, for example, is Gloria's version of *Buttons*:

> We put the buttons into piles called categories. One pile was smooth buttons, and one pile was rough buttons. Some buttons were lumpy. Some were shiny. We made categories for the buttons.

Gloria's version contains the same ideas and the same words as the children's version, but the words have been reorganized into different sentences.

The teacher can also develop questions to accompany dictated texts, such as "How many categories did we have?" or "One pile was smooth buttons. What was the other pile?" Cloze exercises (see Chapter 10) can also be developed from dictated texts, e.g., We put _____ into piles called _____.

Children can illustrate their dictated texts. They can also make books by cutting longer dictations apart. Each sentence can be pasted on a different page and illustrated. Some teachers make story puzzles by cutting dictated texts into sentences and asking children to reassemble the sentences in ways that make sense to them. All these activities involve reading and rereading the texts and, as such, are valuable for building sight vocabulary and developing fluency in reading. Many word- and sound-related activities, which we discuss extensively in other Chapters, are also possible. For example, children can find rhyming words in their dictations or complete sentence frames with as many words as possible, e.g., "The _____ is on the _____."

Dictated texts can be used for teacher-directed instruction as well. Beginning readers need to learn about the conventions of print, the ways written language is similar and yet different from oral language. Oral language is a steady stream of speech, but in writing words are separated from one another on the page. Teachers can show students that words in their dictated texts are separated by spaces. Students can demonstrate this concept by circling or underlining words in the texts.

Other conventions of print can be addressed as well. For example, writers write in sentences and paragraphs; speakers sometimes don't. And then there's directionality: In English letters in a word and words on a line are arranged from left to right, and lines on a page are generally arranged from top to bottom. Readers take all these aspects of written language for granted, but beginners must develop these understandings for themselves.

Much of this learning happens informally. When children watch something being read, they gain knowledge about the conventions of print. This is one reason why it's so helpful to say words while writing them during dictation. Some teachers we know even provide running commentaries about the conventions of print while they record children's words. They say things like, "OK, that's the end of the sentence, so I'll put a period here. This new sentence will need a capital letter." Over time, such informal and incidental learning pays dividends in terms of children's understandings.

More formal instruction can also be planned. In the *Crazy Monster* lesson described earlier, Kay's follow-up activities focused on print conventions. She conducted the lesson the day after the children had built the monster. The children were seated around a large copy of their dictated text.

- Kay asked about the title: "How many words are in the title?" "Where's the first word in the title?" "Where's the last word?" "Who can circle all the words in the title?"
- She asked about the first and last words in the story. The children found them and circled them.
- She asked children to find sentences: "Where does the first sentence begin?" "Where does it end?" "How can we tell when a sentence begins?" "How can we tell when a sentence ends?" "How many sentences are in our story?" "How many lines?"
- She used her word whopper (see Chapter 3) to isolate words in the text that students were asked to read.
- She asked children to match lines from the story with strips of paper that contained the lines. In each case, Kay and the children discussed how many sentences the lines contained and whether or not the lines made sense by themselves.
- She asked children to match words from the story with word cards that contained the words.
- She played word sort games (see Chapter 9). Kay and the children also played word-changing games, which involved changing letters to make new words, e.g., *hats* became *rats* and *bats*; *scary* became *Mary*; *funny* became *fun*. Kay invited all children to participate in these activities; the kindergartners who were beginning to read had the most success with these word-level games. Kay didn't worry about frustrating the others, however, because they found success with other activities more focused on print conventions. In this way she was able to differentiate instruction to accommodate all children's needs and abilities.

In this lesson, Kay's students were working with parts of written language—lines, sentences, and words. Nevertheless, they were also working with familiar and meaningful text, which provided support and allowed them to discover the relationship between the parts and the whole. Over time, activities like these can help beginning readers learn about the conventions of print.

Many of these same activities can serve diagnostic functions. Consider the questions above, for example. Which could Kay use if she were interested in determining students' conceptual knowledge of sentences? Words? Teachers can also gain insight into children's literacy development while they practice reading individual copies of their dictated texts. For example, teachers can see who has mastered directionality, who has mastered the concept of word, who is able to read fluently, and who can use word attack strategies to help them recognize words. Comprehension can be checked by asking children to read old dictations and retell them in their own words. Retellings can be evaluated according to breadth and sequence. Many additional diagnostic suggestions are provided by Ann Agnew (1982); we have used variations of her ideas for more than a decade and have found them helpful for exploring children's growth in literacy.

COPY CHANGE

As we saw with Sue's *Shadow* lessons, children's literature or poetry can be the primary experience or an effective springboard for dictation or writing. After the teacher reads several folk tales or fairy tales to the class, for example, discussion and subsequent dictation can focus on common elements. Children can use these dictated notes to create their own tales, perhaps by changing the characters or updating the plots. In this manner, "Little Red Riding Hood" might become "Dirty Old Baseball Hat" or Goldilocks might visit the home of three roller-bladers.

As we noted in Chapter 3, predictable literature is a good choice for copy change. A book like Margaret Wise Brown's *The Important Book* (1949, 1999) has a readily recognizable pattern that children can easily use to create their own versions. This book is particularly useful during the first days of school. After having read or listened to Brown's descriptions of important things, students can write or dictate descriptions of themselves using the same format ("The important thing about Karen is . . . "). Individual student contributions can be collected to form a class "Introductions" book that will be read and reread throughout the year. Teachers need to be sure to make their own contributions to the book. Copies of the book can also be made for each student to take home to read with family members, perhaps inspiring development of a "Family Important Book."

Poetry is another good choice for copy change activities. Judith Viorst's (1981) poem "If I Were in Charge of the World" is a favorite among teachers and students we know. Its four stanzas follow this pattern:

If I were in charge of the world
I'd cancel oatmeal,

Monday mornings,
Allergy shots, and also
Sara Steinberg.

Marala read this poem several times over several days to her third grade students. Then she asked the children what they noticed about how Judith Viorst created the poem: "What did she say again and again? How did she set up the verses?" As students offered ideas, Marala wrote them on the chalkboard:

Every one starts the same.
She says, "If I were in charge of the world."
The kid wants to change bad things or to get good things.
There are usually 4 things in the verse.

After the students had dictated their thoughts about Viorst's patterns, Marala invited them to create their own versions. Here are a few:

If I was in charge of the universe
I could do anything I want to do.
I could watch TV all day long.
I could fly like a bird.
There would be no school.
    By Patrick

If I was in charge of the school
I would have a computer for each student and teacher.
I would make sure that there are no worksheets.
I would have each teacher make sure their class gets three recesses.
And you would be able to swim in the pool.
    By Amanda D.

If I was in charge of all the holidays
Christmas would be first with all the presents.
Easter would be second,
Third would be Halloween.
Last would be Valentine's Day.
    By Joey

If I was in charge of the barn
I would have electric horse feeders.
I would have electric saddle cleaners.
Horses would always have a big treat dispenser.
Horses would have an electric flyspray hose!
    By Amanda P.

Students can also recast a favorite story in the form of a script to be performed for others. This, too, is a copy change because the original story serves as a framework for the new version. Here, for example, is the beginning of a script based on Bernard Waber's *Ira Sleeps Over* (1972) that was developed and later performed by Bonnie's second grade students:

IRA:	I'm going to sleep over at Reggie's house.
SISTER:	Are you taking your teddy bear?
IRA:	Take my teddy bear? No, I'm not taking my teddy bear!
SISTER:	But you've never slept without your teddy bear. Won't you feel funny?
IRA:	I'll feel fine!
NARRATOR:	Now Ira started thinking. Maybe he did need his teddy bear.

To support children's script development, Bonnie first read the book to them a couple of times. Then the children decided who the characters would be and what they would say. Bonnie took dictation during this discussion.

Like LEAs, students' copy change texts and their scripts can be used to help beginning readers develop concepts about printed language; build a sight vocabulary; and learn about the features of words, sentences, and sounds. Copy change activities encourage careful reading, listening, and thinking so that children can discover and subsequently use the author's pattern. They also provide a structural framework or scaffold that makes writing easier for students. And, like other LEA activities, they yield lots of interesting material to read and perform.

In Conclusion

Language-experience is an elegant and well articulated approach to literacy instruction that is grounded in decades of research and professional practice. Whether dictated texts originate in a classroom experience or are based on a piece of literature, the familiarity afforded by children's own language provides a strong scaffold to support beginning reading success.

Children enter school as competent and creative language users. They already know how to learn. Children will approach reading with the same enthusiasm and problem-solving ability they used in learning to talk if instruction focuses on thinking, communication, interaction, and their own experiences. Experience-based instruction offers all this and more; teachers who use LEA experience a genuine caring for learners and respect for their experiences, interests, and motivations. This caring and respect helps to create self-confident learners who know how to work with one another in cooperative and responsible ways. To us, LEA is more than a reading method. It's a way to help children learn about life inside and outside the classroom. More important, it's a vehicle for helping children develop as informed, confident, and caring human beings.

References

Agnew, A.T. 1982. Using Children's Dictations to Assess Code Consciousness. *The Reading Teacher*, 35: 450–454.

Allen, R.V. 1976. *Language Experiences in Communication*. Boston: Houghton Mifflin.

Ashton-Warner, S. 1963. *Teacher*. New York: Scholastic.

Hall, M. (1985). Focus on Language Experience Learning and Teaching. *Reading,* 19: 5–12.

Huey, E.B. 1908/1968. *The Psychology and Pedagogy of Reading*. Cambridge, MA: MIT Press.

Padak, N., and T. Rasinski. 1996. LEA in ERIC. *Language Experience Forum,* 26: 2, 4–5.

Rippa, S.A. 1984. *Education in a Free Society*. (5th ed.). New York: Longman.

Stauffer, R.G. 1969. *Directing Reading Maturity as a Cognitive Process*. New York: Harper & Row.

Tough, J. 1979. *Talk for Teaching and Learning*. Portsmouth, NH: Heinemann.

Veatch, J. 1986. Teaching Without Texts. *Journal of Clinical Reading,* 2: 32–35.

CHILDREN'S LITERATURE CITED

Behrens, J. 1968. *Who Am I?* Chicago: Children's Press.

Brown, M. 1986. *Shadow*. New York: Aladdin.

Brown, M.W. 1949/1999. *The Important Book*. New York: HarperCollins.

Viorst, J. 1981. *If I Were in Charge of the World and Other Worries*. New York: Atheneum.

Waber, B. 1972. *Ira Sleeps Over*. Boston: Houghton Mifflin.

12

WORD GAMES

Excitement is in the air. It's Friday afternoon and students in Angie's second grade classroom spend the last 30 minutes of the school week playing word games. Angie has introduced students to a number of word games throughout the year, and this afternoon *Wordo* and *Team Scattergories* are on the agenda. Angie has found that her students love to play the word games she has developed. "Many children who show up in my classroom early in the morning or have to wait for their bus after school find word games a good way to spend those few extra minutes. In fact, so many parents have asked about our games that I did two Make-It-Take-It workshops for parents this year. In October we made a reading game and in January we did a math game. My parents find that this is an easy way to help their children and have some fun at the same time."

As proficient adult readers, well over ninety-nine percent of the words you encounter in everyday reading are recognized by sight. How did you achieve this remarkable level of proficiency in your word recognition? The most likely answer is that you began to add words to your sight or automatic vocabulary through repeated exposures to the words. The more you saw certain words, the stronger your mental image became for them, to the point where you can now recognize those words by sight, without any deep conscious analysis.

The goal of any word recognition program is to reach the point where nearly all words a reader encounters in normal reading are recognizable automatically or by sight. Sight vocabulary develops through repeated exposure to words. Gates (1931) determined that learners of average intelligence require approximately thirty-five exposures to a word before it can be easily recognized; less able learners will require about fifty-five exposures to a word before it can be recognized automatically.

Clearly, many exposures to words are necessary before they become part of one's sight vocabulary. Most of these repetitions come from wide reading. Through the process of reading, one is exposed to many words—that is why the most frequent words, e.g., the Dolch list or the Fry Instant Word List are good candidates for sight learning—the reader sees frequent words repeatedly, easily adding those words to his or her sight vocabulary. Lots of contextual reading, including sustained silent reading in school and pleasure reading at home, will gradually help to build one's sight vocabulary simply through repeated exposure to words. Again, then, we return to the notion that the foundation of any good word recognition reading program is lots of reading for real purposes.

There are other ways, in addition to contextual reading, to increase students' exposure to words. One of those ways is through word games. In this chapter we suggest some word games we know work, through our own experience as well as the experience of our teaching colleagues. The main purpose of these games is to provide additional practice for students in learning to recognize and understand written words. Word games can also be devised to reinforce phonics patterns, generalizations, or other significant word recognition skills and strategies.

There is a nearly unlimited number of word games that can be developed or adapted for classroom use. The ones described in this chapter are only a beginning. We encourage you to develop your own word games for your students. The key to word games is to ensure that all students are participating all the time. If only one or two students in a group of twenty-five are attending at any one time, then only those one or two gain from the experience.

WORDO

One of our favorite word games is Wordo, a take-off of bingo. A 5 x 5 game card grid is used, very similar to the one in bingo; however, instead of each box being filled with a number, in Wordo, each box contains a word.

In order to play Wordo you need at least twenty-four or twenty-five words and a Wordo card for each player (see Figure 12.1). The words can be spelling words, words that come from specific word recognition lessons, words from a word bank, words from various content areas, holiday words, or any other set of twenty-five words. The words are listed on the chalkboard and students copy the words randomly on their game cards, one word per box. The center box can be marked Free. It is important that students place the words into the game card boxes randomly; if all students arrange the words in the same order on their cards, all players will win at the same time! The teacher also writes the words on a set of 3 x 5 cards, shuffles them, and spreads them out, written side down, on a table.

Once the game cards are filled out, the game begins. The teacher (or a student) acts as the moderator, draws a word card from those spread out, and calls out the selected word. Students search their cards for the called word and if it appears on their card, they cover it with a marker (dried lima beans, available at most supermarkets, make good, inexpensive markers). The game continues in this way until a student achieves Wordo by getting a line of markers in a row, column, or diagonal. A small prize is often given to the winner, game cards are cleared, and a new game begins.

Rather than simply call out the words as they are selected, the moderator may want to give other clues such as the definition of the selected word, a sentence in which the selected word is deleted, or structural clues, e.g., "the word I selected has two syllables, begins with a consonant blend, and contains a

W	O	R	D	O
		FREE SPACE ☺		

Figure 12.1
WORDO Card

diphthong." These more subtle clues force students to examine the words on their cards in a little more depth.

Younger students may be a bit overwhelmed by games cards that contain twenty-four empty boxes. For students just beginning to learn about words and Wordo, you can use games cards that are made up of a 3 x 3 or 4 x 4 matrix. The 3 x 3 matrix needs only nine words, and the 4 x 4 will require sixteen words to play.

The Wordo concept can also be used to teach initial letters and letter sounds. In this version of Wordo, usually done with a 3 x 3 game card for younger children (see Figure 12.2), students write initial consonant letters or blends on their cards in random fashion—one letter or blend for each box, e.g., *b, br, bl, t, tr, p, pr, pl, s*. Then, the teacher calls out words that contain one of the sounds (e.g., *brother, trap, pet,* or *plant*) or shows a picture that begins with one of the targeted sounds. Students find the appropriate beginning letter or blend and cover it with a marker. The same idea can also be employed with ending letters and sounds, affixes, and vowels and their corresponding sounds.

Students of nearly any age love to play Wordo. It is certainly an enjoyable way to review words you want students to learn and to provide the necessary practice for adding the words to their sight vocabularies.

WORD WAR

Word War is a game played with word cards in much the same way as the card game War. The game is best played by two to four students in a group. A deck of word cards is needed. This can be accomplished by giving each group of students a deck of 3 x 5 cards, asking students to divide them up between themselves, and having them write a word on each card so that it fills a large portion of the card. Students can come up with words from their various areas of study or interest. Once created, the Word War deck of cards can be used for many weeks and new words can be added to the deck as needed.

Another possibility for creating a deck of word cards is for students to use words from their word banks (see Chapter 9 for more on word banks). Of course, if you choose this option you will need for students to mark their own cards in some way (perhaps their initials) so that they can retrieve their cards at the end of the game.

Once the deck is established, all the word cards are put together, shuffled, and distributed to each player, face down. An agreed upon time limit is set, usually five or ten minutes, and the game begins. Each player plays one card face up from his or her deck. The player must be able to pronounce the word in order to continue the play. Once each player presents a card and pronounces it, the player with the longest word wins the round and all the cards that were played. These words go to the bottom of the player's pile.

A new round is then begun in the same manner. If, however, the longest word is shared by two or more players, then a war ensues. Each of the players involved in the tie plays another card face down and then one face up and pronounces it. The player with the longer of the second face-up cards wins all

WORDO

Figure 12.2
WORDO Card

the cards played in that round. Another tie brings on another war with two more cards played by each tied player, one face down and one face up.

Play continues in this manner until the timer bell goes off. At this point, players count the cards they hold. The player with the largest number of cards is the winner. If there is sufficient time, another game can be played.

PICK UP STICKS

Played with two to four students, Pick Up Sticks requires a set of popsicle sticks with words to be practiced written on one end of each stick. One stick has the word ZAP! written at the end. All sticks are placed word-end down, into a can, cup, or some other opaque container.

Play begins with one student pulling a stick up from the container. If the player can pronounce the word he or she gets to keep the stick. If the word cannot be pronounced quickly it must be returned to the container. Each player pulls one stick at a time, followed by the next player. Play continues until the ZAP! stick is pulled. At this point, players count the sticks in their possession and the player with the most sticks is the winner.

A variation of the game requires each player to pronounce the target word as it is pulled. If unable to pronounce the word, the player continues to pull word sticks until one can be pronounced. The player who finally pulls the ZAP! stick is the instant loser (or winner if you need another variation). Students love the suspense that develops as the number of sticks left in the pot becomes smaller and smaller.

MATCH

Match is another game that relies on word cards and is best played in pairs. All word cards in Match are paired. That is, two word cards are made for each word used in the game. Usually, between ten and fifteen words (20–30 cards) are sufficient. Students can make word cards from a clean deck of 3 x 5 cards, or they can be drawn from students' personal word banks. If drawn from word banks, the cards need to be marked for easy return to the owner, and players must ensure that each card has a match.

Once the deck of cards is made, it is shuffled and laid out in a grid, face down. Students take turns turning over two cards at a time. They need to say the words as they are turned over. If the two word cards match, the student wins the pair and continues to play in the same manner. If, however, the cards do not match, the cards are turned back over and the next player takes a turn. Play continues until all pairs or cards have been matched and claimed by a player. Players count the number of cards they have accumulated, and the player with the most cards is the winner.

Variations of the game can be created by changing the criteria for matching cards. In the example given above, the matched pairs were duplicate word cards. Nonetheless, the matched pairs could also be rhyming words, words with the same beginning letter, letter combination, or sound, words with the same ending, words with the same number of syllables, words that are synonyms, or words that mean the opposite.

GO FISH

Another game that involves matching is a variation of the classic card game Go Fish. Like Match, Go Fish requires a deck of word cards in which the words match in some way (e.g., same words, rhyming words, words that begin with the same letters or sounds, words with the same meaning). Ideally played with 4 or 5 players, students are each dealt five cards and the remaining cards are spread out in the middle of the table as the card pond. The object of the game is to find matches to the words in your hand.

A turn begins when a player examines his/her cards and asks a second player for a card that matches a criterion, e.g., "Do you have a word the rhymes with cat?" If the second player has such a card, it's given to the first player, who matches it and lays the pair down face up. The first player then makes another request for a card. If the second player doesn't have the requested card, however, the first player must "go fish." The first player then draws a card from the pond. If he or she can make a match he or she lays it down, face up, and takes another turn. If a match cannot be made, the next player's turn begins. Play continues until one player matches all the cards in his/her hand.

Scoring is variable; usually players get one point for each card matched but must subtract a point for each card that remains in their hands at the end of a round. The game continues until a certain point limit is reached, usually fifty to one hundred.

MAKE WORDS WITH CUBES

Make Words with Cubes requires a set of blank cubes or dice that can be purchased at many teacher supply stores. Individual letters or letter combinations are written on each side of the cube. If cubes cannot be found, you can take a set of dice, white out the dots, and write in individual letters and letter combinations. Alphabet blocks can also be used. Another variation is simply to randomly select six to ten letters or letter combinations to be used in the game and list them on the chalk board.

The game can be played in groups of three to five or with a larger group in which teams of two to three students work together. If cubes are available, they are shaken and spilled out on the table. A timer is set for five to ten minutes and students are challenged to make as many words as they can from the given list of letters. Bear, Invernizzi, Templeton, and Johnston (1996) suggest that a record sheet be used in which students record the words they can make by length (See Figure 12.3). Once time has expired, students check the words they constructed and assign points. Each three-letter word is worth three points, four-letter words are worth four points, and so on.

If you choose to use cubes with only one letter per side, other recording and scoring sheets are possible. For example, rather than having students

2 letters	3 letters	4 letters	5 letters	6 letters	7 letters	8 letters	9 letters	10 letters

Figure 12.3
Cube Word Record Sheet

record their words by number of letters, students can also sort their words by number of syllables, number of consonant blends and digraphs per word, or short and long vowel sounds, with more points given to words with more syllables, more blends and digraphs, or long vowel sounds.

WORD MAKER CUPS

One age-old practice is to have students blend beginning consonants and blends with rimes or word families to determine the words that can be made, e.g., *pr + ay = pray*. Often this involves creating "sliders" in which a strip containing the beginning consonants, consonant blends, and consonant digraphs is slipped through slits in a larger piece of construction paper that contains the rimes. Moving the beginning consonant slider through the rime sheet, the students determines all the words that can be made.

This is a good activity for students learning how to blend onsets and rimes to make words; however, the construction of the sliders or similar items requires considerable time. Furthermore, these constructions are often fragile and tend to fall apart easily when used a lot by young hands.

One alternative to sliders involves the use of Styrofoam coffee cups. The larger cups work best. When two cups are stacked, their lips fit together nicely; they can also be rotated. So, the lips of one set of cups contains beginning consonants and blends (eight to ten per cup should do). And, the lips of the other set of cups show the rimes or word families you want students to work with (two to four rimes per cup seem to work best). Then, have students simply take one of the beginning consonant and blend cups and one of the rime cups, fit them together, and rotate them so that all the combinations of consonants, blends, and rimes can be analyzed (see Figure 12.4). Students

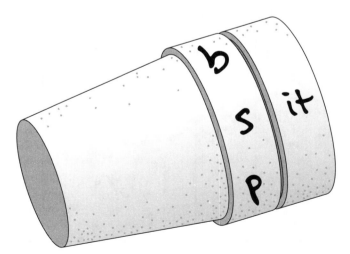

Figure 12.4
Word Maker Cups

should jot down all the words that can be made from the various combinations. Although this is not necessarily a game, it is enjoyable practice in using rimes to decode and spell words. Since cups are inexpensive (usually a hundred or so for a dollar or less), and the word cups are easy to make (even students can make them), this activity is very attractive to those teachers hard pressed for time (isn't that all teachers, all the time?)

SCATTERGORIES

Scattergories can be played with large groups of students; we find it best, however, if students work in teams of two or three at a time. Scattergories is a generative game that is a great way to get students thinking about word patterns. The only requirement is a Scattergory sheet for each student or team (see Figure 12.5).

Along the top row, the teacher (and students) brainstorm about five word patterns—rimes, derivational patterns, and so on. Down the left hand column, the teacher provides a random set of consonants and consonant blends. Then, for the next five to ten minutes students think of words that begin with each consonant or blend and that contain one of the targeted patterns (see Figure 12.6 for an example).

At the end of the given time period students score their sheets. There are a variety of ways to score the game. If students are allowed to put only one word into each box, they can be given a point for every letter used in each acceptable word. This encourages students to think of longer words containing the targeted patterns. In another scoring scheme, students list all the words they can think of that begin with the particular consonant or blend and contain the appropriate blend. One point is given for each acceptable word. In this case, students are rewarded for thinking of many words that fit the given specifications. Still other approaches to scoring can be devised.

The game itself has many variations. Instead of consonants and consonant blends, the left hand column could also contain prefixes. Indeed, the left hand column could also contain semantic categories that require students to orchestrate their knowledge of word patterns with the meanings of words that contain such patterns. For example, word patterns such as *il(l), en, ack, ip,* and *on* could be used on the top row. The left hand columns could contain semantic categories such as *people's names, animals, cities or states,* and *plants*. For *people's names, Bill, Dennis,* or *Jack* could be used. For *animals, killer whale, hen* and *hippo* would work. *Philadelphia, Hackensack,* and *Boston* would fit the *cities and states* category, and *dill* and *tulip* would be in the *plants* category. The many variations of Scattergories that can add depth and interest make it a very useful game for the later primary to middle school grades.

SENTENCING

Word recognition also involves the ability to use context to determine unknown words in texts. One of the best games we have found for supporting this ability is called Sentencing (Hall 1995), a game similar in nature to Wheel of Fortune and

Scattergories

Word Families	ack	ick	at	it
Initial Letters				
t	track	ticker		
p	packet			pitiful
m			Matthew	
d				ditto

Figure 12.6
Scattegories

Scattergories

Initial Letters / Word Families				

Figure 12.5
Scattegories Form

Hangman, except that it uses sentences instead of individual words. Sentencing challenges students to use syntactic and semantic cues to reconstruct a sentence created by the teacher or extracted from an appropriate level text. The game involves teams of three to eight students and can be played with students in grades three and up. Student teams try to determine unknown words in a sentence.

After teams are set, the teacher finds a meaningful sentence of seven to fifteen words that makes strong use of syntax. The sentence should not include proper nouns or contractions. Here are some examples of possible sentences that could be used in the game:

If you are hungry, look inside the refrigerator.
The sun has been shining all week long, and I love it.

Each team is given two "free letter" cards, which allow them to get the first letter of unknown words during the game.

The game begins with the teacher listing the sentence on the chalkboard with only one key word revealed (see Figure 12.7). The revealed word should help students apply their background knowledge in making predictions about the sentence. Also, the teacher should point out to students any clues such as punctuation in the deleted sentence.

One team begins by choosing a blank word from the sentence they would like revealed. Each turn begins with the revelation of one unknown word of the team's choice unless there is only one word remaining, in which case the last word is not revealed. Upon revelation of the word, the team can either guess another word in the sentence, for which they will receive two points if correct, or they can use their "free letter" card in order to get the first letter of any unrevealed word. After seeing the first letter, they must guess any unknown word in the sentence. (The "free letter" card can also be used to guess the second, or any subsequent letter of an unknown word.) Guessing a word that has one or more letters revealed earns one point.

When a team makes an incorrect guess, play goes to the opposing team. With each turn, then, players have one word revealed and must guess one of the unknown words or use a "free letter" card and then guess a word. Correct guesses allow the team to continue. An incorrect guess ends that team's turn. Play is over when the entire sentence is guessed, at which time the score is tallied for each team.

In the example below Team One asked for word five to be revealed. It then used its "free letter" card for the first letter of the first word of the sentence. They correctly guessed *If* after the *I* was given and earned 1 point. They then guessed *the* for word eight and received two more points. Their next guess was the word

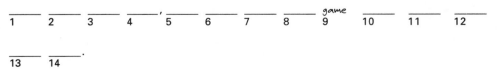

Figure 12.7

we for word two. This was an incorrect guess and the turn went to Team Two. (see Figure 12.8.)

Team Two began by asking for word fourteen to be revealed. The word was *television*. Then they used a "letter card" for the first letter in word four. This was a *t* and Team Two then guessed word two to be *you* and word three to be *are*. These guesses were worth two points. Team Two then guessed *tardy* for word four, which was incorrect. (see Figure 12.9.)

Team One regained its turn and used its last "letter card" for the second letter of word four. This revealed an *i*. Team members correctly guessed the word to be *tired* for one point. From this point, Team One correctly guessed word seven to be *watch,* but missed word six by guessing *will.* (see Figure 12.10.)

Team Two asked for word ten, which was *at* and used its "letter card" for the first letter of word eleven. This was revealed to be an *h*. At this point, Team Two guessed word eleven to be *home* (one point) and then correctly guessed the remainder of the sentence: word six *can* (two points), word twelve *on* (two points), and word thirteen *my* (two points) (see Figure 12.11).

$$\underset{1}{\underline{\text{If}}} \quad \underset{2}{\underline{}} \quad \underset{3}{\underline{}} \quad \underset{4}{\underline{}}, \quad \underset{5}{\underline{\text{we}}} \quad \underset{6}{\underline{}} \quad \underset{7}{\underline{}} \quad \underset{8}{\underline{\text{the}}} \quad \underset{9}{\underline{\text{game}}} \quad \underset{10}{\underline{}} \quad \underset{11}{\underline{}} \quad \underset{12}{\underline{}}$$

$$\underset{13}{\underline{}} \quad \underset{14}{\underline{}}.$$

Figure 12.8

$$\underset{1}{\underline{\text{If}}} \quad \underset{2}{\underline{\text{you}}} \quad \underset{3}{\underline{\text{are}}} \quad \underset{4}{\underline{\text{t}}}, \quad \underset{5}{\underline{\text{we}}} \quad \underset{6}{\underline{}} \quad \underset{7}{\underline{}} \quad \underset{8}{\underline{\text{the}}} \quad \underset{9}{\underline{\text{game}}} \quad \underset{10}{\underline{}} \quad \underset{11}{\underline{}} \quad \underset{12}{\underline{}}$$

$$\underset{13}{\underline{}} \quad \underset{14}{\underline{\text{television}}}.$$

Figure 12.9

$$\underset{1}{\underline{\text{If}}} \quad \underset{2}{\underline{\text{you}}} \quad \underset{3}{\underline{\text{are}}} \quad \underset{4}{\underline{\text{tired}}}, \quad \underset{5}{\underline{\text{we}}} \quad \underset{6}{\underline{}} \quad \underset{7}{\underline{\text{watch}}} \quad \underset{8}{\underline{\text{the}}} \quad \underset{9}{\underline{\text{game}}} \quad \underset{10}{\underline{}} \quad \underset{11}{\underline{}} \quad \underset{12}{\underline{}}$$

$$\underset{13}{\underline{}} \quad \underset{14}{\underline{\text{television}}}.$$

Figure 12.10

$$\underset{1}{\underline{\text{If}}} \quad \underset{2}{\underline{\text{you}}} \quad \underset{3}{\underline{\text{are}}} \quad \underset{4}{\underline{\text{tired}}}, \quad \underset{5}{\underline{\text{we}}} \quad \underset{6}{\underline{\text{can}}} \quad \underset{7}{\underline{\text{watch}}} \quad \underset{8}{\underline{\text{the}}} \quad \underset{9}{\underline{\text{game}}} \quad \underset{10}{\underline{\text{at}}} \quad \underset{11}{\underline{\text{home}}} \quad \underset{12}{\underline{\text{on}}}$$

$$\underset{13}{\underline{\text{my}}} \quad \underset{14}{\underline{\text{television}}}.$$

Figure 12.11

Points were tallied and Team Two won with twelve points. Team One brought up the rear with six points.

Although the game may seem somewhat complex, it is simple to play and, once students become familiar with the format, games tend to take no more than five minutes. Once the game is over, the teacher engages students in a quick debriefing of the game, asking what strategies did you use, and what were the biggest helps to you in figuring out the sentence? Students will inform one another, within teams and later between teams, of significant syntactic and semantic clues that help them determine the words along with the meaning of unknown words.

OTHER GAMES

We have only scratched the surface of the possible word games teachers and students can develop and enjoy. Simple board games based on popular commercial games such as Chutes and Ladders but focusing on words can easily be developed using a card stock file folder as the game board. Games derived from the words on the classroom Word Wall (see Chapter 7) are also possible. Second-grade teacher John has students do word sprints using the sight words on the Word Wall. Throughout the school year John adds five sight words each week to one Word Wall he designated the sight Word Wall. The words came from the second group of one hundred words from the Fry Instant Word List (Appendix B). Once the one hundred words have been introduced, students are paired up about once a week and each pair is given a stopwatch. While one student keeps time and checks for errors, the other student tries to read the wall as accurately and quickly as possible. Scores for accuracy and time are recorded on a "personal best" sheet that each student keeps. After the first student in each pair reads the wall and records his or her scores, the roles are reversed. "It's really only a tiny part of my word study and reading program, ten minutes a week or so, and I want to make sure the students compete against themselves not others," John says, "but the improvement that the students make in the three months that we do this is simply amazing. Based upon their original readings of the wall, students set a goal for themselves for accuracy and speed, and if they can meet or beat their individual goal they win a certificate. The level of intensity as students practice the words on their own is impressive."

Other games for students are possible. The only limits to making word games are teachers' and students' game imagination and their fascination for words.

IN CONCLUSION

Word learning and automatic word recognition require repeated exposures to words. Word games are a great addition to any word learning program and a superb way to add those exposures that build students' sight vocabularies.

Children love to play games and the nature of words themselves—their meaning, their grammatical categories, their orthographic make-up—make them excellent material for classroom and home reading games. Although games should only play a minor part of any reading or word recognition program, they can play a significant role in adding variety, life, and practice to students' word learning.

REFERENCES

Bear, D., et al. 1996. *Words Their Way*. Englewood Cliffs, NJ: Prentice-Hall.

Gates, A. 1931. *Interest and Ability in Reading*. New York: Macmillan.

Hall, A. K. 1995. Sentencing: The Psycholinguistic Guessing Game. *The Reading Teacher*, 49: 76–77.

13

SPELLING AND WORD LEARNING

Jason, age 7, was writing a story (Harste, Woodward and Burke 1984). One of his characters "tried again," which Jason wrote as *chridagen*. Later, while rereading his story, *chridagen* stopped him. He solved the reading problem by thinking about the meaning of the story, but the spelling bothered him. He knew it wasn't right, so, like his character, Jason tried again. His second spelling was exactly the same as his first!

If you look at *chridagen* for a moment and think about Jason's efforts, you will see why we have included a chapter about spelling in a book about word learning. Say the *t* and *ch* sounds to see how your tongue is in the same place for both. Note that Jason has used the letter *i* for the long *i* sound. And *agen* is a pretty good phonetic representation of *again*. Most important is that rethinking the words, which he knew were wrong because they didn't look right, led Jason to the exact same conclusion. Jason's story shows us that children's invented, approximated, or temporary spellings are neither random nor careless errors; instead, these spellings are reasoned and rule-governed—they represent children's best thinking about the relationships between sounds in language and words in writing.

In other chapters of this book, we describe instructional strategies for reading that foster word learning and focus children's attention on important aspects of written language. Writing instruction can also play an important role in children's word learning. Writers learn about writing, reading, and words. Young writers learn how printed language works—how to make letters and words do what they want them to do. And as we can see from the story of Jason, quite a bit of careful thought goes into the decisions children make about how to spell the words they want to write. Thus, a strong focus on unaided writing can help children learn how to work with words.

Our focus in this chapter is not on all aspects of spelling instruction. Others offer more comprehensive discussions of this topic, still a somewhat controversial aspect of language arts instruction (Bear, et al. 1996, Henderson 1990, Rosencrans 1998). We examine spelling from the perspective that learning to spell augments word recognition development. Actually, many of the activities described in this book, such as Making and Writing Words (Chapter 8), support spelling development as well as word recognition.

Scholars have focused on spelling development for decades. Although the stages of children's development as spellers are well understood, there's still lots that we don't know about how to support children's growth in spelling. Fortunately there are some widely accepted guiding principles that teachers can use to integrate spelling instruction into their reading and writing programs (Bear, et al. 1996, Fresch and Wheaton 1997, Heald-Taylor 1998):

- Learning to spell is a complex, developmental process. Spelling proficiency is related to maturation and experience in writing. Knowledge about spelling begins globally and develops gradually as children become able to develop, differentiate, and integrate insights about how letters and sounds are related.
- Spelling instruction should be a functional component of a complete writing program. Of several guiding principles related to instruction (Heald-Taylor 1998), two are particularly important for our purposes in this chapter. Teachers of young children are advised to accept their inventions or approximations, especially initially, and to use the approximations diagnostically. By determining what children know about letter-sound relationships, teachers can determine current understanding about graphophonic relationships and decide on appropriate emphases for instruction.

In this chapter, we address spelling issues that are directly related to children's word learning: what children learn about written language through invented spelling, how teachers can discover what children know about the way that written language works, ways to support word learning through spelling, and how and why to inform parents about this aspect of the reading-writing program.

LEARNING ABOUT WRITTEN LANGUAGE THROUGH SPELLING APPROXIMATIONS

As young children learn to read and write, they begin to think about written language as a system and hypothesize about how it works. They learn that lines of print run from left to right and lines on a page run from top to bottom, for example. Children also develop concepts about units of written language. They learn that print carries meaning and that we use certain rules or conventions of print to represent meaning. Developing a concept of word as a unit of written language is particularly important, and this is no small task. First, the child must think about language as a system, to separate the form of language from its function. Then the child must segment a steady stream of oral speech. Think about this for a moment. Recall the last time you heard someone speaking a language that was foreign to you. Could you segment the oral speech into words? Probably not, because you lack a concept for word in the language. This demonstrates the enormity of children's conceptual learning about written language.

They must learn to separate, think about, and become aware of individual words within spoken language. And then, of course, children must use their knowledge of oral speech to discover that words are also units of written language. As children write (not copy), they must think about written language and about how letters and letter combinations represent sounds in language.

Children learn about written language gradually and informally. The overall learning process is the same as for any other language learning: hypothesis generation and testing. For example, simply telling children that words have spaces around them may not do much good. Children must invent their own concepts and then test them through reading and writing. This same principle applies to sound-symbol relationships in writing. Children who invent spellings get valuable practice with the sound-to-letter system. Moreover, young writers learn that the beginning-to-ending sequences of sounds in words relate, although not exactly, to the left-to-right sequences of letters in words. And this practice pays off in word learning:

> The value of encouraging and allowing young children to invent their spelling has been strongly supported by well-conducted studies. . . . when children attempt to represent their speech with letters, they are applying phonics in a truly authentic context. Along with other meaningful engagements with literacy—shared book experiences, rhyming games, categorization activities focusing on beginning sounds, and so forth—children become aware first of some individual sounds within syllables and then progress to full phonemic awareness. (Templeton and Morris 1999, p. 108)

DISCOVERING WHAT CHILDREN KNOW ABOUT SOUNDS THROUGH SPELLING

Scholars have been exploring the characteristics of young children's spelling since the early 1970s, when Charles Read's (1971) landmark work showed us that young children's spelling errors are predictable and change in predictable ways over time. In brief, this research has helped us understand how spelling develops: from random, incomprehensible strings of letters (and sometimes other symbols) to spellings that show some understanding of sound-symbol relationships to conventional spelling.

Children's spelling ability begins to develop well before they enter school. In this "extended period of emergent literacy . . . children learn much about the forms and functions of print. This understanding lays the groundwork for moving into the exploration of the *alphabetic* layer of spelling" (Templeton and Morris 1999, p. 105). Exploring this alphabetic layer of spelling involves thinking about the relationship between sounds and individual letters of the alphabet. Eventually, children's focus shifts to patterns in language, such as groups of letters, e.g., *-tion*, or conceptually related words, e.g., *act*, *act*ion, *react*or. Thus, children show us their knowledge of words and sounds through their approximations or inventions.

A great deal of this learning occurs during children's preschool through primary years. Below we explain some key features of spelling development for children at these ages, using examples from Ben's writing. Ben was in kindergarten when these samples were written. His ability was average among the children in his urban classroom. Each day Kay, his teacher, encouraged the children to visit the writing center, which was stocked with a variety of writing paper and instruments. The children had access to printed letters of the alphabet, which they could use or not as they wished. Ben had no other writing or spelling instruction.

Figure 13.1 is an example of the prephonemic stage of spelling development. At this stage, children know how letters are formed but not how they work. They have not yet discovered that letters represent speech sounds in words. Some children write random strings of letters, numbers, other symbols, or scribbles. In late October, Ben chose to draw about Halloween. He has memorized the spelling of his name and has added "Boo" from the ghost.

By March (see Figure 13.2), Ben has progressed to the early phonemic stage of spelling development. At this stage, children begin to use letters to represent sounds, but only very sparsely. They sometimes begin words with one or two letter/phonemes and end them with a random string of letters. Or they may represent an entire word with one letter/phoneme. Teachers will see

Figure 13.1
Ben-October

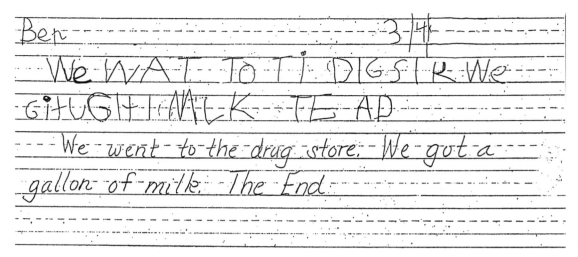

Figure 13.2
Ben-March

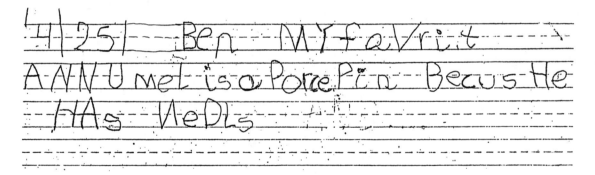

Figure 13.3
Ben-April

more consistency in consonant sounds than vowel sounds. In fact, some early phonemic spellers don't even use vowels yet. Lack of a stable concept of word is another characteristic of early phonemic spelling.

Note that Ben is beginning to write, a sign of growth from October. Note, too, that he knows how to spell *we* and *to* and that he can hear and represent middle consonants, e.g., *drugstore*, as well as beginning and ending consonants. Examine Ben's sound-symbol understanding for a moment. What consonant sounds does he know? Finally, note that Ben's concept of word is not yet stable. He separates some words, e.g., *we went to*, but runs others together, e.g., *got a gallon*.

By April, Ben has progressed to the letter-name stage of spelling development (see Figure 13.3). Letter-name spellers have discovered *word* as a concept, and we can see this in Ben's writing. They spell consonant phonemes with some regularity but may omit (or have difficulty with) vowels. What consonant sounds has Ben learned since March? They spell by breaking words into phonemes and representing the phonemes with letters of the alphabet (e.g., sound of long *e* in *porcepin* and *nedls*).

Some knowledge of children's spelling development helps us examine Ben's writing. We can see growth in his knowledge of the relationship between sounds and letters. Charting this development, as shown in Figure 13.4, can help teachers discover what children have learned through writing that can apply to their reading.

Looking at children's writing in this way underscores the hard work that goes on when they write. Their writing, including their spelling approximations, reflects their ideas about how written language works. Because we use our ideas about how written language works when we read, we can learn a great deal about children as readers by examining what they write.

	Ben	Kathy	Juan
January			
February			
March	D, G, K, M, T, W		
April	B, F, H, L, N, P, R, S, V		
May			

Figure 13.4
Charting Children's Letter-Sound Knowlegde

SUPPORTING YOUNG WRITERS

Perhaps the most important aspect of support for young writers is the classroom atmosphere itself. Children must learn to believe in themselves as writers and to develop confidence in their ability to share what they have to say with others through writing.

Young children, who ordinarily come to school expecting to learn to read and write, may need little more than the suggestion to write. Older children, however, may not take the teacher up on invitations to write. They may have learned negative lessons, such as "I can't write" or "writing is boring" from their previous experiences in school. The teacher's patience, passion, and persistence are critical in order for these negative lessons to be unlearned; so we advise teachers to continue to invite children to write, to praise their attempts, and to establish the expectations that everyone can write and everyone will.

First efforts from all writers, especially young ones, may be drawings rather than writing, but letters and words soon appear. Some children seem to use drawing as a way to think up or refine ideas for their writing. Other children use drawing as a sort of note-taking tool; they sketch the things they want to remember to write about. Whatever its purpose, drawing seems to facilitate writing for many children. So persistent teacher invitations to write, along with patience as children draw or develop the courage to try again, and passion for writing itself, are essential features of the classroom atmosphere.

Opportunities to talk and listen are important. Graves (1983) describes several ways children use oral language when writing. They sometimes plan their writing by talking to themselves or others. They may also read parts of drafts to themselves, as if to get a running start on what should come next. Some children compose aloud and translate their speech into writing rather than use the thought-to-writing process most adult writers employ. Others play with prosodics such as rhythm or intonation. Children may also talk themselves through writing by making procedural comments such as "There! Now I need to write 'The End.'" And of course, children read drafts of their work to others, either to help solve problems they've encountered or to get more general feedback.

Children also need teacher support. Some of this support is mundane, such as having necessary supplies readily available. Children need access to many kinds of paper, lined and unlined, and a variety of writing instruments from which they can choose. These materials can be collected in the classroom writing center. Time to write is another aspect of support. Children need predictable chunks of time every week to write and to share their efforts with interested others.

Other aspects of support, especially the encouragement of spelling efforts, appear to be critical. Teachers who accept invented spellings allow their students to be precise in their use of language and true to their own meanings because they can say what they want to say, not just what they know how to spell. More important, these opportunities to manipulate words and discover spelling principles clarify phonological relationships for children.

So how can teachers support this experimentation with print that yields both word knowledge and writing proficiency? In essence, teachers can foster spelling growth by encouraging independence and accepting the resulting approximations. For example, in response to a child's question about how to spell a word, the teacher might ask the child to say the word, and then ask, "What sound do you hear at the beginning? What letter would that be? Good. Write it down. Now say the word again. What sound do you hear at the end?" and so on. This strategy talks children through the speech-to-print connection and encourages them to develop independence as spellers. Listening for sounds and then representing them with letters supports children's efforts at phonemic segmentation, or separating words into their component sounds. In this way children's first recognizable efforts at spelling will bear strong resemblance to the sounds they hear as they articulate words.

Other classroom activities that focus on sounds and words are also useful for supporting children's invented spellings. Teachers can add a brief comment about spelling when engaging children in phonemic awareness word play, for example (see Chapter 4): "So if you wanted to write a word that begins like *baby* or *ball*, what letter would you use first?" Gentle reminders to use what they know about reading and sounds as they write will help children develop proficiency as spellers.

When children have reached the letter-name stage of spelling development, some more formal attention to spelling is beneficial. The words chosen for focus should be few—perhaps ten or twelve per week. The words should reflect spelling features and patterns that children use but confuse; that is, they should be developmentally appropriate for children. At the primary level, the words selected for spelling instruction should be sight words for children (Templeton and Morris 1999). Many teachers prepare groups of words at different levels of difficulty that represent the same letter/sound patterns so that instruction can be differentiated for children of varying spelling abilities while the entire class focuses on the pattern of interest (Fresch and Wheaton 1997).

In a review of research about spelling instruction, Templeton and Morris comment,

> Of the few methodological studies that have been conducted, none answers to everyone's satisfaction the question of whether spelling is learned primarily through reading and writing or primarily through the systematic examination of words. . . . What does emerge from the research is the suggestion that *some* examination of words is necessary for most students. (1999, p. 108)

The ideal spelling program, then, is a balanced combination of writing for authentic purposes and focused word study. The best word study instruction simultaneously facilitates children's abilities to detect spelling patterns in words and reinforces their memories for the spelling of specific words. Indeed, many of the activities we describe elsewhere in this book, such as word sorts (see Chapter 9) and Making Words (see Chapter 8) are excellent methods for fostering growth in spelling (Templeton and Morris 1999).

Many primary grade teachers struggle with the issue of standard spelling. They express concern that words be spelled correctly if the child's written work will be read by others. As children become more conscious of standard spelling, they too may express concern about their spelling efforts. Then teachers should help them deal with these concerns. Jane Davidson suggests that teachers should reply to students' queries in their initial drafts of "is it right?" with a statement like this: "It's good enough for now. You can read it, and I can read it. We both know what you're saying here. Later, we can change some things, if you'd like, to make them look like they do in other books." This sort of discussion helps lessen concern about spelling when students are generating ideas, yet assures them that their efforts will receive the polish they deserve.

When children's spelling is fairly well developed, perhaps grade three or beyond, spell checkers on word processing programs can be useful. (At earlier stages, the program can't recognize many approximations because they bear so little resemblance to the correct spellings.) Some teachers express concern that spell checkers might become a crutch. This may be, but they're also an aspect of modern life and likely to be even more influential in the future. To ignore their potential does students a disservice. Instead, teachers may want to reserve their use for the final draft stage of writing, when the spell checker can do what teachers have done for decades—identify misspelled words. Unlike teachers' circles of "sp" notations, however, the spell checker also provides options for correcting the error, which promotes independence and the development of visual memory.

To support a young writer, the teacher needs to understand both the child's current thinking about written language and the stages through which spelling knowledge develops. In addition, opportunities to write for reasons the child deems important must be provided. All this, and a consistently positive "you can do it" attitude from the teacher, will yield remarkable results.

PARENTS AND THE SPELLING PROGRAM

Spelling, particularly invented spelling, concerns many parents. Approximations may look like errors to parents; they may wonder why these errors are allowed in the classroom. Through communication and information-sharing, teachers can help parents see the value in invented spellings and the role that writing plays in their children's development as readers.

Parents should be informed about the merits of frequent writing and the integrity of their children's attempts at spelling. They may also need to think about what counts as writing in an early literacy classroom. Indeed, it's quite likely that parents themselves didn't write much as young school children. Most likely they practiced letters and copied words or sentences, but they probably didn't write. So they may need to understand that learning to write is a much bigger, more complex process than learning to make letters.

Many teachers compare written language development to oral language development to help parents see the developmental nature of writing and spelling growth, the importance of children's early efforts to put their ideas in writing, and the critical role that support and encouragement from adults can play in children's development. They ask parents to recall how they celebrated children's first attempts at talking and paid much more attention to what children were trying to say than how they were saying it. And, in fact, they didn't worry that a child would say "Boo Boo" for *grandma* forever; they simply rejoiced in the child's ability to communicate. In other words, parents need to see that learning to read and write like adults takes time, just as does learning to talk like adults. They provided support and encouragement as children learned to talk, and they also accepted their children's approximations. These same principles apply to learning to write and spell.

Some parents may wish to learn about the stages of spelling development; others may worry that spelling accuracy is never stressed and that, as a result, their children will never learn to value correct spelling. Simple charts can be shared with parents to help them learn about both of these issues (Rosencrans 1998). A chart depicting the stages of spelling development, for example, might list characteristics of stages and ideas for supporting children's learning at home. This brief example shows how information might be shared about the prephonemic stage of spelling development.

Prephonemic Spellers	Parents Can
know how writing looks but not how it works	read to children often
use random letters and symbols	play rhyming games
may know their letters but haven't figured out sounds	encourage writing at home

Similarly, a chart can help parents see the role that accurate spelling plays in the classroom:

Levels of Accuracy	Examples
Ideas only	Notes, drafts
Readable	Journals, personal writing, assignments
Good copy	Writing to be displayed and read by others

Communication between school and home can take several forms. Some teachers invite parents to a meeting early in the year to explain their instructional programs. Using writing examples from the previous year's students, they explain how writing develops and show parents the progressive growth in sound-symbol relationships that results from consistent opportunities to write.

Written communication is another good way to share with parents. Some teachers write occasional letters to parents. Others publish weekly or monthly newsletters, often prepared by children through dictation or writing. These are shared with parents throughout the school year and sometimes bound into a book entitled, *Our Year in _____ Grade*, as an end-of-the-year keepsake for children and their families. Dialogue journals between parents and children with or without entries from the teacher are another great way to foster home-school communication (Shockley, Michalove and Allen 1995).

Parent conferences offer valuable sharing opportunities. Dated samples of children's writing can be examined. Teachers can show parents concrete examples of children's growth in word learning as evidenced by changes in their invented spellings. Teachers who chart the development of children's graphophonic knowledge, as we suggest earlier, will want to share this information with parents as well.

Early efforts at writing can seem quite peculiar from a parent's perspective, so helping parents understand instructional goals and children's development as spellers is important. Through communication and information-sharing, parents can come to realize that support and encouragement from interested adults, both at home and in school, will foster word learning that children can apply to both writing and reading.

In Conclusion

Learning to spell is more than just a memory task (Henderson 1990); it is also, and more important for our purposes in this book, "a process of coming to understand how words work—the conventions that govern their structure and how their structure signals sound and meaning" (Templeton and Morris 1999, p. 103). So the process of writing words draws on the same underlying word knowledge as the process of reading words. In a nutshell, this is why unaided writing supports students' phonics and word recognition development; this is also why opportunities to write and spell should be part of word learning programs.

References

Bear, D., et al. 1996. *Words Their Way*. Englewood Cliffs, NJ: Prentice Hall.

Fresch, M.J., and A. Wheaton. 1997. Sort, Search, and Discover: Spelling in the Child-Centered Classroom. *The Reading Teacher*, 51: 20–3.

Graves, D. 1983. *Writing: Teachers and Children at Work*. Portsmouth, NH: Heinemann.

Harste, J., V. Woodward and C. Burke. 1984. *Language Stories and Literacy Lessons*. Portsmouth, NH: Heinemann.

Heald-Taylor, B.G. 1998. Three Paradigms of Spelling Instruction in Grades 3–6. *The Reading Teacher*, 51: 404–413.

Henderson, E.H. 1990. *Teaching Spelling*. (2nd ed.). Boston: Houghton Mifflin.

Read, C. 1971. Pre-School Children's Knowledge of English Phonology. *Harvard Educational Review*, 41: 1–34.

Rosencrans, G. 1998. *The Spelling Book*. Newark, DE: International Reading Association.

Shockley, B., B. Michalove and J.B. Allen. 1995. *Engaging Families*. Portsmouth, NH: Heinemann.

Templeton, S., and D. Morris. 1999. Questions Teachers Ask About Spelling. *Reading Research Quarterly*, 34: 102–112.

14

BEYOND WORD STUDY: READING FLUENCY

Meet Harry, a third grade teacher in a nearby urban school. Harry has some interesting observations about his students. "By the time they come into third grade some of my students are still struggling with decoding words. Others however have gotten this down pretty well—they can decode most of the words they come across while reading. But even these more advanced readers, when reading aloud for me, read without any expression and much of their reading tends to be word-by-word, sometimes even syllable-by-syllable. It's clear to me that even though they can decode, they are not yet proficient readers. They are focusing their attention so much on saying the words, they have little energy left over for making sense of or enjoying what they read. In short, they are readers, but they are not fluent readers yet."

Fortunately Harry uses some of his instructional time for developing reading fluency among his students.

> "We do a lot of things that fit very nicely into the whole curriculum. I like to read poetry to my class, and I try to get my students to read and appreciate poetry themselves. So throughout the school year students choose poems, practice them, sign up for performing them during our poetry breaks, and then read them to the class. I insist that students read their poems with expression, so they have to practice them a lot before they are ready to perform. Sometimes two, three, or even four kids will do a poem together. It's neat to see these students orchestrate and practice their performance so that it is a fun experience for them and their audience."

Harry also does a lot with readers theater. "I think readers theater is one of those special activities that all teachers should know about. Unfortunately, I think few really do know about it, or if they do they rarely try it." Harry has prewritten scripts that groups of students choose, practice, and perform in readers theater style (no memorization, physical movement, costumes, or scenery)—students stand in front of their audience and read their scripts with expression and fluency. He reads to his students everyday and as the school year gets rolling along he eventually shows his students how favorite stories he has read, or ones students have read on their own can be transformed into scripts to be performed as readers theater. "This is the best part for me, to watch these kids turn the class into a writers' workshop as they take a story they like and recast it into a script. Often they have to adapt it for readers theater by cutting out some characters, adding others, adding and deleting lines, making the script work for them. I keep telling them that I am going to send some of their best scripts to Hollywood to be turned into a movie or television show."

In many ways Harry's students don't even know they are working on reading fluency when they do their poetry and script performances. But the results are impressive. "Not only do my students become more fluent in their reading over the year—not just the poetry and script reading, but all their reading—their word recognition improves and so does their comprehension."

Achieving accuracy in word recognition is only the first step in becoming a fully fluent reader. The next step involves developing automaticity in word recognition as well as an awareness of how words work in the context of sentences, that is, syntactic awareness. Fluency refers to the reader's ability to read accurately, quickly, in appropriate syntactic phrases or text chunks, and, above all, with meaningful and appropriate expression.

Fluency is associated with overall proficiency in reading (Pinnell, et al. 1995) and lack of fluency is a significant factor among elementary students who struggle in reading (Rasinski and Padak 1998). Yet, recent studies have found that large numbers of students through the elementary grades, nearly half of all fourth graders, have not achieved even a minimally acceptable level of reading fluency (Pinnell, et al. 1995). One of the reasons for this state of affairs is that fluency is not taught in many classrooms. Allington (1983) has called it the neglected goal of the reading program. In a more recent study, Rasinski and Zutell (1996) found that it is still not given much status in many basal reading programs.

If fluency is an important part of reading, and most reading professionals would agree that accurate, quick, meaningfully expressive, and appropriately phrased reading is important, then it is important that it be taught and nurtured at the elementary and middle school levels. Certainly, wide reading will help develop students' sight vocabularies as well as their syntactic knowledge, but there is more we can do to help students develop as fluent readers. In this chapter we outline several strategies teachers can employ, at nearly any grade level, to promote fluency. These strategies not only work to improve fluency, they also have a positive effect on word recognition and students' own feelings of success as readers.

MODEL FLUENT READING

If we want students to become fluent readers, they need a model of what fluent oral reading sounds like so that they can develop an awareness of the importance of fluent reading. Reading to children helps accomplish this goal, especially if we occasionally follow up with a discussion about the effects and importance of expressive, fluent reading. Even prior to a read–aloud session, a teacher might ask students to listen for variations in voice, phrasing, rate, expression, or volume. After reading, a teacher might ask students, "What did you notice about my voice during the reading? How did it help you understand and pay attention to the reading? How did I communicate love or hate or fear or excitement with my voice during the reading?" Getting students to listen for various aspects of fluency in reading, such as speed of reading, phrasing, pauses within the reading, volume, tone, overall expression, and then to talk about these characteristics is a first step toward getting students to read fluently on their own.

Teachers may also want to experiment by reading a short passage several ways to students—fluently, word-by-word, slow, fast, as a grumpy old man might read it, as a happy distracted teenager might read it, as a comedian might read it, as a clergy person might read it. This will help students see that it is not just the words that carry the meaning, but also how the words are presented. It will also help students develop a sense of point of view for the reading.

Another appropriate practice is for the teacher to fluently read a text aloud to students before asking them to read it on their own. This preview reading helps students develop a sense of how that particular passage should be read; it will also conveniently and unobtrusively introduce students to words they may not have encountered before in print.

REPEATED READINGS

Practice helps develop skills that need to be made automatic in any area of learning—music, sports, or even driving a car. Practice helps in reading as well. Repeated readings is a simple instructional activity in which students practice reading one passage several times until they achieve a degree of fluency, usually defined in terms of rate or word recognition accuracy.

Although the activity itself may be simple, several studies have demonstrated that having students practice read short passages resulted in improved word recognition, fluency, and overall reading performance not only on the passages practiced, but also on passages students had not previously read (Dowhower 1987, Herman 1985, Samuels 1979, 1997). Dowhower has written that repeated readings is a "powerful technique . . . helping both regular and special needs students and young children and adults become better readers; and extremely effective (in) increasing word recognition, fluency, and comprehension" (1997, p. 376). Samuels adds that repeated readings has become the "most universally used remedial reading technique to help poor readers achieve reading skill" (1997, p. 381).

One question that we often hear when talking about repeated readings is, "How can we persuade students to read a passage more than once?" This is an important question, for under most conditions readers have little reason to read a text more than once. Our best response to this concern is to create situations in which students have real reasons to practice. And, it seems to us that students are most likely to read something several times through if they realize that they will be asked to read or perform their text for an audience. Poems, for example, are meant to be shared orally with others (see our list of poetry in Chapter 5), as are play scripts, speeches, and historical documents (see Figures 14.1 and 14.2).

Teachers can use poetry, scripts, or dramatic readings, such as famous American speeches and documents, as texts for repeated reading practice.

We know teachers, such as Harry, who regularly feature poetry or readers theater in their classroom. In Darlene's third grade class, Poetry Club happens every other week. Students select poems or scripts, practice them on their own or with a group of readers throughout the week, and perform their poems or scripts for classmates and parents on Friday afternoon. Students love the authenticity that comes from being able to read aloud and with expression to an audience. Darlene adds to the authentic atmosphere by turning off the overhead lights in her classroom for the poetry performance and using a reading lamp on stage as the spotlight. Students can read from a stool that is set on the classroom stage. Refreshments such as hot apple cider and popcorn

---

Books already written in script format

Fleischman, P. 1997. *Seedfolks*. New York: HarperCollins.

Fleischman, P. 1993. *Bull Run*. New York: Harper Trophy.

Hall, D. 1994. *I Am the Dog, I Am the Cat*. New York: Dial.

(The form of the book can also be used for students to write their own books that compare and contrast characters, events, or things—e.g., I am a Democrat, I am a Republican).

Hoose, P. and H. Hoose. 1998. *Hey, Little Ant*. Berkeley, CA: Tricycle Press.

Johnson, A. 1989. *Tell Me a Story, Mama*. New York: Orchard.

Raschka, C. 1993. *Yo! Yes?* New York: Orchard.

Easy books for recasting as scripts

Eastman, P.D. 1960. *Are You My Mother?* New York: Random House.

Fox, M. 1987. *Hattie and the Fox*. New York: Bradbury.

Marshall, E. 1994. *Fox in Love*. New York: Puffin.

Minarik, E. H. 1957. *Little Bear*. New York: Harper and Row.

Moderately challenging books for recasting as scripts

Brown, M. 1992. *Arthur Babysits*. Boston: Little Brown. (All the Arthur books are good candidates for recasting as scripts.)

Caseley, J. 1991. *Dear Annie*. New York: Greenwillow.

Champion, J. 1993. *Emily and Alice Again*. San Diego: Harcourt Brace.

Naylor, P. R. 1992. *King of the Playground*. New York: Atheneum.

Stevens, J. 1995. *Tops and Bottoms*. San Diego: Harcourt Brace.

Challenging books for recasting as scripts

Blume, J. 1974. *The Pain and the Great One*. New York: Bradbury.

Karlin, B. 1992. *Cinderella*. Boston: Little, Brown.

Kimmel, E.A. 1994. *Anansi and the Talking Melon*. New York: Holiday House.

Figure 14.1
A sampling of texts adaptable for readers theater.

complete the coffee house setting. Students in Darlene's class have even learned to snap their fingers (as a less noisy and much "cooler" alternative to clapping) to express their appreciation for each poetry reading.

Readers theater involves the performance of a script without costumes, props, movement, scenery, or memorization of lines. Performers simply stand in front of the audience in their normal attire and read the script to the audience. Readers theater is very similar to the dramas and comedies broadcast over the radio in the 1930s through 50s. The actors simply stood around a microphone, script in hand, without costumes, scenery, props, or movement. They didn't even have to memorize their lines—they read them from the script. Of course, in order for the script to have any impact on the audience it needs to be read with expression—hence readers theater is a superb activity for promoting practiced or repeated readings.

Nearly any script can be used for readers theater; however, we have found that scripts written by students are among the best. To make a script, students simply find a favorite short story or story segment and recast it in the form of a script, deleting unneeded parts and adding parts and lines that will contribute to the script. Usually a four to five page (double-spaced) script will result in a ten to fifteen minute performance. This is also a great way to encourage those reluctant writers—script writing from a existing story provides a plenty of support for novice writers.

Martinez, Roser, and Strecker (1999) describe a weekly classroom routine in which second graders, formed into repertory groups, hear the story on which their assigned script is based read by the teacher on Monday, work on their scripts throughout the week, and perform their scripts before an audience on Fridays. In just ten weeks of doing readers theater, the second graders made reading rate increases that were 2.5 times greater than two similar classes of second graders who did not have readers theater included into their reading instruction. Other measures of reading, including informal reading inventories, also demonstrated significant gains for the readers theater students. Mrs. Carter, one of the second grade teachers said that readers theater helped her students in two ways: "The first is comprehension that results from having to become the characters and understand their feelings, and the second is the repetition and practice" (p. 333).

Hanson-Harding, A. (ed.) 1997. *Great American Speeches*. New York: Scholastic.

King, M. L. 1999. *I Have a Dream*. New York: Scholastic.

Lincoln, A. 1997. *The Gettysburg Address*. New York: Scholastic.

Web Address: http://curry.edschool.virginia.edu/curry/centers/currycommunity/resources/links/hisspeeches.html

Historical speeches are archived at this University of Virginia website.

Web Address: http://www.history plance.com/speakers/

The History Place, A Repository of over 50 Historic Speeches.

Figure 14.2
A sampling of speeches and documents for repeated readings and perfomances

Another approach to repeated reading is to encourage students to practice reading short stories so that they can share them with reading buddies in lower grade level class. Students love being able to perform for their younger buddies and help them in reading. The younger students, also, are motivated to read by the example demonstrated by their older buddies. Gregg's fourth graders have a date once a week with Lisa's first graders. They alternate classrooms for their visits and bring blankets, pillows, and stuffed animals for their literary rendezvous. The fourth graders practice their reading throughout the week so that the first graders will hear fluent and meaningful presentations of their stories. Both groups of students have come to love their meetings. With the advent of classroom e-mail, the first and fourth graders have been corresponding about books to be read and responding to the readings.

If you want your students to become reading buddies to a younger classroom of readers but cannot find an appropriate time to meet, your students can read their books on tape for their younger buddies to read and listen to when time is available. Before the older students are allowed to record their readings, they will need to have practiced them several times so that the taped reading is read with expression, meaning, and minimal word recognition errors. Older students love to insert personal introductions, sound effects and audible cues for page turns into their tapes. The younger students benefit from a growing library of favorite books on tape.

Many students are motivated by the opportunity to read with a friend in their own class. Pat Koskinen and Irene Blum (1984, 1986) found that repeated readings work very well in what they called paired repeated reading. In this version of repeated readings students read a passage to a partner several times. The partner's role is to provide positive feedback and assistance. After several readings, the roles are reversed. Koskinen and Blum found that students enjoyed the alternative format and demonstrated strong gains in fluency, word recognition, and comprehension doing the paired repeated reading as little as 15 minutes, three times per week for a little over a month.

SUPPORTED READING

Fluency is also developed when a student has the opportunity to read along with a more fluent reader. In this way, the more fluent reader provides ongoing support and encouragement for the less fluent reader and allows the less fluent reader to achieve success, even on more difficult passages.

One of the most common forms of supported reading is choral reading. Although used mainly in the primary grades, choral reading can be adapted for use at any grade level. When reading as a group, the less fluent readers gain from reading and listening to their more fluent classmates at the same time. Moreover, since they are reading as a group, the less fluent readers are not exposing themselves to embarrassment. With continued choral practice on the same passage, the less fluent readers will eventually achieve fluency on it and become more fluent on new texts they encounter as well.

Variety can be added to choral readings by bringing in poems, song lyrics, and raps for choral reading. Also, teachers can create variety by occasionally dividing up the choral group into groups that read various parts of the text (antiphonal reading) or by encouraging students to decide beforehand where in the text to change the volume, pitch, or speed of their voices. Of course, making these decisions requires rereading, an authentic form of practice in itself.

PAIRED READING AND SHARED READING

Paired reading is a supported reading activity in which a fluent reader and a less fluent reader (parent-child, teacher-student, student-student, etc.) sit side by side and simultaneously read one text aloud. The more fluent reader provides a model and support for the less fluent partner. The partner reads in a moderately loud voice at a pace that tends to pull the less fluent reader along. In easier parts of the reading or when the less fluent reader wants to read on his or her own, he or she signals the partner who then stops reading aloud or reads in a whisper at a rate that shadows or slightly trails the voice of the less fluent reader. As soon as the child begins to experience difficulty, the partner returns to the original role of leader.

Keith Topping (1987, 1989) has found that this sort of paired reading practice, for as little as ten to fifteen minutes daily, can result in extraordinary gains in students' fluency and overall reading. Students' reading progress accelerates three to five times faster than their earlier progress. Paired reading is a wonderful supplemental activity for classroom use. Parent volunteers can be asked to pair read with selected students and higher achieving students can pair read with less fluent or younger students. Indeed, the buddy reading we described earlier can easily be altered into a paired reading format.

Shared reading is a somewhat more elaborate version of paired reading. In shared reading the teacher, tutor, or parent introduces the student, or small group of students, to a text and reads it to them. Then the students read the text with the teacher, tutor, or parent. This is followed by the students reading the text to the teacher. Over the course of several days the students and teacher return to and reread the text, examine words and other features of the text, and engage in other extension activities based on the text. The essential feature of shared reading is the read to, read with, listen to the student read, and the rereadings of the text by student and teacher.

A two-year study of shared reading versus traditional reading instruction found that the shared reading students improved at twice the normal rate in reading and out-performed the traditional instruction group on measures of reading, writing, vocabulary, and grammar (Smith and Elley 1997). The shared reading group doubled the usual pass rate on a standardized test of reading.

TAPE-RECORDED PASSAGES

An alternative to paired-reading is to provide students with an audiotape of the text to be read so that they can listen to the text on tape while reading the written version. Marie Carbo (1978) calls the approach "talking books." In Carbo's research, students who read a book while they listened to it on tape made exceptional gains in reading, well beyond what would have been expected based on their previous progress. Using this approach, students learned to read fluently what they were previously unable to read at all.

In one study, students who listened to high-interest stories at their instructional levels until they felt they could read the selected story on their own made an average gain of 2.2 years in reading achievement in about three-fourths of a year's participation (Smith and Elley 1997). Moreover, students who participated in this talking books program maintained their reading progress over a two-month summer break.

As we mentioned earlier, older students can make talking books for younger students. The process of making talking books can be very productive for the older readers. When the talking books reach their intended audience, a significant fluency benefit will be accrued by the younger readers as well. This seems to us to be a great one-two punch for improving students' reading at more than one grade level.

Tape-recorded books also have superb potential for use with ESL (English as a Second Language) students. Pat Koskinen and her colleagues (1999) found that having ESL students take home books and their accompanying audio tapes for reading practice resulted in increased reading achievement and interest as well as greater self-confidence in students. Those children who were the least proficient readers reported practicing their reading more often than their more proficient classmates. Koskinen et al. (1999) created two readings for each story on each tape. The first reading was a slower, more deliberate presentation while the second was a faster, more fluent rendition. This permitted students to move from an initial focus on words and phrases to a more fluent presentation of the stories.

An interesting variant to talking books is captioned television (see Chapter 17). Televisions now sold in the United States must have built-in captioning capability. When students watch television with the captioning on and the volume low, they must focus on the printed words in order to understand the program. The spoken text along with the television pictures provide the students with support to read successfully. Some recent research has suggested some very promising results with captioned television (Koskinen, et al. 1993, Postlethwaite and Ross 1992). In addition to captioned television programs, videos of favorite children's songs from animated musicals, with the lyrics presented in a captioned format, are available at most popular department stores and for checkout in many public libraries. From our own observations, young children love watching, singing, and reading these video texts.

FOCUS ON PHRASE BOUNDARIES

An important part of reading fluency is the ability to read in phrases, as opposed to word-by-word reading (Schreiber 1980, 1981). Consider the following sentences:

The principal said the teacher was very helpful.
Woman without her man is nothing.

Depending upon how you phrase the first sentence, the principal or the teacher was thought to be helpful. And in the second, either woman or man could be interpreted to "be nothing" depending on how the sentence was phrased. In many cases, punctuation will help readers phrase the text properly, but not always. Actually, the noun and verb phrases are hardly every separated by punctuation. It is up to the reader to separate these two meaningful elements of a sentence. But this is not easily done or learned by all readers. Many younger readers, especially those who have developed a word-by-word reading habit, may have difficulty in seeing that meaning in a sentence is carried by phrases more than it is carried by individual words.

All the activities we have described in this chapter, along with wide reading, will help students develop sensitivity to phrase boundaries. Another approach is to mark or highlight phrase boundaries in the text itself, using a slash mark or vertical line to specify the boundary (see Figure 14.3). A considerable amount of research has demonstrated that marking phrase boundaries can improve fluency, reading performance, and comprehension, especially with less able readers (Rasinski 1990).

When marking a text for reading, keep the text reasonably short—no more than two pages at a time. Have students read the text once or twice in one day. On the following day have students read the same text without the phrase markings. This will give students repeated reading practice and help them transfer their syntactic understandings of text phrasing to texts that are in a conventional, non phrase-marked, format.

In addition to marking phrase boundaries, word recognition practice can also take on a phrased nature. Rather than always presenting sight words or word bank words in isolation, they can occasionally be taught in the form of phrases.

> In the car
> My old dog
> When it rains
> By the river
> Inside the house

Not only does this add a bit of variety to word practice activities, it also emphasizes the notion that words are rarely read in isolation, but almost

Simply embedding slash marks into a passage / at phrase and sentence junctures / can have a positive effect / on students' own phrasing, / fluency, / and comprehension. For students who do not have a good understanding / of how sentences are phrased or chunked /, the slash marks provide direct visual cues / that enable students' own phrased reading.

Figure 14.3
Example of Phrase-Cued Text

always in the context of phrases and sentences. If you introduce five to ten words each week to be learned as sight words, you may also want to list them in the context of a sentence or phrase, on the chalk board or on sentence or phrase strips, for students to practice as part of a longer syntactic chunk.

CHOOSE YOUR TEXTS CAREFULLY

The texts chosen for reading can help or hinder fluency. Any reader, including you or me, becomes less fluent when asked to read a difficult or unfamiliar text. Often, students with fluency difficulties attempt to read texts that are too difficult. Such texts ensure a lack of fluency, perpetuating the students' self image as poor readers.

When teaching fluency, teachers should always choose texts that are relatively easy in terms of word recognition and syntactic complexity. If the text is difficult, be sure to provide sufficient support before and during reading to ensure success. For example, introduce new and difficult words, build background, and read the text to students before they read it solo. Also, use paired reading, listening to text on audio tape while reading, phrase marked text, and repeated readings of the text. Reading easier texts helps students develop power and confidence in their reading.

Predictable or patterned text (see Chapter 3) is particularly well suited to helping students develop fluent reading. These texts are written in a distinct and easily detected pattern that makes them not only easy to read but also requires readers to attend to the pattern through phrasing and expression. Bill Martin's *Brown Bear, Brown Bear* and *Polar Bear, Polar Bear* are among the best-known examples of predictable or patterned books. The texts follow a clear pattern that most beginning readers will discover and employ after as little as one reading.

Poetry and song lyrics for children are patterned texts that have the advantage of being short and rhythmic, thus lending themselves to repeated readings while appealing to many grade levels. Every elementary teacher should have several poetry anthologies in order to celebrate poetry every day of the school year. Teachers and children can also compose original verse or verse modeled after favorite poems, which can be put together into class collections.

Predictable and readable texts for older students come in the form of stories with highly predictable plots and characters—plots and characters with which they are familiar. Contemporary fiction often contains highly predictable elements that students can easily tap into. Despite (or perhaps because of) their predictability, most students find great enjoyment in these fictional accounts of lives that are, in many ways, similar to their own. The predictable nature of these books make them easy to read, excellent choices for fluency development.

Series books for older students are also highly predictable. Beverly Cleary's *Dear Mr. Henshaw* and *Slider*, Lynn Reid Banks' *Indian in the Cupboard* series, or the *Babysitters* books, for example, all contain the same or similar characters, writing styles, and plots. Reading one book in the series provides the background knowledge for subsequent stories, adding to the predictable nature of the books.

Synergistic Instruction—The Fluency Development Lesson

Up to this point, we have presented individual aspects of fluency instruction; these are made even more potent when teachers design lessons incorporating multiple aspects of good fluency instruction. We have done this with a lesson we have developed and tested called the Fluency Development Lesson (FDL) (Rasinski et al. 1994). We originally devised the FDL for teachers who work with primary-grade children experiencing difficulty in achieving even initial stages of fluent reading. The FDL combines several aspects of effective fluency instruction in a way that maximizes students' reading in a relatively short period of time. The FDL is intended as a supplement to the regular reading curriculum. The lesson takes ten to fifteen minutes to complete. We have found the beginning of each day is a good time to do the FDL, as a sort of warm up for school. Teachers make copies of brief passages, usually poems of 50–150 words, for each child.

A typical Fluency Development Lesson looks like this:

1. The teacher passes out copies of the text to each student.
2. The teacher reads and rereads the text to the class while students follow along silently with their own copies.
3. The teacher discusses with the class the content of the text as well as the quality of his or her reading.
4. The entire class reads the text chorally several times. The teacher creates variety by having students read different verses or portions of the text in groups.
5. The class divides into pairs. Each pair finds a quiet spot, and one student practices reading the text to a partner three times. The partner's job is to follow along in the text, provide help when needed, and give positive feedback to the reader. After the first three readings, the roles are switched. The partner becomes the reader and reads the text three times as well.
6. Students regroup, and the teacher asks for volunteers to perform the text. Individuals, pairs, and groups of up to four perform the reading for the class. The teacher makes arrangements for students to perform the text for the school principal, secretary, custodian, and other teachers and classes. The performing students are lavished with praise.
7. Students and teachers choose words from the text for closer examination (e.g., rhyming words) and addition to word banks. Words can be practiced and sorted at various times throughout the school day.
8. Students take a copy of the text home and read it to their parents and other relatives. Parents are asked to listen to their child read as many times as they would like and to praise their child's efforts.

Our experience with the FDL indicates that, when employed three to four times a week over several months, it is easily implemented by teachers and parents, enjoyed by students, and leads to significant improvements in students' fluency and overall reading, considerably beyond their previous progress. We have also found that by changing the text that students read, the FDL can be adapted for a variety of grade levels in the elementary school.

Our goal in describing the FDL to you is not to suggest that you use it as described here in your own classroom. Rather, we hope you will see what can happen when a lesson format is created using informed practices as building blocks. Thus, we challenge you to adapt the FDL for use in your own classroom, with whatever modifications fit your own particular needs or the needs of your students. We think that the FDL would also work well, with modifications, in certain middle school classrooms. Finally, we hope you will develop your own lesson format for fostering fluency and overall reading growth among your students.

In Conclusion

Fluency should be an important goal of the reading curriculum. It is not enough for students to become proficient in word decoding. They need to read *with* meaning, not just read *for* meaning. And reading with meaning is what reading fluency is all about. Fluent reading is accurate, quick, expressive, and above all, meaningful. Fluency is a bridge between word recognition and comprehension. Unfortunately, it is a bridge that is often not sufficiently dealt with in the reading curriculum.

The activities we have described in this chapter share a common purpose: to help students develop the ability to read fluently. Fluency can be taught in such a way that it is woven seamlessly into other areas of the reading and school curriculum—it does not need to be turned into a skill and drill activity. Nonetheless, if fluency is to be taught and fostered, it needs to be taught by informed and dedicated teachers who recognize its importance in the total reading curriculum. This chapter provides a starting place for making fluency instruction an integral part of your reading curriculum.

References

Allington, R. L. 1983. Fluency: The Neglected Goal of the Reading Program. *The Reading Teacher*, 36: 556–561.

Carbo, M. 1978. Teaching Reading with Talking Books. *The Reading Teacher*, 32: 267–273.

Dowhower, S. L. 1987. Effects of Repeated Reading on Second-Grade Transitional Readers' Fluency and Comprehension. *Reading Research Quarterly*, 22: 389–407.

Dowhower, S. 1997. Introduction to "The Method of Repeated Readings." *The Reading Teacher*, 50: 376.

Herman, P. A. 1985. The Effect of Repeated Readings on Reading Rate, Speech Pauses, and Word Recognition Accuracy. *Reading Research Quarterly*, 20: 553–564.

Koskinen, P. S., and I.H. Blum. 1984. Repeated Oral Reading and the Acquisition of Fluency. In J. A. Niles and L. A. Harris (eds.), *Changing Perspectives on Research in Reading/Language Processing and Instruction, Thirty-Third Yearbook of the National Reading Conference*, pp. 183–187. Rochester, NY: National Reading Conference.

Koskinen, P. S., and I. H. Blum. 1986. Paired Repeated Reading: A Classroom Strategy for Developing Fluent Reading. *The Reading Teacher*, 40: 70–75.

Koskinen, P. S., et al. 1993. Captioned Video and Vocabulary Learning: An Innovative Practice in Literacy Instruction. *The Reading Teacher*, 47: 36–43.

Martinez, M., N. L. Roser and S. Strecker. 1999. "I Never Thought I Could Be a Star": A Readers Theater Ticket to Fluency. *The Reading Teacher*, 52: 326–334.

Pinnell, G. S., et al. 1995. *Listening to Children Read Aloud: Data from NAEP's Integrated Reading Performance Record at Grade 4*. Washington, DC: U.S. Department of Education, Office of Educational Research and Intruction.

Postlethwaite, T. N., and K. N. Ross. 1992. *Effective Schools in Reading: Implications for Educational Planners*. The Hague: International Association for the Evaluation of Educational Achievement.

Rasinski, T. V. 1990. *The Effects of Cued Phrase Boundaries in Texts*. Bloomington, IN: ERIC Clearinghouse on Reading and Communication Skills (ED 313 689).

Rasinski, T. V., and N. D. Padak. 1998. How Elementary Students Referred for Compensatory Reading Instruction Perform on School-Based Measures of Word Recognition, Fluency, and Comprehension. *Reading Psychology: An International Quarterly*, 19: 185–216.

Rasinski, T. V., et al. 1994. Effects of Fluency Development on Urban Second-Grade Readers. *Journal of Educational Research*, 87: 158–165.

Rasinski, T. V., and J. B. Zutell. 1996. Is Fluency Yet a Goal of the Reading Curriculum? In E. Sturtevent and W. Linek (eds.), *Growing Literacy, The Eighteenth Yearbook of the College Reading Association*, pp. 237–246. Harrisonburg, VA: College Reading Association.

Samuels, S. J. 1979, 1997. The Method of Repeated Readings. *The Reading Teacher*, 32: 403–408. Reprinted in *The Reading Teacher*, 50: 376–381.

Schreiber, P. A. 1980. On the Acquisition of Reading Fluency. *Journal of Reading Behavior*, 12: 177–186.

Schreiber, P. A. 1991. Understanding Prosody's Role in Reading Acquisition. *Theory into Practice*, 30: 158–164.

Smith, J., and W. Elley. 1997. *How Children Learn to Read*. Katonah, NY: Richard C. Owens.

Topping, K. 1987. Paired reading: A Powerful Technique for Parent Use. *The Reading Teacher*, 40: 608–614.

Topping, K. 1989. Peer Tutoring and Paired Reading: Combining Two Powerful Techniques. *The Reading Teacher*, 42: 488–494.

15
INSTRUCTIONAL ROUTINES FOR
WORD STUDY AND FLUENCY

Throughout this book, we have presented instructional strategies and ideas that help young readers develop fluency, learn words, and learn how to solve problems related to words. These are fine strategies and ideas. They work. But effective instruction is more than simply the sum of all these ideas; teachers must also consider how they fit together into a coherent and effective curriculum. In this chapter we offer some suggestions for planning a word-learning, fluency-building curriculum.

Teachers' teaching styles and preferences vary. So do students' learning needs and preferences. Other important aspects of learning environments differ from classroom to classroom, even at the same grade level in the same school building. Because of these differences, teaching must involve planning curriculum. Nobody knows the situation and children's learning needs better than the teacher who interacts daily with children.

PLANNING A WORD-LEARNING CURRICULUM

The curriculum planning process often begins with some careful thought about broad aims for literacy learning. Teachers might consider such questions as

- What do I believe about literacy learning?
- What do I believe about children as learners?
- What is the role of the teacher?
- What sort of physical and psychological environment best promotes learning?
- How would I characterize an excellent learning activity?
- What role should word learning play within an overall literacy program?

Questions like these help teachers articulate their philosophies of teaching, learning, and literacy. We recommend making notes about beliefs because they are useful for guiding curriculum planning, selecting instructional activities, and evaluating the impact of programs on children as learners. Moreover, the beliefs can be used to double-check existing programs—to see if children have sufficient opportunities to learn what's important, and whether literacy instruction features a balance among various important aspects of reading and learning to read.

The next stage in curriculum planning is to establish a few broad goals for children as learners. These goals should reflect the teacher's beliefs or philosophy by articulating expectations for children in a particular grade. Goals provide the foundation for a reading program; they describe the general areas within which literacy instruction occurs. Here, for example, are Lyndell's goals for his kindergarten students:

- to develop interest in and appreciation for books and reading.
- to develop and extend understanding of stories and informative text.
- to learn concepts of print and an awareness of key features of books and printed language.
- to develop phonemic awareness.

In contrast, June's goals for her second graders include:

- to develop interest in and appreciation for books and reading.
- to develop and extend comprehension abilities with a variety of genre.
- to read fluently.
- to solve word-related reading problems successfully.

Note that both sets of goals are comprehensive. Lyndell and June develop their entire reading programs, based on these goals, by ensuring that children have daily opportunities to develop proficiency in the targeted areas. Note, too, that the first and second goals on their lists are similar. Indeed, teachers throughout their school have the same goals for students. This makes sense because positive attitudes about reading and the continued development of comprehension abilities are all teachers' responsibilities.

The next stage in the curriculum planning process involves selecting or developing instructional routines. A routine is a regular block of time during which a predictable set of activities occur. Teacher read-aloud is an instructional routine, or should be. So are sustained silent reading and readers workshop. Routines are helpful for teachers in curriculum planning—together the routines constitute the reading program. Routines are also helpful for students because within them students can behave independently—they don't have to rely on the teacher to figure out what to do next.

Our focus in this chapter (and book) is on fluency development and word learning, so our discussion of routines will focus on these important aspects of reading programs. Nonetheless, an effective reading curriculum aims for much more. Developing routines that, as a whole, provide sufficient opportunities for children to achieve curriculum goals will ensure a balanced reading program.

PRINCIPLES FOR ROUTINES

Some routines, like teacher read aloud, are features of most classrooms. Others may be unique to the teacher or particular group of children. A few years ago in our summer reading program, for example, one child wanted to write a riddle on the chalkboard one day. This idea quickly caught other students' interest—

soon everybody was looking for riddles, and the chalkboard was covered with a new set each morning. So finding, writing, reading, and solving riddles became a much anticipated routine for this group of children. This riddle mania happened quite by accident and probably wouldn't have been as effective if teachers had planned it. Despite the occasional serendipity, effective routines for promoting word learning are generally based on several important principles. In this section we comment briefly on each.

BASE ROUTINES ON WHAT CHILDREN NEED

Routines should be based on what children need, not on a skills list or sequence of lessons in materials. Think back on your own early years in school for a moment. Were there times when you were taught things you already knew? Boring, wasn't it? How about times when the focus of the lesson was beyond your ability to benefit from it—too abstract, say, or not immediately useful for you? If you can't think of anything, try rules for dividing words into syllables, determining accents in words, for using semicolons. How many times did well meaning teachers try to help you learn these rules? And when—if ever—did you finally figure the rules out so that you could use them in your reading and writing? Our point here is not to criticize past educational practices; rather we wish to underscore the importance of basing instructional routines on what children need.

Needs-based instruction sounds good but can be tricky to implement. First, teachers must develop good ways to determine needs. Observing students and especially listening to them read are good ways to do this. As we mentioned in Chapter 13, analyzing children's invented spellings is another good way to find out what they know about sounds and symbols and where instruction may be beneficial. Finally, talking to children can offer useful insights. We frequently ask children, What do you do when you come to a word that you don't know? What do you do if that doesn't work? What does good reading sound like? We find that children's answers, especially when considered along with samples of their oral reading, provide on-target direction for instruction.

Next, classroom management issues must be resolved. The odds are slim that every child will have the same needs at the same time, so teachers must think about how to coordinate several classroom activities simultaneously. We offer two pieces of advice here. First, remember that the predictable nature of routines enables children to behave independently as learners. Second, remember that the best way to practice reading, frequently what the rest of the children do while the teacher works with some, is to read.

An effective record keeping system is also necessary to implement needs-based instruction. Some teachers make notes on index cards or large computer labels. Others keep charts with children's names down one side and skills or strategies across the top. Another alternative is to keep lists of words or skills in children's reading portfolios and to indicate the dates on which children demonstrate proficiency. The sight word list in Appendix B, for example, could be used in this manner to keep track of children's sight word acquisition. The format of the records is a matter of personal preference, but the existence of records is not. Teachers need a way to keep track of what children know and what instruction can promote word learning growth.

Is all this effort worth it? We believe that it is, for two major reasons. First, for decades scholars have searched in vain for the single best way to teach all children to read. Nothing works for everyone so attention to individual readers' needs is warranted. The second reason is, most likely, related to the first: children are different. Here's how Cunningham and Allington put it:

> Anyone who has ever observed how different children from the same family behave knows that all children do not learn, respond, and think in the same manner. Successful parents recognize the differences in their children and adjust their rules, routines, and interactions accordingly, in order to maximize the potential of each of their children. (1999, p. 15)

We believe that teachers can take a lesson from parents in this regard. Providing effective instruction in word learning or any other area of the curriculum depends on the teacher's ability to determine both what children need to know and how they can best learn. No list of skills or sequence of instructional material can provide this insight.

MAXIMIZE TIME ON TASK

Time is another important consideration in establishing instructional routines. It goes almost without saying that children need time to read in order to become readers. We say *almost* because sometimes instructional time is spent doing lots of reading-related and reading-like activities but very little reading. Surely children enjoy and can benefit from opportunities to respond to their reading. Just as surely, instruction in word-learning skills and strategies may involve working with words or even parts of words. These activities are important, but most important is time on task—reading connected text. Time spent reading is related to achievement in reading (Anderson, Wilson and Fielding 1988, Postlethwaite and Ross 1992, Rupley, Wise and Logan 1986).

The focus of children's attention during instructional time with the teacher is another issue related to time. This is especially true for children who struggle as readers. Descriptions of instruction for struggling readers show lack of opportunity for and emphasis on meaningful reading (Allington 1977, 1980, McDermott 1978). In these studies, less able readers were asked to focus almost exclusively on decoding. As Allington (1977) has asked, "If they don't read much, how they ever gonna get good?"

Sometimes we're so busy teaching that we ignore this critical issue of time on the task of reading. Observing three readers for a couple of days is one way to begin to understand how much time students spend reading. A high-achieving reader, an average reader, and a low-achieving reader might be selected, and the teacher might tally minutes spent reading—not engaging in reading-related activity, but actually reading. This quick check is sometimes a real eye opener.

Word-learning activities are important; however, it's essential that children have plentiful and daily opportunities to read and listen to texts read aloud. After all, that's what all the word learning is for. Besides that, both reading and listening foster fluency development.

Make it fun

Ensure that children will be successful. Many of the word-learning activities we have described in this book have a game-like feel to them. This is purposeful. Children learn best when they enjoy what they are doing and when they are able to complete tasks successfully. Even as adults, most of us are drawn to activities that we enjoy, especially if we are successful; so it is with our students. We want them to be readers, to see the value in reading for their lives in and out of school, and to feel confident in their abilities to solve the inevitable problems readers encounter. Enjoyable, success-oriented word learning activities can support the achievement of these goals.

What makes an activity enjoyable for children? Competition can be enjoyable, but only for the winners. Struggling readers, particularly, may not enjoy competitions. Opportunities to win small prizes or other forms of external motivation can also be enjoyable; however, unlike internal motivation—doing something for personal reasons—external motivation ceases when the particular task is concluded (Sweet and Guthrie 1996). Too many competitions or activities dependant solely on external motivation, then, are probably not advisable. Aside from these general guidelines, each teacher will probably have to answer the question of what makes an activity enjoyable to students. But remember, a teacher's enthusiasm for an activity contributes to its allure and enjoyment.

Opportunities to complete activities successfully are also important. The repeated readings characteristic of fluency practice has success built in. Tape-recording a child's first and, say, fifth reading can provide concrete evidence of success. Also, divergent thinking activities like open word sorts (see Chapter 9) invite success because of the many ways in which the activity can be completed. One way to ensure success, then, is to provide frequent opportunities for children to engage in open-ended word learning activities. An additional benefit is that divergent thinking activities pose problems for children to solve and, therefore, engage children actively as learners. The level of difficulty of an activity also affects the likelihood that children will complete it successfully. Here teachers should strive for activities that are challenging but not frustrating, neither too easy nor too difficult.

Develop Home-school Connections

One clear conclusion from five years of research supported by the National Reading Research Center relates to this principle: "Literacy learning occurs both at school and home, and connections between home and school enhance children's learning in both environments" (Baumann and Duffy 1997, p. 21). Effective teachers realize the importance of inviting the home and community into the classroom. They know that reading is not just for school; it's for life. Effective teachers invite parents' substantial involvement in their children's education. The Fast Start program described in Chapter 17 is an example of a routine for home involvement with school support.

Research is clear about the uniformly positive effects of promoting home-school partnerships. In one multinational study, parental involvement and support was the most important characteristic of schools where children achieved exceptionally well as readers (Postlethwaite and Ross 1992). Another research project looked at the relationships among classroom support, home support, and low-income children's achievement in reading (Snow 1991). The results of this study show the enormous impact of both of these factors on children's achievement (see Table 15.1). Chapter 17 offers many ways to nurture home-school partnerships that can benefit children's word-learning growth.

USE A WHOLE-TO-PART-TO-WHOLE MODEL FOR TEACHING SKILLS AND STRATEGIES

Throughout the book we have emphasized that learning about words and parts of words is most successful and meaningful if students first focus on whole text. A narrower highlight on the words or word parts of interest follows, after which teachers and students explore the usefulness of new knowledge—how knowing about the *-it* family, for example, can help students solve word-related problems in reading. This focus on problem-solving for authentic purposes seems natural to children because it mirrors the way they learned oral language:

> Babies use a variety of strategies to discover relationships about language and thinking. . . . They find ways to distinguish the sounds of language from the sounds of cars, cats, and fire engines. In order to learn they do not have to isolate these sounds. . . . As a consequence of using language and thought authentically children have learned to sample, infer, predict, confirm, and integrate new information into their existing linguistic and pragmatic schema. These same strategies are used by students learning to read if they are permitted to capitalize on them in the classroom and if significant written context is available. A student's own strategies are the strengths on which a reading program must be built. (Goodman, Watson, and Burke 1996, p. 53)

A skill becomes a strategy when the knowledge represented by the skill can be used purposefully. Certainly we use word learning activities to develop students' skills, but in the final analysis these skills are only useful if students can apply them when they need to, as in the case of an unknown word. Routines designed to foster word learning should seek to develop both skills and strategies.

| | Home Support | |
Classroom Support	High	Low
High	100%	100%
Mixed	100%	25%
Low	60%	0%

Table 15.1
Home Support, Classroom Support, and the Percentage of Children Who Achieve Success*
* Based on Snow, 1991, adapted from Cunningham and Allington 1999, p. 2

Enhancement of children's sight vocabularies—those words they recognize immediately without thought—is another goal of word learning activities. (See Appendix B for a list of commonly used sight words.) Essentially this is a memorization process that happens as a result of many meaningful encounters with words. We do not foster sight vocabulary growth by solely and extensively asking children to look at words in isolation, as on flash cards; instead, words become known by sight because children have seen and used them successfully in multiple contexts. Also, teachers should look for opportunities to focus children's attention on the visual features of the words. Here are several ways to do this (also see word bank activities listed in Chapter 9):

Ask children to locate and circle all examples of a sight word in a story they are reading.

Place the words on Word Walls (see Chapter 7).

Record the words in personal or class dictionaries.

Add the words to students' word banks.

Make word collages—cut the word out of old magazines and paste on construction paper.

Construct the words with magnetic letters; write the words in the sand tray, in finger paint, or in shaving cream.

Play word games with the words (see Chapter 12).

REMEMBER THE OVERALL GOAL: GROW READERS

The final principle for establishing word-learning routines reminds us to keep word learning in perspective, not to lose the forest for the trees. As Baumann and Duffy note, "reading skills and strategies can be taught effectively and efficiently when instruction is systematic and integrated with quality children's literature" (1997, p. 17). In other words, instruction in words and word learning is one important component of a reading program but should not be the focus of the program. Reading aloud to children, guiding children to read texts themselves, and encouraging students to read and write independently and with one another are also essential. In the next section we explore some ways to plan instruction so that all these features receive the emphasis they deserve.

TYPES OF ROUTINES

Designing a classroom reading program involves making some decisions about how space will be used. For example, some teachers create centers, such as a book nook for independent reading, a writing center filled with writing tools including computers, and a words center where children can complete word-related activities either independently or with partners. Others prefer for children to work at their tables or desks. In either case, we recommend that the classroom be organized so that children can behave as independently as possible. Daily lists of things to do or simply written charts posted around the classroom can save lots of time. Children won't have to wait for instructions from the teacher; they will be able to get about the business of learning.

Teachers must also decide how to break up the larger block of reading time. In part, this decision may involve thinking about how large the instructional group will be—whole class? Small groups? Individual activity? Many of the activities we describe in this book can work well within any of these formats. We offer a word of caution, however, about whole group instruction—for this organizational scheme to work effectively, all children must be appropriately engaged all the time. This is a time on task issue.

The Four Blocks curriculum design is a particularly promising way to divide a large amount of language arts time. Pat Cunningham and her colleagues created this curriculum framework. Nearly a decade of research into its usefulness has shown its effectiveness with all young learners, particularly those who struggle with learning to read (Cunningham, Hall and Defee 1998). We find the model useful for teachers at all grade levels. Devoting approximately equal time (Cunningham and colleagues suggest about 30 minutes each day) to each of the four blocks ensures a balanced reading and writing program that gives children ample opportunities to achieve the goals that the teacher has set.

The self-selected reading block is time for children to participate in teacher read-alouds, sustained silent reading, and other reading that they choose themselves. Fluency activities can occur here. Literature circles may also be a self-selected reading activity. Comprehension instruction occurs during the guided reading block. The writing block is time for writers' workshop. The fourth block, working with words, provides opportunities for instruction and practice in reading and writing words and word parts fluently—what this book is all about.

The Four Blocks is a large scale routine that characterizes an entire reading program. Within each block teachers design smaller scale routines that are made up of related activities. For example, in one classroom the daily self-selected reading routine may consist of ten minutes of teacher read-aloud, fifteen minutes of student silent reading, and five minutes of writing in response journals. In another classroom, the same block has a different routine: student silent reading for twenty minutes followed by ten minutes of oral sharing and response.

The routine working with words block might consist of a weekly set of activities described in this book. Here's one example:

Monday	Tuesday	Wednesday
1. Read the Word Wall	1. Read word family poems	1. Read Word Wall
2. Mini-lesson	2. Student word-family poems	2. Mini-lesson
3. Making & Writing Words (MWW)	3. Word sorts	3. MWW
4. Cloze		4. Cloze

Thursday	Friday
1. Poetry festival	1. Word games
2. Word sorts	

Teachers do not need to march children through the blocks each day. Indeed, some of the most effective lessons may even involve several of the blocks simultaneously. The Fluency Development Lesson, a routine we describe in Chapter 14, is one example of how this might work. In a brief ten to fifteen minute period, children participate in both guided reading and word-related activities. Predictable books and poetry (see Chapter 3) can be used for word family instruction, word sorts, Word Walls, repeated readings, and paired readings. So the point is not to shift reading-related gears every thirty minutes; rather, when thinking about children's learning opportunities over the course of a few days or a week, teachers should see that the four areas have received approximately equal emphasis.

WHEN READERS STRUGGLE

Young children struggle with the learning-to-read process for many reasons. Some have language barriers; others have special needs. Some may have had little exposure to books and print prior to school entrance. Still others may simply be late bloomers—children who are not yet developmentally ready to learn what the school system has designated for their grade levels. Regardless of the reasons for the struggle, these children need all the support we can provide. Below we offer several guidelines and adaptations that may help struggling readers to succeed (Cunningham and Allington 1999, Five and Dioniso 1999).

Chief among the guidelines is, we believe, to forget about the child's age or what other children are doing and to focus instead on the struggling reader's needs. Successful learning experiences, important for all, are doubly important for children who find reading difficult. Teachers must focus on students' strengths, not their weaknesses, and must plan many daily opportunities for children to experience success in reading and reading-related activity. Sometimes this involves slowing down, allowing children time to grow and progress at their own rates. Often teachers must find books and other material that the child can read successfully. Other times, instructional adaptations may be necessary. For example, children might listen to a tape-recorded version of a book the class is using while reading the book. Or a buddy or tutor may read to or with the child. These strategies allow the child to be an active and successful participant in classroom activities.

Another general principle for working with struggling readers is to approximate the real act of reading as much as possible. Sometimes we think that breaking reading down into minute skills or subskills will make it easier for children to learn. Not so. Some instructional programs for struggling readers, for example, even focus on shapes, pictures, or nonsense words. These, too, are not effective: "Numerous studies have shown that matching shapes and pictures as preliminary instruction for letter and word discrimination is useless. . . . If we want students to visually identify the distinguishing features of letters and words, [lessons] should include letters and words, not nonword forms" (McCormick 1999, p. 477).

So what might a routine for struggling readers look like? In the regular classroom, teachers might take special care to ensure that most materials will be easy for students to read. More invitations to read familiar books may accomplish this goal. Moreover, careful observation, including numerous opportunities to listen to the child read and analyze his or her reading strategies, will help the teacher determine how to focus instruction; such a focus may differ from mini-lessons prepared for other students. Multiple opportunities to read successfully coupled with instruction designed to meet specific needs (and frequent celebrations of success) will go a long way toward ensuring that struggling readers achieve.

Coordination is another guideline. Coordinating with other teachers, such as a Title 1, special education, bilingual education, or Reading Recovery teacher, is absolutely essential. Without joint planning, what begins as an effort to provide additional assistance may result in a "confusing and unhelpful conglomeration of reading lessons and activities" (Cunningham and Allington 1999, p. 202). Some teachers accomplish coordinated instruction by team-teaching in the classroom; others plan jointly. All keep in close contact about what's happening in the child's classroom and what needs the child appears to have.

> What is common among the very best programs is that children spend most of their time actually reading and writing in a way that supports classroom success. The support children receive from the specialist teacher provides immediate returns in improved reading and writing during classroom instruction. (Cunningham and Allington 1999, p. 203)

Volunteers, such as parent helpers, tutors, older students, or senior citizens, can also provide extra support for struggling readers. Before eliciting tutors' assistance, however, teachers should give some thought to what tutors might do and how to teach them what they need to know to work successfully with children. Many of the activities we describe in this book can be easily and successfully adapted to a tutoring situation. For example, tutors and children can play word games together, or the tutor can listen to the child read a poem, dictated account, or pattern book. Most children can make considerable progress in reading if their strong classroom program is supplemented with the extra opportunities that one-on-one tutoring can provide. So the time it takes to plan these tutoring opportunities and to help tutors learn about their roles is well worth it in the long run.

Finding ways to teach a young child who struggles with reading is sometimes a challenge, but it can also be one of the most rewarding aspects of a teacher's job because doing so gives a child the gift of literacy. Although we have no easy answers or sure-fire remedies for assisting struggling readers, we agree with Five and Dionisio, who note that nearly all children "can succeed when we include them as valued members of [the classroom], enable them to work and learn collaboratively with peers, build on their strengths and knowledge, and meet their individual needs through explicit instruction" (1999, p. 5).

In Conclusion

Children will learn what they have the opportunity to learn. Moreover, no one knows children's needs and interests as readers better than their classroom teacher. For these reasons, curriculum planning must be part of the teacher's responsibility. Effective instruction in word learning is more than just the sum of interesting and engaging activities. To plan effective instruction, the teacher must first look at the big picture—think about beliefs and establish instructional goals. These ideas are used to develop complete programs, which are designed to make the best use of children's time and to help them achieve the goal of proficient reading.

REFERENCES

Allington, R. 1977. If They Don't Read Much, How They Ever Gonna Get Good? *Journal of Reading*, 21: 57–61.

Allington, R. 1980. Teacher Interruption Behaviors During Primary Grade Oral Reading. *Journal of Educational Psychology*, 72: 371–377.

Anderson, R., P. Wilson, and L. Fielding. 1988. Growth in Reading and How Children Spend Their Time Outside of School. *Reading Research Quarterly*, 23: 285–303.

Baumann, J., and A. Duffy. 1997. *Engaged Reading for Pleasure and Learning: A Report from the National Reading Research Center*. Athens, GA: National Reading Research Center.

Cunningham, P., and R. Allington. 1999 . *Classrooms that Work* (2nd ed.). New York: Longman.

Cunningham, P., D. Hall and M. Defee. 1998. Nonability-Grouped, Multilevel Instruction: Eight Years Later. *The Reading Teacher,* 51: 652–664.

Five, C., and M. Dionisio. 1999. *School Talk: Teaching the Struggling Reader and Writer* vol. 4, no. 2. Urbana, IL: National Council of Teachers of English.

Goodman, Y., D. Watson and C. Burke. 1996. *Reading Strategies: Focus on Comprehension* (2nd ed.). Katonah, NY: Richard C. Owen.

McCormick, S. 1999. *Instructing Students Who Have Literacy Problems* (3rd ed.). Upper Saddle River, NJ: Prentice Hall.

McDermott, R. 1978. Pirandello in the Classroom: On the Possibility of Equal Educational Opportunity in American Culture. In M. Reynolds (ed.), *Futures for Exceptional Children: Emerging Structure*, pp. 41–64. Reston, VA: Council for Exceptional Children.

Postlethwaite, T., and K. Ross. 1992. *Effective Schools in Reading*. The Hague, Netherlands: International Association for the Evaluation of Educational Achievement.

Rupley, W., B. Wise and J. Logan. 1986 Research in Effective Teaching: An Overview of its Development. In J. Hoffman (ed.), *Effective Teaching of Reading: Research and Practice*, pp. 3–36. Newark, DE: International Reading Association.

Snow, C. 1991. *Unfulfilled Expectations*. Cambridge, MA: Harvard University Press.

Sweet, A., and J. Guthrie. 1996. How Children's Motivations Relate to Literacy Development and Instruction. *The Reading Teacher,* 49: 660–662.

16
ASSESSING WORD RECOGNITION AND READING FLUENCY

Carol works as a third grade teacher in a school with high student turnover. "We are always getting students coming in and leaving the school. In my classroom alone last year I had ten students leave and thirteen new ones come in during the school year." When new students enter her classroom Carol needs to assess where they are in reading. "Rather than try some standardized test, I use some of the informal instruments I have learned about over the years. I ask students to read for me for a few minutes from a grade-level book. From that reading I can get a sense for their ability to decode words, I can estimate their reading efficiency or reading fluency, and by the student's recall of what they read, I can get a pretty good sense for how well they understand what they read."

Not only does Carol's informal assessment provide her with how to work with the new child, she also uses the data as a baseline against which to determine how well children are responding to instruction and progressing in reading. Actually, Carol's assessments aren't just for new students who come to her classroom during the school year. "I assess everyone in my classroom during the first week of school, and I do a quick assessment for all my children about every two or three months throughout the school year. The information from these quick assessments truly helps me see if I am doing my job and guides me in planning instruction that meets the needs of all my students."

No book on word recognition and reading fluency would be complete without providing the reader with some guidance on assessing progress. This is particularly important for those students who are older and who still struggle in these areas. It is important for teachers to be able to determine what areas in word recognition and fluency are concerns for the struggling reader.

In this chapter, then, we provide several approaches for assessing students' word recognition and fluency. We divide our discussion of assessment into three portions: initial assessment, measuring continuous progress, and diagnostic assessment. Please remember that although these areas may be presented in distinct segments, there is considerable overlap among them. Diagnostic assessment, for example, should include information about students' early assessments as well as information gathered periodically to measure progress in word recognition and fluency. Moreover, assessments listed here as diagnostic can also be used to measure students' progress in each of the areas assessed by the diagnostic instrument.

INITIAL ASSESSMENT

Before beginning instruction in phonics and word recognition with young students, it is important to know just where students are in terms of some basic understandings with print and how it works. Fortunately, there are several types of information about students that will be helpful for teachers and parents and that are fairly easily obtained.

PHONEMIC AWARENESS

Phonemic awareness was discussed in some detail in Chapter 4. Phonemic awareness is an important predictor of early and continual success in reading. In Chapter 4 we presented an adaptation of the Yopp-Singer Test of Phonemic Awareness. This test of twenty-two items, which can be administered in minutes, provides teachers with a good understanding of individual students' ability to perceive and manipulate speech sounds in words.

LETTER–NAME KNOWLEDGE

Letter–name knowledge is an important part of early reading instruction simply because teachers make reference to letters using their names. If students do not know the names of the letters, they have a much greater chance of experiencing difficulty in word recognition instruction. Letter–name knowledge is easily assessed by printing the letters, upper and lower case, on index cards, shuffling the deck, and asking students individually to name the letters.

LETTER–SOUND KNOWLEDGE

Letter–sound knowledge is also an important part of early word recognition instruction. Phonics instruction usually begins with the sounds associated with individual letters. As with letter names, letter sounds can be assessed by presenting individual children with letter cards (primarily consonants) and asking them to identify the sounds associated with the letters.

Another way to assess students' knowledge of letters and sounds is to examine their unaided writing or writing from dictation. Especially when students invent spellings for words, we can see much about their letter-sound knowledge in their efforts.

For any of the above assessments, if it becomes clear that individual children have little or no knowledge of the concepts being tested, halt the assessment. After several items are missed in a row the examiner can safely conclude that the child does not have understanding of the concepts and that those concepts need to taught. In any type of assessment situation, try to limit the child's frustration. You do not need to go through every letter name to come to the conclusion that letter name knowledge is largely present or absent in individual children.

BASIC PRINT CONCEPTS

Basic print concepts refer to ideas that are essential to reading and reading instruction. They are the stuff around which reading instruction revolves. Ideas such as letter, word, sentence, beginning, and end are concepts that can easily be assessed in individual students.

In order to assess basic print concepts we suggest having individual students dictate a brief story to the examiner. The story could simply be about what the child did earlier in the day or the previous day. Two to four sentences should be sufficient. The examiner prints the story verbatim on a blank sheet of paper as it is dictated. Then, the examiner reads it back to the student, pointing to individual words as they are read. Once the story is written the examiner can ask the student questions about basic print concepts:

- Point to the *beginning* of the story or line of text.
- Point to the *end* of the story or line of text.
- Point to the *top* of the story.
- Point to the *bottom* of the story.
- Circle *one letter* in the story. Circle *two letters* together in the story.
- Circle a *capital* or *uppercase* letter in the story.
- Circle *one word* in the story. Circle *two words* together in the story.
- Point to a period; ask the child if she knows its name and purpose.
- Ask the child to point to and say any words she may know in the story.

If the child is not reading conventionally yet, you may also want to check the child's knowledge of one-to-one correspondence between words spoken and written as well as the child's ability to learn words on sight. Rewrite the first sentence from the story and read it several times to the child with the child looking at the text. Point to the words as they are read. After having read the sentence several times slowly, invite the child to read the text back to you, pointing to the words as they are read. Does the child make a one-to-one match between the written and spoken words? Ask the child to find certain words from the sentence. Is the child able to do so? Does the child find the words by immediate recognition or rereading the sentence from the beginning? Write one of the words from the sentence on a card or another sheet of paper. Ask the child to identify the word. If unable to do so, can the child match it with the same word in the sentence? If the child can match the written word in isolation with the word in context, can he or she then say the word?

BOOK AWARENESS

A particular type of print awareness is children's knowledge of how books work. Since so much of reading and other content area instruction centers on books, it is critical that even young students have some basic understandings about books. An easy way to assess book knowledge is to have a child examine a picture book and answer specific questions about the book. For example, hand the picture book to the child so that the child receives it with the back cover facing up and the spine facing the child. The child's responses to the following directives and questions should provide you with a good idea of what the child knows about books:

- Show me the front of the book.
- Open the book up to where you start to read.
- (With the book open) On what page should you start to read?
- (Looking at one page) Where do you start reading on this page?
- What do you do when you come to the end of each line?
- What do you do when you come to the end of the page?
- (After looking at both pages of an open book) Now where do you go next in this book?

While it is not necessary for children to have mastered all the assessments above, some knowledge of letter names, letter sounds, sound segmentation and manipulation, and basic print concepts will surely facilitate students' word recognition learning. Those students who experience severe difficulty in these assessments may need some extra help, in the classroom and at home, in these important early stages of reading and word recognition. Because these assessments can be given quickly, they may be administered periodically to those students who have difficulty in order to chart individual students' progress.

MEASURING CONTINUOUS PROGRESS

Instruction will benefit students at different rates and in different ways. In this age of increased accountability, it is important for teachers to document students' progress periodically throughout the school year. Not only will this provide evidence of student progress, but regular assessment will provide clear and quick indications of those students who may not be getting optimal benefit from instruction.

A fairly simple way to document progress in word recognition is to take periodic samples of students' oral reading or what has been termed curriculum based assessment (CBA) in order to document progress and note any areas of concern (Salvia and Hughes 1990). To do a CBA that focuses on word recognition and fluency, simply take a short passage of 200-400 words from a text that students will soon be reading in their school curriculum. Ask individual students to read the text to you at their normal reading rate for one or two minutes. Either record each student's reading for later analysis or mark any errors while you listen and time each student's reading. From each reading you should be able to determine the number of word recognition errors, quality of errors (do they retain or disrupt meaning of the passage), and overall rate of reading (words per minute). If students are asked to recall what they read in the two minutes, you should also get a sense for their reading comprehension.

The procedure takes only a matter of minutes per student. When your students' reading is sampled in this way every month or so and charted, you should get a good picture of each child's progress in word recognition and fluency over time (see Figure 16.1). Those students who are experiencing difficulty in word recognition and fluency will be evident as will those students who begin to experience difficulty during the school year.

CBA allows teachers to continuously monitor their students in word recognition and fluency. Students experiencing difficulty in word recognition

Date	Text Source and Grade Level	Number of Errors Per 100 Words	Number of Meaning Changing Errors Per 100 Words	Reading Rate (wpm)	Comprehension 1 = poor 2 = adequate 3 = good

Figure 16.1
Student Reading Progress Chart (Curriculum-Based Assessment)

and fluency may require more detailed or diagnostic analysis of their reading in order to identify those areas in which they most need corrective instruction.

DIAGNOSTIC ASSESSMENT

WORD RECOGNITION

Diagnostic assessment provides teachers with further information about individual students' word recognition and fluency so teachers can tailor instruction to meet each student's individual needs. Nonetheless, the assessments we present in this chapter can also be used to measure ongoing progress in these areas.

Sight vocabulary are words that readers recognize instantly and automatically. One way to measure growth in this area is to keep a running tally of the contents of students' word banks (see Chapter 9). As we mentioned earlier, the best words to have in one's sight vocabulary are those that appear with the greatest frequency in reading. The Fry Instant Words (see Appendix B) are a list of high frequency words that are good candidates for any reader's sight vocabulary. The first 300 words in the list make up approximately two-thirds of all the words elementary school readers will encounter in their contextual reading.

In addition to guiding instruction, the Fry Instant Word List can also be used diagnostically. As a rule of thumb, we can expect students to have added the first 100 words to their sight vocabularies by the end of first grade, the first 200 words to their sight vocabularies by the end of second grade, and all 300 words by the end of third grade. So, by the beginning of fourth grade and beyond, students should have fairly accurate and automatic command of the first 300 words in the Fry Instant Word List.

We have created a diagnostic sight word assessment by sampling twenty words from each of the first three groups of 100 (see Figure 16.2). Put these words on index cards, one per card, and present them to individual students. Students should read the words accurately and quickly in order to be given credit. Since the words should be part of one's sight vocabulary and this assessment measures one's sight vocabulary, accurate but slow recognition should not be counted correct. Second graders should have the first group of 20 mastered (90% immediate accuracy, 18 of 20); third graders should have the first two groups of 20 mastered; and fourth graders and above should have all three groups of 20 mastered.

PHONOGRAMS/WORD FAMILIES/RIMES

In Chapter 5 we noted that word patterns, particularly rimes or phonograms, were an excellent focus for teaching phonics. In addition, we shared the thirty-eight most common rimes (Fry 1998) that should be taught initially to students. In order to assess students' mastery of the most common rimes, we developed an informal word list test (see Figure 16.3) that contains the thirty-eight rimes in one syllable and multisyllable words. Asking students to read the words in the lists should provide teachers with an indicator of those stu-

Group 1	Group 2	Group 3
the	give	city
have	sound	country
was	work	earth
you	sentence	saw
they	know	thought
were	where	few
your	through	group
their	around	might
each	follow	always
said	show	important
would	another	children
about	large	white
them	because	river
time	went	carry
write	move	second
people	picture	enough
water	play	almost
who	animal	mountain
down	mother	young
over	America	family

Students should have, by the end of first grade, automatic mastery (90% or better immediate recognition) of Group 1 words, automatic mastery of Group 2 words by the end of second grade, and automatic mastery of Group 3 words by the end of third grade.

Figure 16.2
Fry Instant Word List Sample for Sight Word Assessment

dents who have mastered these rimes and those who are still in the process of learning them, indicating which students are in need of more thorough instruction on particular rimes.

The Common Phonogram Assessment provides information on the phonograms or rimes students know and may not yet have mastered; however, neither it nor the Fry Instant Word List Sample provides information on students' developmental level in word recognition or their mastery of some of the more traditional phonics concepts. The enhanced version of *The Names Test* provides this information (Cunningham 1990, Duffelmeyer, et al.

Ask students to pronounce each of the following words in Group 1 and 2. Make note of any errors or patterns of errors that occur.

Group 1	Group 2	Group 1	Group 2
say	playmate	bug	dugout
spill	willful	stop	popcorn
ship	skipping	chin	tinsel
bat	satisfy	Stan	flannel
slam	hamster	nest	Chester
brag	shaggy	think	trinket
stack	packer	grow	snowplow
crank	blanket	chew	newest
quick	cricket	score	adore
yell	shellfish	red	bedtime
got	hotcake	crab	dabble
king	stacking	knob	robber
clap	kidnap	block	jockey
junk	bunker	brake	remake
nail	railroad	shine	porcupine
chain	mainstay	light	sighted
weed	seedling	brim	swimming
try	myself	stuck	truckload
spout	without	chum	drummer

Figure 16.3
Rasinski-Padak Common Phonogram Assessment

1994). *The Names Test* is a word list test in which the words are presented as names that students are asked to read. The seventy words, or names, present students with a variety of phonics elements that they must know in order to read the list correctly. The names are shown in Figure 16.4. Students "take roll" by reading the names on the list. The teacher listens and marks any errors, transcribing errors as read by the student. In Figure 16.5 we present average October scores on the seventy names by grade level (Duffelmeyer, et al. 1994). We have interpolated their findings to add expected average scores for the March-April period. Students who score significantly below their appropriate grade and month averages (eight items or more below the average) should be considered at risk in word recognition.

Student sheet for the Names Test

Jay Conway	Chuck Hoke
Kimberly Blake	Homer Preston
Cindy Sampson	Ginger Yale
Stanley Shaw	Glen Spencer
Flo Thornton	Grace Brewster
Ron Smitherman	Vance Middleton
Bernard Pendergraph	Floyd Sheldon
Austin Shepherd	Neal Wade
Joan Brooks	Thelma Rinehart
Tim Cornell	Yolanda Clark
Roberta Slade	Gus Quincy
Chester Wright	Patrick Tweed
Wendy Swain	Fred Sherwood
Dee Skidmore	Ned Westmoreland
Troy Whitlock	Zane Anderson
Shane Fletcher	Dean Bateman
Bertha Dale	Jake Murphy
Gene Loomis	

Figure 16.4
The Names Test

The errors of students who perform poorly on *The Names Test* can be further analyzed using the scoring matrix in Figure 16.6. The scoring matrix can be used to categorize the error by type (initial consonant, initial consonant

Record sheet for the Names Test

Name_____ Grade____ Teacher_____ Date_____

Jay Conway	Chuck Hoke
Kimberly Blake	Homer Preston
Cindy Sampson	Ginger Yale
Stanley Shaw	Glen Spencer
Flo Thornton	Grace Brewster
Ron Smitherman	Vance Middleton
Bernard Pendergraph	Floyd Sheldon
Austin Shepherd	Neal Wade
Joan Brooks	Thelma Rinehart
Tim Cornell	Yolanda Clark
Roberta Slade	Gus Quincy
Chester Wright	Patrick Tweed
Wendy Swain	Fred Sherwood
Dee Skidmore	Ned Westmoreland
Troy Whitlock	Zane Anderson
Shane Fletcher	Dean Bateman
Bertha Dale	Jake Murphy
Gene Loomis	

Figure 16.4
The Names Test (cont'd)

Grade	Average Percentage (# correct)
2 (Oct)	63% (44)
2 (March–Apr)	68% (48)
3 (Oct)	73% (51)
3 (March–Apr)	81% (57)
4 (Oct)	89% (62)
4 (March–Apr)	91% (63)
5 (Oct)	92% (64)
6 and beyond	100% (70)

Figure 16.5
Average Grade Level Scores on The Names Test

Name:_____ Date of testing:_____

Grade Level:_____   Raw Score (70 items total):_____

Secondary analysis by phonics category:

Phonics category	*Errors*
Initial consonants	/37
Initial consonants blends	/19
Consonant digraphs	/15
Short vowels	/36
Long vowels/VC-final *e*	/23
Vowel digraphs	/15
Controlled vowels	/25
Schwa	/15

Additional comments:

Figure 16.6
Recording Sheet—The Names Test

Scoring matrix for the Names Test

Name _____ Date _____

Name	InCon	InConBl	ConDgr	ShVow	LngVow/VC-e	VowDgr	CtrVow	Schwa
Anderson				A			er	o
Austin						Au		i
Bateman	B				ate			a
Bernard	B						er, ar	
Bertha	B		th				er	a
Blake		Bl			ake			
Brewster		Br					ew, er	
Brooks		Br				oo		
Chester			Ch	e			er	
Chuck			Ch	u				
Cindy	C			i	y			
Clark		Cl					ar	
Conway	C			o		ay		
Cornell	C			e			or	
Dale	D				ale			
Dean	D					ea		
Dee	D					ee		
Fletcher		Fl	ch	e			er	
Flo		Fl			o			
Floyd		Fl				oy		
Fred		Fr		e				
Gene	G				ene			
Ginger	G			i			er	
Glen		Gl		e				
Grace		Gr			ace			
Gus	G			u				
Hoke	H				oke			
Homer	H				o		er	
Jake	J				ake			
Jay	J					ay		
Joan	J					oa		
Kimberly	K				y		er	
Loomis	L					oo		i
Middleton	M			i				o
Murphy	M		ph		y		ur	

Scoring matrix for the Names Test (cont'd)

Name _____ Date _____

Name	InCon	InConBl	ConDgr	ShVow	LngVow/VC-e	VowDgr	CtrVow	Schwa
Neal	N					ea		
Ned	N			e				
Patrick	P			a, i				
Pendergraph	P		ph	e, a			er	o
Preston		Pr		e				
Quincy				i	y			
Rinehart	R				ine		ar	
Roberta	R			o	o		er	a
Ron	R			o				
Sampson	S			a				o
Shane			Sh		ane			
Shaw			Sh				aw	
Sheldon			Sh	e				o
Shepherd			Sh	e			er	
Sherwood			Sh			oo	er	
Skidmore		Sk		i			or	
Slade		Sl			ade			
Smitherman		Sm	th	i			er	a
Spencer		Sp		e			er	
Stanley		St		a		ey		
Swain		Sw				ai		
Thelma			Th	e				a
Thornton			Th				or	o
Tim	T			i				
Troy		Tr				oy		
Tweed		Tw				ee		
Vance	V			a				
Wade	W				ade			
Wendy	W			e	y			
Westmoreland	W			e			or	a
Whitlock			Wh	i, o				
Wright					i			
Yale	Y				ale			
Yolanda	Y			a	o			a
Zane	Z				ane			

Figure 16.6 (continued)
Recording Sheet—The Names Test

blend, consonant digraph, short vowel, long vowel, vowel digraph and diphthong, r controlled vowel, and schwa). Adding up the errors by category may indicate particular patterns of difficulty which may then be addressed through corrective instruction.

The *Cloze Procedure* is used to assess students' use of context to decode words in text. Although we presented the Cloze procedure in Chapter 10 as a way for teaching contextual word recognition, it can also be used to provide information on students' ability to use context in word recognition. Cloze assessments are created with a few more rules than Cloze texts for instruction.

To create a Cloze assessment you need to find a text of at least 150 words from material appropriate to students' grade level (use materials from students' reading curriculum). Retype the passage leaving the first sentence intact. Then, delete every fifth word, leaving a blank space where the word was deleted. After at least twenty-five deletions, add a final sentence with no deletions. Students are then asked to write in the words they believe fit the deletions. If students find the text too difficult to read on their own, you may wish to read it to students, making sure you don't read the deleted words.

An alternative (and easier) construction involves making a copy of the target passage, deleting every appropriate word by lining through it with a marker, and numbering each deletion by hand. Then, make sufficient copies for use. Provide students with the Cloze text and a numbered answer sheet on which to write the deleted words.

Scoring is fairly simple. Any word used by students that closely fits the context should be counted correct. A score in the range of 40–60% correct is considered instructional work. Less than 40% correct may suggest that the student has difficulty in using context to determine unknown words.

READING FLUENCY

Fluency is the ability to read expressively, meaningfully, with appropriate phrasing, and with appropriate speed. Given that assessing expressiveness, meaningfulness, and phrasing may be a bit of a judgment call makes assessing fluency somewhat enigmatic. Nevertheless, since it is an important part of reading, we need to have some ways of assessing it among students.

Perhaps the easiest way of assessing fluency is through reading rate. Although this may seem a rather gross measure, several studies have indicated that rate is a predictor of overall reading proficiency. At the very least, reading rates provide some indication of the degree to which students can decode words by sight or at least through efficient analysis. Rate can be measured by having students read an instructional level text orally for sixty seconds and then counting the number of words read or by having students read a longer passage and calculating rate using the formula below. When students read in order to measure rate, be sure to ask them to read in their normal manner. You should probably make several rate calculations over a couple days and determine each student's average reading rate.

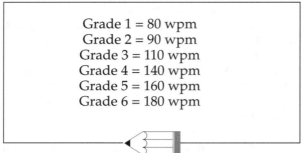

Grade 1 = 80 wpm
Grade 2 = 90 wpm
Grade 3 = 110 wpm
Grade 4 = 140 wpm
Grade 5 = 160 wpm
Grade 6 = 180 wpm

Figure 16.7
Estimated Second Semester Instructional Reading Rates

Reading rate in words per minute = (# words in passage / # seconds to read passage) × 60

Students' reading rate may be compared to second-semester instructional oral rate estimates by grade level (see Figure 16.7). Students who read well below these rates may have some difficulty in reading fluency.

A second method for assessing fluency involves listening to students read a text at their instructional levels and rating their oral performance against some standards. Several useful fluency scales have been developed (Zutell and Rasinski 1991). In Figure 16.8, we provide the Oral Reading Fluency Scale that was used in the National Assessment of Educational Progress Fluency Study that was field tested on 1,100 fourth grade students (Pinnell, et al. 1995). Rasinski (1985) found that rating students' oral reading on a version of this scale significantly predicted third and fifth-grade students' overall reading proficiency. When conducting this type of fluency assessment,

Level 4	Reads primarily in larger, meaningful phrase groups. Although some regressions, repetitions, and deviations from text may be present, these do not appear to detract from the overall structure of the story. Preservation of the author's syntax is consistent. Some or most of the story is read with expressive interpretation.
Level 3	Reads primarily in three- or four-word phrase groups. Some smaller groupings may be present. However, the majority of phrasing seems appropriate and preserves the syntax of the author. Little or no expressive interpretation is present.
Level 2	Reads primarily in two-word phrases with some three- or four-word groupings. Some word-by-word reading may be present. Word groupings may seem awkward and unrelated to larger context of sentence or passage.
Level 1	Reads primarily word-by-word. Occasional two-word or three-word phrases may occur—but these are infrequent and/or they do not preserve meaningful syntax.

Source: U.S. Department of Education, National Center for Education Statistics. *Listening to Children Read Aloud*, 15. Washington, DC: 1995

Figure 16.8
NAEP Oral Reading Fluency Scale

Child's Name_____ School Year_____

Teacher's Name_____

	No Evidence	In Process	Well Developed
Letter Name Knowledge			
Letter Sound Knowledge			
Basic Print Concepts			
One-to-One Correspondence			
Word Recognition			
Sight Vocabulary			
Phonograms			
Context (Cloze)			
Fluency			

Figure 16.9
Continuum for Word Recognition and Fluency Assessment

Student Name:_____

Grade:_____

School Year:_____

Date	Sight Vocab.	Phonograms	Word Rec. (Names Test)	Cloze	Text Read	Fluency Rating	Rate (WPM)

Figure 16.10
Student Reading Summary

allow students to read the passage silently first, then have them read it orally. When listening to students read, we suggest not looking at the text they are reading. Simply attend to their oral reading expression, phrasing, and rate. You will only need to listen to the reading for a minute or less. Students who you rate at levels one or two may be at risk in fluency. For these students we recommend that you go into further analysis of oral reading (and other reading assessments) and provide corrective fluency instruction if warranted.

Some method of summarizing results and keeping track of students' growth over time is desirable. Many teachers we know use continuum or summary forms like those depicted in Figures 16.9 and 16.10. Periodically, say every month or grading period, the teacher evaluates the accumulated assessment information and marks each child's progress on a copy of the continuum or summary form. Assessment data regularly recorded on a continuum or summary form provides an easy and understandable way to track progress over time. The forms are useful for conferences with students and parents as well.

In Conclusion

Assessment is an important part of a total reading program. Assessment should provide us with measures of students' progress as well as directions for further instruction. Certainly there are other measures of word recognition and reading fluency available; if you find some that work especially well for you and your students, we recommend that you use them. The assessment instruments and approaches in this chapter provide you with some of the measures we have found useful in our own practice for determining progress and identifying areas for further instruction. For the most part, the assessments are quick, informal, easy to learn and administer, controlled by the teacher or examiner (not some disembodied test manual), and can be analyzed in a variety of ways to get a better understanding of readers' word recognition and fluency. This combination of attributes provides you with an assessment foundation that will help you better understand your students' word recognition and fluency and design instruction that most effectively meets their needs.

References

Cunningham, P. M. 1990. The Names Test: A Quick Assessment of Decoding Ability. *The Reading Teacher*, 44: 124–129.

Duffelmeyer, F. A. et al. 1994. Further Validation and Enhancement of the Names Test. *The Reading Teacher*, 48: 118–128.

Fry, E. 1998. The Most Common Phonograms. *The Reading Teacher*, 51: 620–622.

Pinnell, G. S., et al. 1995. *Listening to Children Read Aloud*. Washington, DC: U. S. Department of Education, Office of Educational Research and Improvement.

Rasinski, T. V. 1985. *A Study of Factors Involved in Reader-Text Interactions That Contribute to Fluency in Reading.* Unpublished doctoral dissertation. Columbus, OH: The Ohio State University.

Salvia, J., and C. Hughes. 1990. *Curriculum-Based Assessment: Testing What is Taught.* New York: Macmillian.

Zutell, J. B. and T. V. Rasinski. 1991. Training Teachers to Attend to Their Students' Oral Reading Fluency. *Theory into Practice,* 30: 211–217.

17
INVOLVING PARENTS IN WORD STUDY AND READING FLUENCY INSTRUCTION

Recently we had the chance to talk with Maureen, a second grade teacher in an urban school who has worked hard over the years to involve parents in their children's reading. We caught up with her after a long school day and her first response when asked to tell us about parental involvement was "It's hard! It is really hard!" But after a pause that lasted a few seconds she added, "But you know it is worth the effort. Of all the things I have done to help kids learn to read over the years, I think the most important and powerful has been to get parents involved." Maureen told us that she has done a variety of programs, some aimed at just getting parents to read with their children and others that have been more directive, such as having parents of children who struggle do paired reading with their children daily. "Sometimes I have had great success and sometimes the program has fallen flat on its face."

We asked Maureen what was most effective in promoting active parental involvement. Her response was immediate,

"You've got to have patience and persistence. Look at parental involvement as a long–term process; continue to make improvements on the program that you use. When I first started my paired reading program only about ten percent of the parents showed up for my training session, and only about half of them did the paired reading for the suggested three months. But every year the program seems to get better. The second year I had about twenty-five percent participation, and today it's more like seventy-five percent. I don't know what it is—word of mouth between parents that the program really works, the improvements I have made in the program, or just the fact that I have learned to become more comfortable working with parents over time. Whatever the reason, I will tell you this—getting parents involved does work. Those kids who are lucky enough to have parents who will read to and with them are the kids who make the most progress in reading each year. If I were a school principal, I would insist that we have a school-wide parent-child reading program in my school."

In many ways parents and home involvement are the secret weapon in learning to read. Research over the past several decades has demonstrated empirically what Maureen has found among her students—that home involvement invariably improves students' school performance (Epstein 1984, 1987, Henderson 1987, 1988). More specifically, a recent international study of second and eighth grade students' reading achievement found that parental involvement and cooperation and the amount of reading students did at home were the two most powerful variables associated with student achievement, higher than any school–specific variable or instructional activity (Postlethwaite and Ross 1992). Any exemplary program aimed at improving students' overall reading achievement, fluency, and word recognition must include a parent/home involvement component.

ADVISING PARENTS

One of our foremost roles as teachers in working with parents is to communicate with and advise parents on how they can help their children progress in reading. Oftentimes, parents are seduced by the new phonics programs advertised on television or radio promising unbelievable (and usually unsubstantiated) gains in reading for children who participate in the program. Parents do not need to spend oodles of dollars for such programs, workbooks, and phonics kits to help their children in reading and we need to tell them so.

We need to advise parents of what they do need, and it is usually around the home already. Access to books and other material at the local library, as well as to books, magazines, and newspapers around the home is all that's needed to effectively support children's home reading. We also need to teach parents how to use these materials to help their children read. This is what this chapter is all about.

LITERACY AT HOME

Learning to read takes time—time, especially, for reading. And with the school day already nearly filled with various curricular components, we must look at the time after the school day when students can read and receive additional support in their learning to read. We know that simply reading is associated with higher levels of reading achievement. Moreover, we also know that the act of reading provides students with practice in recognizing words and helps develop students' sight vocabulary. Thus, one of most important things teachers and schools can do to improve students' reading and word recognition is to develop a program to promote reading at home. In one study, just twenty minutes of reading outside school each day was associated with above average reading performance (Anderson, Wilson and Fielding 1988). Promoting twenty minutes or more of reading at home will go a long way to promote reading growth.

We have several examples of schools that have developed programs, involving parents, to encourage students to read at home (Baumann 1995, O'Masta and Wolf 1991, Shanahan, Wojciechowski and Rubik 1998). In these schools, teachers agree at the beginning of the school year that parental and family involvement in reading is a goal for their school. And, the nature of that involvement is for parents to ensure that their children read a specified period of time (usually twenty-thirty minutes per day at home) for pleasure. The school year then becomes a campaign to get parents and children reading at home and keep them reading at home. The school year begins with a school assembly in which the home reading campaign is introduced. The principal and teachers challenge students to read, as a school community, a specific number of minutes over the course of the school year. An impressive goal is one million minutes of reading (a school of 300 students would accumulate 1,080,000 minutes of reading if each student read 20 minutes, five days a week, over a 36-week school year). Parents are invited to the assembly as well as to an informational session, early in the school year, in which the home reading campaign is introduced. Information is also sent home to parents periodically throughout the school year.

Beginning with the first week of school, each student gets a weekly log sheet on which he or she records the number of minutes read each day during the week (see Figure 17.1). These log sheets are returned every Monday and are tallied by an aide. A spread sheet computer program can be very helpful in entering data and updating each students' home reading progress; classroom, grade level, and school updates are also made in order to give students a sense of the school's progress and to encourage friendly rivalries between classrooms and grade levels.

The importance that the school has placed on the home reading campaign is evident in the school lobby. Visitors to the school are greeted by a large chart that explains the home reading campaign and provides an update on the progress of the school as a whole. In one school a huge cardboard thermometer displayed the school's progress as the mercury rose during the school year. Periodic assemblies to promote reading, book fairs, author studies and visits, posters placed throughout the school reminding students to read, and personal notes and words of encouragement from teachers and the school principal help many students catch the reading habit and bootstrap themselves to proficient reading. With such wonderful support from the school staff, it is inevitable that the school will reach and surpass its goal. Ultimate attainment of the reading goal is celebrated with a school parade, author visit, picnic, ice cream social or some other special event.

Students in the home reading campaign who are not yet reading conventionally may be read to by a parent for twenty minutes each day in lieu of reading on their own. We know that reading to students can have a dramatically positive effect on various aspects of students' reading achievement. One of the first scholars to note the importance of parents reading to children, Dolores Durkin (1966), found that children who learned to read before beginning formal schooling had parents who read to them in such a way that their children could see the text, could follow their parents' reading, and could ask and answer questions about the words encountered in the reading. Apparently, through this particular format for reading aloud, children were beginning to develop a sight vocabulary and examine the spelling and structure of words. More important, perhaps, is that they were picking up the reading habit.

Name _____   School _____

Please return this log to your child's teacher at the beginning of the week.

Day of Week	Date	Time Spent Reading (minutes)	Name of Passages Read	Other Reading Activities Done	Comments
Mon.					
Tue.					
Wed.					
Thu.					
Fri.					
Sat.					
Sun.					

Figure 17.1
Weekly Reading Log

READING TO CHILDREN

Parents are reminded to read to their children all the time. Perhaps we should add a bit of additional information to parents of those children who are beginning to read, or who are in need of extra practice in developing word recognition skills and sight vocabulary—*read to your child in such a way that your child can see what you are reading.* Furthermore, we need to encourage parents to direct their children's eyes toward the text itself by pointing and informally asking questions about the words that are encountered during the read aloud session. This is in no way meant to imply that parents turn the very affective and bonding activity of reading to their children into a reading lesson. Nonetheless, informal chats about the text may help children develop more quickly as readers and ease some of the difficulty in learning to recognize and analyze words that many young children experience.

In addition to using the read-aloud experience as a way for children to examine the visual nature of words and match the oral representation to them, read aloud can also help children develop the phonemic awareness skills that we mentioned in Chapter 4. Parents can contribute to their child's phonemic awareness from preschool through first grade, by reading, simply telling, or singing children's stories, songs, rhymes, or other texts that have a strong language sound component. The books we listed in Chapter 4 are excellent choices for parents. Familiar songs printed for parent and child use are another great choice. Some of the best texts for phonemic awareness development are nursery rhymes. Encouraging parents to read and reread nursery rhymes with children will inevitably lead to wonderful discussions about sounds and children's development in sound awareness.

Since traditional nursery rhymes are in the public domain, they can be copied freely for parents. In an attempt to get young children on the right track in reading, the Ravenna, Ohio Even Start program, a family literacy program connected to the local public schools, has made its own Nursery Rhyme book, complete with illustrations. It is given to parents of young children in the hopes that they will begin reading to their children early in life, and that some of that reading will help children develop abilities critical to their growth in phonics and word recognition.

Technology has expanded the possibilities for literacy learning and parent involvement. The World Wide Web is another superb source of parent-child reading material. Parents and children can together explore the web, parents working at the keyboard and children in control of the mouse. As they visit different sites, parents can read when requested, and parents and children can read together when appropriate.

WRITING AT HOME

We mentioned previously that opportunities for children to engage in invented or phonemic spelling allows them to apply their emerging phonics knowledge in their own writing. Parents can foster their children's writing development and their phonics knowledge by encouraging their children to write at home. Usually, this means using writing at play to make recipes, create menus, and make lists. Journal or diary writing, also, is an exceptional way for children to write at home in an authentic way.

Dialogue journals are particularly well suited for parental involvement and for developing students' writing and word knowledge. A dialogue journal is simply a written journal that is kept by two people in order to communicate. In essence, it is a conversation between parent and child that takes place in writing. One person writes in it one day, asking his partner questions or making observations, and then passes the journal to his partner. The partner writes in the same journal on the following day, replying to the questions and comments, and then adding questions, comments, or observations for the first writer. Over time, the journal is an exceptional way to learn about the other person and to communicate in ways that are often difficult or superficial when done orally, for instance, offering explanations for one's behavior or making apologies. In addition, the very nature of a dialogue journal at home means partnering a developing writer with a more proficient writer. As the more proficient writer provides an immediate model for the child, the child begins to emulate the parent's writing.

Tim began a dialogue journal with his son, Mike, in April. It was Mike's seventh birthday. The journal passed between Tim and Mike a couple times a week when they first began. Mike's early written entries were at an emergent level. Mike and Tim kept their journal going over the summer months when school was not in session. By September Mike's written entries were longer and significantly more conventional. This was due mainly to the writing and modeling that took place during the summer—no formal instruction took place. His writing became much more conventional in format, and his knowledge of how words are spelled grew greatly as he responded to his dad's writing by using the words his dad used. Parents and teachers never know just how much they influence their children's development. Mike is now a college student, and apparently his love for writing has not ceased. As of this writing he has been the basketball team beat writer, and sports and assistant managing editor for the *Kent Stater*, Kent State University's daily newspaper.

CAPTIONED TELEVISION

Recently, reading researchers have been looking into the effects of captioned television on children's reading development; what they have found is very promising. Captioned television has been found to help children learn words and increase the reading performance of readers who struggle (Adler 1985, Koskinen, et al. 1987, Koskinen, et al. 1993, Neuman and Koskinen 1992). As children watch the visual image on the screen and hear the words spoken, they also see the words printed on the screen. The dual presentation of words, in visual and oral formats, helps children develop their sight vocabulary and decoding skills as they read the screen. With the spread of captioned televisions, and the addition of captions to most commercial programs and advertisements, the potential for captioned television to affect children's reading at home is enormous. Moreover, parents have to do little to make this work.

Teachers who want to encourage parents to turn their children on to reading through captioned television might send home a letter explaining the potential and encouraging parents to ensure that whatever television their children might view is done with captions (see Figure 17.2). Remind parents to discuss with their children the possibilities of captioning. Remind parents too that children may find the captions obtrusive and bothersome for the first few days. But parents should persevere with the captioning, and it won't be long before it becomes a natural part of children's television experience.

September 15

Dear Parents:

Now that the school year is underway, I'd like to inform you of an exciting and easy way to help your child in reading. Recent research has shown that children who view television that contains captions improve their word learning as well as their overall reading. Seeing the words on the screen while at the same time hearing the words helps readers learn to recognize words and read with fluency.

All televisions currently sold in the United States must have the ability to display captions on the television screen. If you have one of these televisions, please make sure that the captioning "switch" is turned on when your child watches television. Actually, it would be a good idea to have the captioning on all the time. Talk to your child about how paying attention to the captions will improve their reading. Encourage your child to "read the screen" as he or she watches TV.

Your child may find the captions distracting and bothersome at first. This will only last a few days until you and your child become comfortable with captioned television. It won't take long before the captions become an accepted part of the television experience.

Captioned television is a very easy way to help your child in reading. Since most elementary school children spend a considerable amount of time watching TV everyday, the amount of reading students do will increase significantly just from the addition of captioned television viewing. And, the more students read, the better readers they will become.

Please feel free to call me if you have any questions about captioning television. Thank you for your assistance in helping your child become a better reader.

Sincerely,
Mr. Rasinski

Figure 17.2
Letter to Parents Explaining Captioned Television

The activities we described above should be recommended to parents by all teachers, preschool through grade six. For most children, especially those experiencing difficulty in reading, more directed activities at home may provide essential reinforcement to the word recognition instruction they receive at school. The remainder of this chapter examines more specific ways in which parents can help their children learn how words work.

MORE HOME ACTIVITIES FOR IMPROVING WORD RECOGNITION

Often teachers give students lists of words to learn to spell or read. These might be the weekly spelling list or the words that are introduced in a story or entire basal book. One way teachers can reinforce children's learning of these words is to send home weekly word lists and ask parents to work with their children on the words. This work may include daily practice reading the words, spelling the words, or using the words in word games that the teacher has introduced to children and parents (see Chapter 12). Indeed, many of the previously described activities for developing phonemic awareness, word recognition, and reading fluency can be easily adapted for home use. Many parents would jump at the chance to help their children in these more directed ways. Even for those parents who are unable to work with their children every night, any additional practice they give their children is helpful.

Two weeks prior to the end of summer vacation in the years that Tim's children's were entering first and second grades, the teachers mailed home a list of ten to twenty words that would be taught during the initial weeks of school and used in the children's reading early in the school year. Tim and his wife Kathy were glad to get the words and to briefly introduce them to their children for ten to fifteen minutes a day on those waning days of summer. It created a bit of a transition for the children from vacation to school and eased some of their fears of what to expect in their new classrooms. For Tim and Kathy, it was a specific way to help their children succeed as they began a new school year. Of course, in addition to this mini-word study, Tim and Kathy continued to read to and write with their children daily.

In Chapter 5 we described a classroom routine in which students learn about rimes and phonograms by writing poems that feature a particular rime. As you will recall, children brainstorm words belonging to a particular rime pattern, read poems and other texts containing the targeted rime, and are then encouraged to make a short poem of their own featuring the rime. Although students can do this final writing task on their own, with classmates, or with an older reading buddy, we have found that the activity works best when parents work with their children to make the short poems. Not only does this give children expert help (even low literate parents can be quite successful with the activity), it demonstrates to children that their parents are readers and writers also and that they should emulate their parents' writing. Later, when children read their compositions in school, parents can occasionally be invited to share the spotlight with their children as the original poems are read and celebrated by the class.

We also mentioned paired reading in Chapter 14 as a direct way to improve students' word recognition and overall fluency. Topping's (1987) original application of paired reading was as a parent tutorial. Parents of elementary students were given a brief training session in which paired reading was described and modeled. The activity is simple—a parent and a child sit side by side and simultaneously read aloud a text of the child's choosing, with either the parent or child pointing to the text as it is read. When the child experiences difficulty with a word, the parents supplies the word and the partners continue reading. When ready to try reading without assistance, the child signals the parent who then either follows the text silently or reads in very soft voice, following the child's reading.

Topping (1987) found that about ten minutes per day of this sort of parent-child activity could accelerate children's reading progress significantly. We know of many teachers and schools who have developed paired reading as a parent involvement program with great success and wide participation.

SYSTEMATIC ROUTINES

One of the best ways for teachers to involve parents in their children's word recognition learning is to develop a systematic word recognition and fluency routine for the home. A systematic routine is simply a set of learning activities designed to be regularly implemented in a preordained sequence. We have worked with many schools and teachers in our local area to develop and implement such routines with parents. One is called Fast Start (Rasinski 1995), and it is based on research indicating the potential of parents reading to their children, reading with their children, and then listening to their children read on their own.

In the Fast Start routine, teachers provide parents with texts to be read and practiced each evening, usually five per week. Along with the pack of texts (see Figure 17.3), which are often rhymes, poetry, or other short passages of no more than 200 words, is a weekly log sheet (see Figure 17.4) that is to be placed on the refrigerator at home as a reminder for parents and children to do the routine daily. For younger children, short poems, jokes, and nursery rhymes may be most appropriate. For older students, more sophisticated poetry may work best. The lesson is based on previously described individual activities. Each lesson takes approximately 15 minutes and goes like this:

1. Parents read the text to their children, one to three times.
2. Parents chat with their children about the passage and how it was read.
3. Parents and children read the text together orally. Again, this may be done several times until the child feels comfortable and confident in reading it.

Dear Parents:

1. Read the rhyme below to your child several times; point to the text as you read.

2. Read the rhyme with your child several times.

3. Listen to your child read the rhyme to you several times.

4. Point to and read individual words in the text.

5. Identify rhyming words (e.g. hot, pot) and write out several other words that follow the same rhyme pattern on this sheet.

Pease-porridge hot,

Pease-porridge cold,

Pease-porridge in the pot,

Nine days old.

Some like it hot,

Some like it cold,

Some like it in the pot,

Nine days old.

Figure 17.3
Fast Start Text

4. When ready, the child reads the passage independently with the parent providing support and encouragement. Again, the text can be read several times by the child, perhaps to different listeners each time.

5. After having read the passage several times through, the parent and child can engage in some word learning activities. These can involve adding words from the text to a home word bank and doing word bank activities such as word sorts, flash cards, word games (see Chapters 9 and 12) or finding words from the text that belong to a

Name _____

Date	Time Spent on Lesson	Name of New Passage Introduced	Other Reading Activities
10-27			
10-28			
10-29			
10-30			
10-31			
11-1			
11-2			
11-3			
11-4			
11-5			
11-6			
11-7			
11-8			
11-9			
11-10			
11-11			
11-12			
11-13			
11-14			
11-15			
11-16			
11-17			
11-18			
11-19			
11-20			
11-21			
11-22			
11-23			
11-24			
11-25			
11-26			
11-27			
11-28			

Figure 17.4
Fast Start Monthly Reading Log

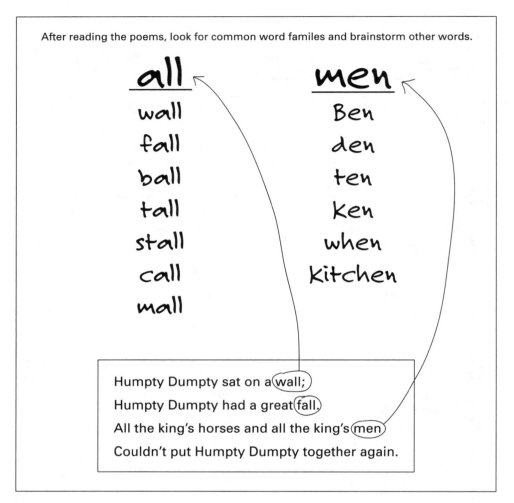

After reading the poems, look for common word familes and brainstorm other words.

all
wall
fall
ball
tall
stall
call
mall

men
Ben
den
ten
Ken
when
Kitchen

Humpty Dumpty sat on a wall;
Humpty Dumpty had a great fall.
All the king's horses and all the king's men
Couldn't put Humpty Dumpty together again.

Figure 17.5
Fast Start Text with Word Study

particular word family (rime group) and brainstorming and practicing other words that fit into the word family (see Figure 17.5).

6. To make a good connection to the school, teachers can add a chance for students to read, reread, and perform the passage at school the next day. The topic of the original text may lead to other passages on a similar topic or theme at school.

Fast Start is inexpensive, easy for parents to learn, and quick for them to implement. Parents report that they and their children enjoy the quick-paced activities. We have also found that the Fast Start program, implemented at several grade levels and with parents whose children attend our reading center clinic, results in significant improvements in word learning and overall reading proficiency.

Fast Start is a good example of the kind of program that can be designed at any grade level to help students become better at word recognition and reading at home. Although we have no hesitation in recommending it for any elementary classroom, we encourage you to develop your own systematic routine, or an adaptation of Fast Start, for your own students and parents that will maximize their learning.

In Conclusion

The home is a wonderful place to support children's literacy learning, and teachers and schools should support parents in helping their children become readers and writers. But, in our efforts to encourage home reading, we need to remember that home is not school, nor should it be turned into school. When we ask parents to read to and with their children or to engage in activities such as Fast Start, we must emphasize the importance of the ambiance that parents create around the activity. Home reading should be natural and enjoyable for children and parents. Parents and children should feel at ease throughout their reading and writing. We need to remind parents to praise their children lavishly for their reading efforts and to focus attention on children's success. And, we need to help parents understand that parent-child learning can be emotionally taxing for both parent and child and that any parent-child reading activity should stop at the first sign of frustration.

There is no doubt in our minds that parents are absolutely necessary to children's reading development. And, effective parent involvement can take a variety of forms—from a fairly explicit type of intervention like Fast Start, to simply encouraging children to read twenty to thirty minutes at home every-day for pleasure. Either way, students get more exposure to, and practice with, the written word. The extra reading students do at home will help them significantly in becoming proficient readers. If achieved early in children's education, parental involvement leads to reading success and ongoing support for schools and teachers. Getting parents involved may be a tough nut to crack for some teachers, but if you are truly interested in maximizing your students' development in decoding, fluency, and overall reading, it is essential that you get parents involved their children's reading.

References

Adler, R. 1985. Using Closed-Captioned Television in the Classroom. In L. Gambrell and E. McLaughlin (eds), *New Directions in Reading: Research and Practice: Yearbook of the State of Maryland International Reading Association*, pp. 11–18. Silver Spring, MD: State of Maryland International Reading Association.

Anderson, R. C., P. Wilson, and L. Fielding. 1988. Growth in Reading and How Children Spend Their Time Outside of School. *Reading Research Quarterly*, 23: 285–303.

Baumann, N. 1995. Reading Millionaires—It works! *The Reading Teacher*, 48: 730.

Durkin, D. 1966. *Children Who Read Early*. New York: Teachers College Press.

Epstein, J. 1984. School Policy and Parent Involvement: Research Results. *Educational Horizons*. vol. 62, pp. 70–72.

Epstein, J. 1987. Parent Involvement: What Research Says to Administrators. *Education and Urban Society*, 119–133.

Henderson, A. T. 1987. *The Evidence Continues to Grow: Parent Involvement Improves Student Achievement*. Columbia, MD: National Committee for Citizens in Education.

Henderson, A. 1988. Parents are a School's Best Friend. *Phi Delta Kappan*, 70: 148–153.

Koskinen, P. S., et al. 1987. *Using the Technology of Closed-Captioned Television to Teach Reading to Handicapped Students*. Performance Report, United States Department of Education Grant No. G–00–84–30067. Falls Church, VA: National Captioning Institute.

Koskinen, P. S., et al. 1993. Captioned Video and Vocabulary Learning: An Innovative Practice in Literacy Education. *The Reading Teacher*, 47: 36–43.

Neuman, S. B., and P. S. Koskinen. 1992. Captioned Television as Comprehensible Input: Effects of Incidental Word Learning in Context for Language Minority Students. *Reading Research Quarterly*, 27: 95–106.

O'Masta, G. A., and J. A. Wolf. 1991. Encouraging Independent Reading Through the Reading Millionaires Project. *The Reading Teacher*, 44: 656–662.

Postlethwaite, T. N., and K. N. Ross. 1992. *Effective Schools in Reading: Implications for Educational Planners*. The Hague: International Association for the Evaluation of Educational Achievement.

Rasinski, T. V. 1995. *Fast Start: A Parental Involvement Reading Program for Primary Grade Students*. In W. Linek & E. Sturtevent (eds), *Generations of literacy. Seventeenth Yearbook of the College Reading Association*, pp. 301–312. Harrisonburg, VA: College Reading Association.

Shanahan, S., J. Wojciechowski and G. Rubik. 1998. A Celebration of Reading: How Our School Read for One Million Minutes. *The Reading Teacher*, 52: 93–96.

Topping, K. 1987. Paired Reading: A Powerful Technique for Parent Use. *The Reading Teacher*, 40: 608–614.

Appendix A
Common Rimes (Phonograms or Word Families)

ab: tab, drab
ace: race, place
ack: lack, track
act: fact, pact
ad: bad, glad
ade: made, shade
aft: raft, craft
ag: bag, shag
age: page, stage
aid: maid, braid
ail: mail, snail
air: hair, stair
ain: rain, train
ait: bait, trait
ake: take, brake
alk: talk, chalk
all: ball, squall
am: ham, swam
ame: name, blame
amp: camp, clamp
an: man, span
ance: dance, glance
and: land, gland
ane: plane, cane
ang: bang, sprang
ank: bank, plank
ant: pant, chant
ap: nap, snap
ape: tape, drape
ar: car, star
ard: hard, card
are: care, glare
ark: dark, spark
arm: harm, charm

arn: barn, yarn
arp: carp, harp
art: part, start
ase: base, case
ash: cash, flash
ask: mask, task
ass: lass, mass
at: fat, scat
atch: hatch, catch
ate: gate, plate
aught: caught, taught
ave: gave, shave
aw: saw, draw
awn: lawn, fawn
ay: hay, clay
ax: wax, sax
aze: haze, maze
ead: head, bread
eak: leak, sneak
eal: real, squeal
eam: team, stream
ean: mean, lean
eap: heap, leap
ear: year, spear
eat: beat, cheat
eck: peck, check
ed: bed, shed
ee: tee, tee
eed: need, speed
eek: leek, seek
eel: feel, kneel
eem: deem, seem
een: seen, screen
eep: keep, sheep

eer: beer, peer
eet: feet, sleet
eg: leg, beg
eigh: weigh, sleigh
eight: weight, freight
ell: fell, swell
elt: felt, belt
en: Ben, when
end: tend, send
ent: sent, spent
ess: less, bless
est: rest, chest
et: get, jet
ew: flew, chew
ib: bib, crib
ibe: bribe, tribe
ice: rice, splice
ick: kick, stick
id: hid, slid
ide: wide, pride
ie: die, pie
ief: thief, chief
ife: wife, knife
iff: cliff, whiff
ift: gift, sift
ig: pig, twig
ight: tight, bright
ike: Mike, spike
ile: mile, tile
ill: fill, chill
ilt: kilt, quilt
im: him, trim
in: tin, spin
ince: since, prince

217

ind: kind, blind
ine: mine, spine
ing: sing, string
ink: sink, shrink
ip: hip, flip
ipe: ripe, swipe
ire: tire, sire
irt: dirt, shirt
ise: rise, wise
ish: dish, swish
isk: disk, risk
iss: kiss, Swiss
ist: mist, wrist
it: hit, quit
itch: ditch, witch
ite: bite, write
ive: five, hive
ix: fix, six
o: do, to, who
o: go, no, so
oach: coach, poach
oad: road, toad
oak: soak, cloak
oal: coal, goal
oam: foam, roam
oan: Joan, loan
oar: boar, roar
oast: boast, coast
oat: boat, float
ob: job, throb
obe: robe, globe
ock: lock, stock
od: rod, sod
ode: code, rode
og: fog, clog
oil: boil, broil
oin: coin, join
oke: woke, spoke

old: gold, scold
ole: hole, stole
oll: droll, roll
ome: dome, home
one: cone, phone
ong: long, wrong
oo: too, zoo
ood: good, hood
ood: food, mood
ook: cook, took
ool: cool, fool
oom: room, bloom
oon: moon, spoon
oop: hoop, snoop
oot: boot, shoot
op: top, chop
ope: hope, slope
orch: porch, torch
ore: bore, snore
ork: cork, fork
orn: horn, thorn
ort: fort, short
ose: rose, close
oss: boss, gloss
ost: cost, lost
ost: host, most
ot: got, trot
otch: notch, blotch
ote: note, quote
ough: rough, tough
ought: bought, brought
ould: could, would
ounce: bounce, pounce
ound: bound, found
ouse: house, mouse
out: pout, about
outh: mouth, south
ove: cove, grove

ove: dove, love
ow: how, chow
ow: slow, throw
owl: howl, growl
own: down, town
own: known, grown
ox: fox, pox
oy: boy, ploy
ub: cub, shrub
uck: duck, stuck
ud: mud, thud
ude: dude, rude
udge: fudge, judge
ue: sue, blue
uff: puff, stuff
ug: dug, plug
ule: rule, mule
ull: dull, gull
um: sum, chum
umb: numb, thumb
ump: bump, plump
un: run, spun
unch: bunch, hunch
une: June, tune
ung: hung, flung
unk: sunk, chunk
unt: bunt, hunt
ur: fur, blur
urn: burn, churn
urse: curse, nurse
us: bus, plus
ush: mush, crush
ust: dust, trust
ut: but, shut
ute: lute, flute
y: my, dry

APPENDIX B
FRY INSTANT WORD LIST

These are the Fry 600 most often used words in reading and writing. The first 300 words represent about two-thirds of all the words students encounter in their reading. Students should be able to recognize these words instantly and accurately (i.e., become part of their sight vocabularies) in order to read with fluency. We recommend, as a rule of thumb, that the 1st 100 words be mastered by the end of 1st grade and each succeeding group of 100 mastered by the end of each succeeding grade (i.e., by the end of grade 6 all 600 words should be part of students' sight vocabularies.)

FIRST 100 INSTANT WORDS

the	had	out	than
of	by	many	first
and	words	then	water
a	but	them	been
to	not	these	called
in	what	so	who
is	all	some	oil
you	were	her	sit
that	we	would	now
it	when	make	find
he	your	like	long
was	can	him	down
for	said	into	day
on	there	time	did
are	use	has	get
as	an	look	come
with	each	two	made
his	which	more	have
they	she	write	from
I	do	number	their
at	how	no	if
be	will	way	go
this	up	could	see
or	other	people	may
one	about	my	part

FRY INSTANT WORD LIST *(cont.)*

SECOND 100 INSTANT WORDS

over	say	set	try
new	great	put	kind
sound	where	end	hand
take	help	does	picture
only	through	another	again
little	much	well	change
work	before	large	off
know	line	must	play
place	right	big	spell
years	too	even	air
live	means	such	away
me	old	because	animals
back	any	turned	house
give	same	here	point
most	tell	why	page
very	boy	asked	letters
after	following	went	mother
things	came	men	answer
our	want	read	found
just	show	need	study
name	also	land	still
good	around	different	learn
sentence	form	home	should
man	three	us	American
think	small	move	world

FRY INSTANT WORD LIST *(cont.)*

THIRD 100 INSTANT WORDS

high	saw	important	miss
every	left	until	idea
near	don't	children	enough
add	few	side	eat
food	while	feet	face
between	along	car	watch
own	might	miles	far
below	close	night	Indians
country	something	walked	really
plants	seemed	white	almost
last	next	sea	let
school	hard	began	above
father	open	grow	girl
keep	example	took	sometimes
trees	beginning	river	mountains
never	life	four	cut
started	always	carry	young
city	those	state	talk
earth	both	once	soon
eyes	paper	book	list
light	together	hear	song
thought	got	stop	being
head	group	without	leave
under	often	second	family
story	run	later	it's

FRY INSTANT WORD LIST *(cont.)*

FOURTH 100 INSTANT WORDS

body	order	listen	farm
music	red	wind	pulled
color	door	rock	draw
stand	sure	space	voice
sun	become	covered	seen
questions	top	fast	cold
fish	ship	several	cried
area	across	hold	plan
mark	today	himself	notice
dog	during	toward	south
horse	short	five	sing
birds	better	step	war
problem	best	morning	ground
compete	however	passed	king
room	low	vowel	fall
knew	hours	true	town
since	black	hundred	I'll
ever	products	against	unit
piece	happened	pattern	figure
told	whole	numeral	certain
usually	measure	table	field
didn't	remember	north	travel
friends	early	slowly	wood
easy	waves	money	fire
heard	reached	map	upon

FRY INSTANT WORD LIST *(cont.)*

FIFTH 100 INSTANT WORDS

done	decided	plane	filled
English	contain	system	heat
road	course	behind	full
half	surface	ran	hot
ten	produce	round	check
fly	building	boat	object
gave	ocean	game	am
box	class	force	rule
finally	note	brought	among
wait	nothing	understand	noun
correct	rest	warm	power
oh	carefully	common	cannot
quickly	scientists	bring	able
person	inside	explain	six
became	wheels	dry	size
shown	stay	though	dark
minutes	green	language	ball
strong	known	shape	material
verb	island	deep	special
stars	week	thousands	heavy
front	less	yes	fine
feel	machine	clear	pair
fact	base	equation	circle
inches	ago	yet	include
street	stood	government	built

FRY INSTANT WORD LIST *(cont.)*

SIXTH 100 INSTANT WORDS

can't	picked	legs	beside
matter	simple	sat	gone
square	cells	main	sky
syllables	paint	winter	glass
perhaps	mind	side	million
bill	love	written	west
felt	cause	length	lay
suddenly	rain	reason	weather
test	exercise	kept	root
direction	eggs	interest	instruments
center	train	arms	meet
farmers	blue	brother	third
ready	wish	race	months
anything	drop	present	paragraph
divided	developed	beautiful	raised
general	window	store	represent
energy	difference	job	soft
subject	distance	edge	whether
Europe	heart	past	clothes
moon	sit	sign	flowers
region	sum	record	shall
return	summer	finished	teacher
believe	wall	discovered	held
dance	forest	wild	describe
members	probably	happy	drive

From Fry, E., Kress, J., and Fountoukidis, D.L. (2000), *The Reading Teacher's Book of Lists*, Fourth edition. Englewood Cliffs, NJ: Prentice-Hall. Reprinted with the permission of Edward Fry, copyright holder.

APPENDIX C
PREFIXES

Letter patterns added to the beginning of words that change their meaning.

Prefix	Meaning	Example
after-	after	afternoon
ambi-	both, around	ambidextrous
amphi-	both, around	amphibian
ante-	before	antebellum
anti-	against	antiwar
auto-	self	automatic, automobile
bene-	good	benefit
bi-, bin-	two	bicycle
by-	near, aside	bystander
cent-	hundred	century
circu-	around	circulate
co-	together	coauthor
col-	with	collaborate
contra-	against	contraband
de-	from, down	decay
dec-, deci-	ten	decade, decimal
di-	two	digaph
dia-	through, across	diameter
dis-	opposite	disagree
re-	back, do again	recall, rewrite
semi-	half	semicircle
sept-	seven	September
sub-	under	submerge
super-	more than, over	supernatural, supervisor
syn-	together	synonym
tele-	distant	telephone
trans-	across	transcontinental
tri-	three	tricycle
ultra-	beyond	ultramodern
un-	not, opposite	unhappy, unable
under-	below, less than	underground, underage
uni-	one	unicorn

APPENDIX D
SUFFIXES

Letter patterns that when added to the end of a word change the word's meaning.

Suffix	Meaning	Example
-ance	state or quality of	repentance
-ancy	state or quality of	vacancy
-ant	one who	servant
-ar	one who	beggar
-arium	place for	aquarium
-ary	place for	library
-ation	state or quality of	inspiration
-cle	small	particle
-cule	small	miniscule
-cy	state or quality of	accuracy
-d	change of verb tense	baked
-dom	state or quality of	freedom
-ed	change of verb tense	talked
-en	change tense of verb	taken
-en	made of	golden
-ence	state or quality of	absence
-ency	state or quality of	frequency
-er	comparative	smaller
-er	one who	teacher
-ern	direction	eastern
-ery, ry	state or quality of	bravery
-ery	trade or occupation	surgery
-ess	female	hostess
-ess	one who	actress
-est	comparative	smallest
-ette	small	cigarette
-eur	one who	chauffeur
-ful	full of	careful
-hood	state or quality of	childhood
-ier, yer	one who	lawyer
-ily	in what manner	speedily

-ing	change of verb tense	singing
-ion	state or quality of	champion
-ism	state or quality of	heroism
-ist	one who practices	biologist
-itis	inflammation of	laryngitis
-ity	state or quality of	civility
-ization	state of quality of	civilization
-less	without	worthless
-let	small	islet
-ling	small	duckling
-ly	in what manner	strangely
-man	one who works with	craftsman
-ment	state or quality of	amazement
-most	comparative	innermost
-ness	state or quality of	kindness
-ology	study of	biology
-or	one who	doctor
-orium	place for	auditorium
-ory	place for	laboratory
-phobia	fear of	claustrophobia
-ry	trade or occupation	dentistry
-s	more than one	dogs
-ship	state or quality of	ownership
-ship	art or skill of	swordsmanship
-sion	state or quality of	tension
-t	change tense of verb	slept
-tion	state or quality of	fascination
-ty	state or quality of	loyalty
-ward	direction	backward
-wright	one who works with	playwright

Appendix E
Greek and Latin
Word Patterns

Root	Meaning	Examples
act	do	react
aero	air	aerate
agri	field	agriculture
alt	high	altitude
alter	other	alternate
ambul	walk, go	ambulance
amo, ami	love	amiable
ang	bend	angle
anim	life, spirit	animal
ann, enn	year	annual
anthr, anthro	man (people)	anthropology
aqua	water	aquarium
arch	chief	archbishop
archae, arche	ancient	archaeology
art	skill	artist
ast	star	astronaut
aud	hear	auditorium
belli	war	belligerent
biblio	book	bibliography
bio	life	biology
brev	short	brevity
cam, camp	field	campus
cap	head	captain
cardi	heart	cardiac
center, centr	center	egocentric
cert	sure	certain
chron	time	chronological
cide	cut, kill	suicide
cogn	know	recognize
common	common	community

corp	body	corporation
cosm	universe	cosmonaut
crat	rule	democrat
credit	believe	incredible
cycl	circle, ring	bicycle
dem	people	democracy
dict	speak	contradict
div	divide	divorce
doc	teach	indoctrinate
don, donat	give	pardon
dont, dent	tooth	orthodontist
dox	belief	orthodox
esth	feeling	anesthetic
fac	make, do	factory
flex, flect	bend	reflex
form	shape	uniform
fract, frag	break	fracture
frater	brother	fraternity
fric	rub	friction
gam	marriage	polygamy
gen	birth, race	generation
geo	earth	geology
gon	angle	pentagon
grad	step	gradual
gram	letter, written	telegram
graph	write	telegraph
grat	pleasing	gratitude
homo, hom	man	homicide
hydr	water	hydrant
ject	throw	reject
junct	join	juncture
jud	law	judge
jur	law, swear	perjury
jus	law	justice
lab	work	labor
lat	side	collateral
liber	free	liberty
loc	place	location
log, logue	word	monologue
luc	light	elucidate
lum	light	illuminate
luna	moon	lunar
lust	shine	luster
man	hand	manual
mand	to order	command
mania	madness	maniac

mar	sea	marine
mater, matri	mother	maternity
max	greatest	maximum
mech	machine	mechanic
mem	mindful	remember
ment	mind	mental
meter	measure	thermometer
migr	move	migrate
min	small,lesser	minimize
miss	send	missionary
mob	move	automobile
morph	shape	polymorphous
mort	dealth	mortal
mot	move	motor
mut	change	commute
narr	tell	narrate
nat	born	innate
nav	ship	naval
neg	no	negative
neo	new	neoclassic
nov	new	novel
ocu	eye	binocular
opt	eye	optometrist
opt	best	optimal
onym, nym	name	pseudonym
orig	beginning	origin
ortho	straight, right	orthodontist
paed, ped	child	pediatrician
pater	father	paternal
path	feeling, suffer	sympathy
ped	foot	pedal
phil	love	philosophy
phob	fear	claustrophobia
phon	sound	phonograph
photo	light	photograph
phys	nature	physical
plur	more	plural
pod	foot	tripod
poli, polis	city	metropolis
pop	people	popular
port	carry	transport
pos	place	position
psych	mind, soul	psychology
pug	fight	repugnant
quer, ques	ask, seek	inquiry
rupt	break	bankrupt

scend	climb	ascend
sci	know	conscience
scop	see	microscope
scribe, script	write	inscribe
sect	cut	dissect
serv	save, keep	reservoir
sign	mark	insignia
sol	alone	solitary
son	sound	unison
soph	wise	philosopher
spec	see	inspect
spir	breathe	spirit
stell	star	constellation
strict	draw tight	restrict
struct	build	structure
sum	highest	summit
tact	touch	contact
temp	time	temporary
term	end	exterminate
terr	land	terrain
tex	weave	texture
the, theo	god	theology
therm	heat	thermos
tract	pull, drag	tractor
urb	city	suburb
vac	empty	vacant
vag	wander	vagrant
var	different	variety
ven	come	advent
ver	turn	convert
ver	truth	verify
vict, vine	conquer	victory
vid	see	video
viv, vit	live	survive
voc, vok	voice	vocal
void	empty	voided
volv	roll	revolver
vor	eat	voracious

APPENDIX F
WEB SITES FOR WORD STUDY

Use these web sites as a personal resource to help nurture the love of words in your students. Be sure to examine the sites yourself before having students visit them.

A Word A Day — http://www.wordsmith.org/awad/
Introduces readers to a new word every day; provides readers with interesting information about each day's word.

Wordly Wise Word Games — http://www.in.on.ca/~hoad/
Creative word puzzles.

Wordsmyth — wysiwyg://126/http://wordsmyth.net/
An online educational dictionary and thesaurus.

Word Puzzler's Corner — wysiwyg://186/http://wwwniagara.com/~wrdpuzlr/default.html
A source for crossword and other word puzzles.

Wordwatch — http://titania.cobuild.collins.co.uk/wordwatch.html
Weekly examination and commentary of interesting words or phrases from English.

Verbivore — http://pw1.netcom/~rlederer/index.htm
Richard Lederer's website for "wordaholics, logolepts, and verbivores" (people who devour words). Many links to other word related web sites.

Vocabulary.com — http://www.vocabulary.com/
The home of Vocabulary University. Source for a multitude of word puzzles.

Language/Etymology	http://www.heimbaugh.com/language/etymology/ Provides origins to common words and phrases.
Origin of Phrases	http://members.aol.com/MorelandC/PhrasesData.htm Provides answers to the question, "Why do certain phrases mean what they do?" Examines how common phrases came to be.

Author Index

Subject Index